A HOUSE ON THE OCEAN,
A HOUSE ON THE BAY

A HOUSE ON THE OCEAN, A HOUSE ON THE BAY

A Memoir

FELICE PICANO

Faber and Faber
Boston · London

Library of Congress Cataloging-in-Publication Data

Picano, Felice, 1944–
A house on the ocean, a house on the bay : a memoir / Felice Picano.
p. cm.
ISBN 0-571-19913-5
I. Title.
PS3566.I25H68   1997
813'.54—dc20
[B]   96-43419
CIP

Jacket design by Adrian Morgan
Printed in the United States of America

To Donna Lieberman

Acknowledgments

Thanks to those who read over this manuscript beforehand—Will Meyerhofer and Donna Lieberman—and for their useful reactions and comments. Much thanks to Valerie Cimino for finely and tactfully helping to make it a reality. And of course, thanks to Malaga Baldi, a constant star.

BOOK ONE:

Apprentice Without a Master

I wondered how far I should turn out faithful
to that ideal conception of one's own personality
every man sets up for himself secretly.

JOSEPH CONRAD

"Five Islands," the old maps have it: seventeenth-century navigational charts with their fine, faded, clear penmanship on yellowing parchment. And there they are, the five sketched-in little oval isles, all in a row, somewhere below the bulk of "The Long Island" and the wavier mass of water called "The Great South Bay," distinguishing that body from a dozen smaller bays and inlets.

Five Islands, quite clearly written. As clearly as the names of the Indian tribes Peconic and Conanicut and Shinnecock are labeled on strategy maps of the Revolutionary War; as clearly limned on nineteenth-century maritime charts as the "New Light," the just-erected lighthouse at the eastern end of "Rocks-Away."

As clear as the North Port and the East Port and the Free Port, which was exactly that when clipper ships would stop for the night on their long journey back from Yokohama and Manila and the Spice Islands, not sail on to their final destination of New York Harbor until they'd been lightened a bit. The booty was stashed among the dunes on one of the five, by now quite long, nearly abutting sandbars, to be retrieved a few days later. This might explain the proliferation of Japanese maple trees in Freeport, Sayville, and the surrounding towns first populated by those seamen, and their enormous Victorian houses, with verandas extending along the lawn to roof over a folly upon which to sit in one's duty-free Chinese bamboo chair and sip one's duty-free Assam tea and take the ocean breezes.

Once, at a dinner at the Last House in Fire Island Pines, I was shown a photograph of one such clipper ship that arrived home far too late in the year. It was embedded in ice, mizzenmasts and furled sails and sailors all frozen together, looking like swirls of sugary frosting you'd put atop a homecoming cake. I was reminded of Thoreau's journals, of how he traveled to that same "bleak beach" to visit—somewhere not far from the Last House in the Pines—the sight of the shipwreck that had spewed forth the broken bodies of Margaret Fuller, her husband, and their child who Thoreau had come to meet—and remained to mourn. And of Margaret Fuller herself, that ever-questioning bluestocking, whose last words to Emerson before she went to Europe were about God and Fate and Destiny, Emerson's own topics. She'd said, "Though it is difficult, I accept!" and as she'd walked up the gangplank, Emerson had been heard to sputter, "She'd damned *better* accept!"

An old man who'd worked for my father told me that in the 1920s the lighthouse was relocated to the western end of the by-now connected five narrow isles, and how during Prohibition, the long sandbar was used by gangsters to cache their bootleg Canadian whisky when Coast Guard cutters drew too close for comfort. By then, someone's misreading of an old map had become common-place, turning Five Islands into Fire Island, and besides the Cosa Nostra hideouts, there were already a few small early summer communities.

In the 1930s there were more, most of them called "artists' colonies" whenever they were mentioned in the *New Yorker* or the original *Vanity Fair*. A rather naughty one seldom mentioned in print was named Cherry Grove and was located a third of the way along the thirty-five-mile-long sandbar. Auden and Isherwood and Gypsy Rose Lee photographed each other with Brownie cameras camping and smooching on the sands. Behind them you can see the familiar tiny wooden cabins.

In the days after the great hurricane of 1938, Fire Island temporarily became three islands again, but soon mended itself. Even so, a half century later I could tell where the ocean had breasted the land, leaving "downs" and little swamps. One such spot, between Cherry Grove and Fire Island Pines, later became known as the Meat Rack, sometimes affectionately called the "Judy Garland Memorial Park."

A remarkable overhead shot—doubtless photographed from a small plane—hangs in the front of the Pines Pantry showing Fire Island Pines in the 1950s and 1960s when it was the island's newest "family community."

By then I was a teenager, living in Twin Ponds, where the New York City line met Nassau County. My older brother and I would take our two-seater fiberglass Sunfish sailboat out from the end of Long Beach Island into South Oyster Bay. On a good day we'd sail east, far beyond the Fire Island Lighthouse. One time, as we attempted to turn around and return, we were caught by strong crosswinds and knocked over three times. That was when I first stepped foot on Fire Island, as, tired from fighting bad winds, soaked to the skin, our tipped boat at last righted upon the muddy shingle of a tiny bay beach at Sea View, we waited for someone with a motorboat to pull our kit-built ketch out into the middle of the bay where we hoped a strong, straight current would glide us back home before sunset.

In February of 1965, Billy Lee, a friend at the East End Welfare Center, came into my unit office, sat down, and said, "Uh, uh, a coupl'a people you know are taking a house at Ocean Beach on Fire Island, and uh, uh, we're looking for people to share a room. Glenn and, uh, Dennis are looking for a third."

That midsummer I began my share on a late Friday afternoon. I drove out with a co-worker, Ellen Voight, who was sharing Kitty's or someone else's room in our house that weekend. We parked her car at Bay Shore and took a small, snaillike ferry directly into a thick white fog, buffeted by rain and gales all the way to Ocean Beach. We debarked in darkness and mist and found the house only after knocking on several wrong doors. The next day was sunny and hot, perfect beach weather. Among friends I warmed in the sun. The following summer, I took my own room with the group in a larger place.

This bunch of twenty-five-year-old middle-class Maoists at their peak of vigor and bloom spent Friday nights together in our Ocean Beach weekend home, and Saturday nights out, sex hunting. Flynn's, in the abutting community of Ocean Bay Park, was our main hangout, but after a while some of us wanted to go elsewhere. Lucy (by then of Lucy-and-Dennis) declared the Ocean Beach/Ocean Bay park singles scene "too boring. Hey guys! I've got an idea," Lucy said. "Why don't we take a beach taxi down to the Grove and go dancing? I hear they have great dancing there. And they're always looking for girls."

"Not from what I heard about the Grove," Billy Lee said.

"No, really, Billy, they are. Because this great dance place has so many more guys than girls and there's this sign on the dance floor that says No More than Four Men per Woman. They'll love us!"

Somehow eight of us managed to arrive at Cherry Grove that night. The dance place was right off the beach, with a raised terrace for dining and inside a professional-sized dance floor and lights and real—not plastic—rock music. And men, lots of single men. But our LSD had taken hold during the fifteen-minute-long, bumpy, swerving ride in yellow jeeps along the sand and all I noticed at first were the colored pennants on poles along the beach, the twirling colored lights, the good music. Once inside, I was more concerned with not appearing as high as I really was and with staying with my friends (who always seemed to be disappearing) than I was in checking out the scene. I'd still not come out yet and I was with a woman. And, just as Lucy had predicted, since our group contained five women, we proved to be quite popular: several people even bought us rounds of drinks.

I went to Europe and returned a year or so later. I've written extensively about this trip in *Men Who Loved Me*. In 1966, the painter Jay Weiss, my close friend at the time, told me he'd wangled an invitation to someone's house in the Pines, a community I'd never been to. I'd heard about the Pines, of course. That was where many of the gay celebrities Douglas and Miss Sherry gossiped about spent their summers. It had a reputation for being chic and, compared to the Hamptons, rather more private.

For some arcane yet typically Weissian reason, and despite the fact that neither Jay nor I had a regular job, we couldn't manage to leave Manhattan until late Friday afternoon, and we either missed our connecting train at Babylon or (more likely) he got the times mixed up, so we didn't step foot in the little Pines harbor until long after dark. Jay had only been there a few times before and he had only the sketchiest of directions. Once away from the harbor there was no light on the wooden walkways. It seemed to take us forever to follow a tortuous path. With far greater knowledge today I can reconstruct our path: we went around the west side buildings of the tiny "downtown," past the Boatel and Blue Whale, almost up to the yacht slip, took a sharp turn left through an endless darkness of trees with intermittent light from houses along what I now know to be Bay Walk West, and advanced almost up to the crossing Coast Guard Walk, where we stepped onto an upward curving path to a fence-enclosed house, terrace, and pool.

It turned out the person who'd invited Jay was himself a guest of a guest: and it didn't take me long to figure out that this sneeringly handsome porn actor/model had invited Jay out to be his weekend date. I had not been expected at all. Completely misreading Jay's and my relationship, this surly fellow was barely restrained toward me, and after some coffee and a bit of conversation in which it became clear that Jay was not going to sleep with him, he reduced Jay's invitation to a single night. He might not have even done that, but the last ferry back to Sayville had already left. Jay and I went without supper and slept inside the unheated, unweatherproofed pool cabana on tiny old mattresses with ancient beach towels as blankets. But the next day was beautiful and we spent it on the beach and hunting up and visiting others of Jay's acquaintance, where he managed to get us breakfast, lunch, and dinner. We were home by late Saturday night, but the memories of our surly host and bad arrival conditions had by then been utterly replaced by a great subsequent day filled with sun, beach, food, drinks, grass, and general bonhomie from everyone else.

A decade later, I would walk that same, once mysterious, first night's path late at night from the harbor to Bayside Six, an unextraordinary house that somehow or other became a noted weekend orgy haven once the local disco closed at 3 A.M. I can still recall my surprise and pleasure when I was first invited. I was inside the Sandpiper, alone among the crowd, dancing in place on that section we'd nicknamed "The Widow's Walk" because it was the main cruising drag of the club, when someone passing by suddenly leaned over and whispered into my ear over the sound of Gladys Knight and the Pips those magical four words: "Orgy at Bayside Six."

Some years after that, when I was living on Midway Walk on the west side of the Pines, I would take that same stretch of Bay Walk every day to go to the harbor for groceries and to Tea Dance or just to avoid the crowds getting off the ferry along the more populated Fire Island Boulevard. I determined to search for the house where I'd spent my first chilled night at the Pines and I looked for weeks, peering over fences and through foliage, until I finally happened upon the place by chance. Its seven-foot-high gate was open for a delivery of butane gas, so I could make out the round central pool, the walls of the encircling house, even the distinctive little cupola-roofed cabana we'd slept in. It turned out to be directly across Bay Walk from a house friends of mine had rented for several years in the late 1970s and had named "Grey Gardens" because of its age, color, and state of dilapidation. (A new owner had since freshened it up considerably and renamed it "Annie Hall.") The little cabana Jay and I had slept in, huddling for warmth that night, was barely a hundred yards from where I was now living for the summer.

Jay Weiss was also responsible for my second visit to the Pines the following summer. This time it was a bona fide invitation for both of us to spend the weekend in Sam Plaia's house, Como La Playa, on the ocean side of the island where Ocean Walk met Tarpon. Not only was it on the opposite side of the little Pines harbor from my first visit, east rather than west, but it was on the ocean, rather than the bay. Even so, it also entailed another trek. This time it was in daylight but again almost endless, climaxing in a great hill we barely managed to get over, me and Jay lugging his many paint supplies, several bags of beach togs, his cat carrier, his cat, and about fifty pounds of cat litter. All without benefit of a wagon. Once arrived, however, we were warmly received, and we spent the weekend amid flowers and incense, good food and fine wines, surrounded by bright and talented people. That Saturday, Arnie Deerson arrived and, with Messiaen's *Turangalila* playing on the stereo, we "tripped" on the beach.

When I first came to live on the Island for an entire April-to-November season (rather than merely going out on weekends or even for several weeks' vacation), it would be here, ocean side east, in a house perched high upon that same hill on Tarpon Walk that Jay and I had struggled over; a tiny gray house with a white roof and red front door from which I could easily see Sam's house, by then being rented by someone else.

Bay side and ocean side: two very different experiences for me from the very beginning. Later on, rereading Proust, I would almost think of them as Marcel had thought of two paths he'd taken as a child in Combray. Not that these *côtes* were socially distinct as the Guermantes Way had been from Swann's Way. No, rather I thought of them as being distinctive in two main ways, the first atmospheric, the second emotional.

The bay side was fragrant, heavily wooded, nocturnal, obscure, somewhat bewildering, a place filled with unclarities of location, not to mention relationship. Beyond a doubt quite sensual, even if somewhat contrarily so, a bit excessive somehow, tinted by feelings not quite fully understood or under control. The omnipresent flutter of mosquitoes and moths hovering on screened windows somehow dovetailed in my mind with unmet expectations and tiresome disillusionments.

Contrarily, I'd think of the ocean side as brightly sunny by day, wide open to the sweep of the Milky Way by night. Periodically cleaned by ocean breezes and the salted tang of the briny air, everything around—people, houses, hedges—seemed so sharply outlined, clear cut, and my days and nights were defined by comfortable friendships and easily handled amours, by Whitmanlike athletic sexual encounters, some publicly out of doors upon decks and amid dunes, others in never quite completely shuttered or shaded afternoon bedrooms. Here storms could be frighteningly sudden and dramatic: lightning struck this high spot both literally and figuratively. But all was cleared up in a few hours.

Some years later, I would understand that even these categorizations were false, even treacherous.

But those first visits to Fire Island are mere blurs in my memory compared to my third, in the summer of 1971. Edward and I sat on the large, almost empty, open upper deck of one of the wide new ferries just put into service. It was a moonless night, the ebony sky silvered with stars, warm and balmy enough so we were only wearing shorts, not even shirts. The bay water formed an expanse of black mirror barely disturbed by the boat's fore and aft wakes. As for me, who'd not been back to the Pines in years, not only was I there for a week, I also believed I was about to begin a long-delayed honeymoon with the man I thought I loved.

* * *

I have to thank—or blame—Jon Peterson for the circumstances that led up to that magical nighttime ferry ride to the Pines. Thank—or blame—Jon for introducing me to that man I thought I loved: Edward Armour. It was Jon who called me some ten months before that ferry ride, one raw, wintry afternoon in late November of 1970, when summer and Fire Island were the last things on any of our minds. Jon's call quite innocently, quite inadvertently brought Edward into my life. For everything else that happened, Jon bears no responsibility at all. It was all my and Ed's doing. After all, Jon merely asked if I had any LSD.

Not an unusual question at the time, certainly, except that it was coming from Jon, who liked his Scotch to be Black Label with an inch of water and who otherwise seemed to have no use at all for the drugs my friends and I used. I'd known Jon only a few years, enough to be aware of his involvement in various kinds of business, most strikingly, the theater. He was a producer and was somehow connected with Israel Horovitz's off-Broadway success, *The Line*, and—it was said—in discovering the actor Al Pacino, who starred in the play.

Jon quickly explained that the acid wasn't for him (no surprise here) but for a good friend. Or rather for not such a good friend so much as for someone Jon would like to do a favor for. He spoke about it so casually I didn't know how to respond. So I told Jon the truth. I had perhaps four tabs of acid that I kept around in case I and my pals decided to trip. I didn't like selling it, even though Jon assured me his friend was completely okay. "He was even at the Carmen Miranda party at the Pines last summer, done up as a toreador!" Would I at least let Edward phone me so I'd be able to explain my compunctions directly?

Ed Armour phoned the next afternoon. He understood my feelings about drugs and strangers, he said, but asked if I'd make an exception this one time. His regular grass connection wasn't able to come through with the stronger drug. Ed and a friend were going to Los Angeles, and they knew no one there. They were driving directly down to Disneyland, spending the day, then flying home the following morning. They wanted the LSD for Disneyland. They'd planned this for months and had suddenly hit this single snag.

The whimsy in it piqued my interest. I said he could come by that afternoon. I'd sell him the two tabs of acid at cost: $5 a hit.

Ed arrived an hour later. From the open doorway of my first-floor apartment on Jane Street I could see him behind the multipaned inner glass front door. When I buzzed him in, he walked, slightly bowlegged in his close-fitting jeans and square-toed boots, along the narrow corridor toward me like a real-life cowboy. He had broad shoulders, but not the heavy torso to go with them. Instead he seemed somewhat wiry. His hair was short for those years and neat, but wavy, fine, chestnut. His face as he came closer was square, with a cleft chin. The immediate impression was "ruggedly handsome," Marlboro Man, except for his offbeat, slightly canted eyes.

He left a half hour later with the LSD, following coffee and enough coversation for me to tamp down any paranoia I still might have about the transaction. The minute he was out of the building, I phoned Jon Peterson.

"He's gorgeous!" I gushed. "He's the sexiest man I've ever met. Tell me everything about him."

Jon told me next to nothing. They'd met a year before. Like everyone else who met Ed, Jon had been smitten by his combination of modesty, intelligence, charm, and looks. Ed was an artist—a painter—and lived on lower Seventh Avenue in the West Village not a dozen blocks away from me.

"Who's this friend he's going to L.A. with?" I asked. "Are they lovers? Does Ed have a lover?"

The friend, according to Jon, was indeed just a friend. Someone named Ben. Jon had seen them going around together a great deal, including at the Carmen Miranda party. But the way Ed had flirted with others, Jon included, Jon didn't think sex was part of their relationship. To Jon's knowledge, Ed did not have a lover, although "God knows, I and every sane man in town would like to be."

A House on the Ocean, A House on the Bay

I asked for Ed's phone number. Sensing my seriousness of purpose now, Jon immediately began to waffle. The competition was heavy, he said. "Who besides yourself?" I provoked him. Ed might admittedly be sexy and gorgeous and smart, but he might also be into some heavy scenes: he'd been known to frequent the Eagles Nest, a leather bar under the West Side Highway up in Chelsea. Shouldn't I reconsider what was after all mostly a momentary physical attraction?

I reminded Jon that his own lover—a French gymnasium instructor—was due to arrive from Paris and move in with Jon in two weeks' time and that I was twenty-six years old and could handle myself. Besides, I'd settle for a momentary physical attraction.

Jon reminded me that I might not be completely over the recent short yet disastrous affair I'd just had. I was still vulnerable, Jon warned, my emotions still atumble.

This was undoubtably so. But all I wanted really was to get this man alone with his clothing off.

"I'll take my chances," I told Jon. So he broke down and gave me Ed's phone number, all with such a rare ungraciousness that when I remarked on what a spoilsport he was being, Jon said, "I've warned you!"

Phone number in hand, I waited.

Jon of course was right to warn me. Oh, I didn't know then if he should have warned me away from Ed specifically—how can anyone determine what anyone else's relationship will be with someone else, never mind what anyone's fate will end up being because of that person? But he was right to warn me because the past year or so of my life had been so generally disastrous. Not merely my love life, although that had come in for its share of the dismal honors. I suspected I really ought to slow down and not follow my impulses, but instead carefully consider any moves I might make in my life.

Indeed, the past year had been the most difficult I could remember having since I was a child of eleven. I was currently living a hand-to-mouth existence, encountering great resistance on almost every level. Looking back on this time with the hindsight of astrological prediction in hand, I'd later see that it was a truly dangerous time for me, emotionally, financially, and spiritually. Not physically dangerous . . . that would come a bit later on.

Not a week before Jon's phone call, I'd walked out onto the Bank Street Pier late one unseasonably warm November afternoon, sat down, and assessed my life. I had no companion since my sudden, unhappy breakup last summer and few friends since Jan Rosenberry and Arnie Deerson had moved to California, effectively ending the Twelfth Street commune that had become my second home for the past few years. So my closest friends, my moral and mental supports, were gone. I possessed little in the way of earthly goods. I had no money, no job, and no apparent future.

Not long before, everything had been different.

*   *   *

In late 1969, I'd again run out of cash and in my lighthearted usual fashion since my intense bouts working at *Graphique* magazine and with mononucleosis, I'd looked around for work fitting one who'd followed Timothy Leary's dictum to "tune in, turn on, and drop out"—i.e., work I could leave behind the moment I stepped out of the workplace door.

Although I'd unquestionably been physically trashed by the mono, it hadn't at all affected my spirits. I was still young, rapidly recovering my health, relatively good looking, and with little in the way of responsibilities. My immediate aim was to experience life and have fun. Whenever I ran out of cash, I'd work long enough to pay back bills and expenses, and—given my low rent—to save up for another few months to come, after which I would once again quit work. This modest program had so far served me fairly well in my attempts to separate myself from my bourgeois background and fit myself more closely into my bohemian new Greenwich Village neighborhood. Oh, and, by the way, to also transform me into a writer.

On reflection, my output wasn't much for a year and a half: three playlets, each barely ten pages long, and a dozen poems as I slowly taught myself how to write lyrics, songs, sonnets, sestinas, all in various rhythm and rhyme schemes. Even a few cantos of a mock-epic à la Pope, titled "The Hootiad," a foolish attempt to "send up" a sometime boyfriend, a blond hunkette of a hustler from Kentucky named Lee Gipson, and naturally nicknamed Hoot after the cowboy character actor. Indifferently alexandrined, canto 1 of my poem opened:

> Spaced on speed, hair popper-yellow,
> Lies my Lee on golden pillows,
> Jerks off for an old John's fancy . . .

And so on. I was also writing in my hardbound journals, following the advice of the *I Ching* on how to become a writer, to wit, "Practice chariot driving daily." These were short entries, and longer essays, extended book reports, detailing my thoughts on authors—James, Balzac, Mann, Tolstoy, Dinesen—whose work I admired and from whom I hoped to learn particular aspects of the craft: point of view, narrative rhythm and speed, organic use of symbol and metaphor. I'd also written what I thought might be the opening of a novel. Barely eight pages, and clearly leading to something large, but what exactly I'd still not figured out.

The earliest of my notebooks I titled "Journals of an Alchemist." The immediate source derived from a popular book among my friends of the time called *Morning of the Magicians*. Like several other books people were reading then—Carlos Castaneda's *Don Juan* books, Heinlein's *Stranger in a Strange Land; Black Elk Speaks, Autobiography of a Yogi,* and *The Tibetan Book of the Dead*—this book gave me examples and hints and ideas about how I could change myself from the middle-class postgrad with a little work experience into an entirely new person: totally individual and never before seen on earth. It turned out that the legend of turning dross to gold was merely metaphorical (though one's fortune might also await on the other side of that change). Not ore but I myself was to be the material that was changed, and I myself would select both the alembic and the conditions within it in which I would be transformed. Hopefully too I'd also be able to guide myself during the difficult states of the metamorphosis.

If all this sounds very much of the late 1960s and like many of the artifacts of the time, rather quaint nowadays, let me merely point out the obvious: it worked. Aside from two women I knew from college, there are few from my past I can have even a ten-minute conversation with as an equal. Meanwhile, however, the process had its ups and downs, ins and outs. During the time I'm writing about, I was apparently moving away from the glamour of my last high-paying and fancy job at the magazine, a time of wide-spread friendships, many social contacts, and various love affairs and into a more inward, interior kind of life, limited in many ways.

My new job, for instance, was as a clerk in a tiny bookstore, a single link in a large nationwide chain. Although it was located on the main level of Grand Central Station, it was situated on a lower side corridor of the huge terminus, near the Times Square shuttle—hardly a major thoroughfare. The shop was only active during a few hours in the morning, at lunchtime, and again briefly during the evening rush hour. Even then it was never terribly busy. Once the commuter traffic had passed, it was empty. The shop opened at 8 A.M. and was shut again by 7. I was to come at 11, just before the hoped-for "lunchtime crunch" and remain to help close.

I'd been hired as temporary help for the Christmas holidays, exactly the type of off-hours, noninvolving work I wanted. And the hours were perfect. Ever since junior high, when to accommodate the early baby-boom, students were placed on three time levels and went to school in shifts, I'd gotten used to staying up late at night, waking up late, having a leisurely morning to myself before having to be anywhere. With the return of these hours, I could now read and write as long into the night as the spirit took me, and after breakfast still have time to revise any previous night's work.

When I first arrived at the shop—directly from my formal interview at the chain's posh Fifth Avenue main office—I wondered why such a tiny store needed help. True, the manager, Mr. Harris, was at or very near retirement age. He moved slowly, even within the confines of the store, and aside from those periods when customer traffic was deemed to be heavy, he was away from the shop, passing most of his time in the "office," which Jim O'Shea, his assistant manager, always spoke of as though it were enclosed in quotation marks: a bit of typical light irony, I was eventually to discover.

O'Shea was a short, heavy-set, prematurely balding fellow no more than thirty-five years old. At first glance, with his baby face, tiny nose, round button-blue eyes, and Gerber baby flushed cheeks, unruly dun-colored hair barely covering his ginger jar head, O'Shea looked like nothing so much as a cheerful Irishman out of a 1950s Hollywood musical or maybe an illustration for an early Dickens novel.

But as soon as O'Shea and I began to talk during those long after noons when Mr. Harris was at his "office" and there was only occasional drop-in business, I found out he was quite different: an extreme realist, indeed, a complete cynic. After further acquaintance I fabricated a sort of past for O'Shea: he'd surely suffered some major disappointment in life, whether romantic or career related, I never found out. Whichever, it had affected him so as to completely color his future. He'd backed out of even the possibility of fulfilling any ambition in life. He saw his poorly paid job in this hole-in-the-wall shop as a refuge from the world. He was content with his lot, although ready to gently chide others for avarice and hypocrisy—and for selling out.

It was O'Shea who told me that this shop was a known dead end in the company, and that Harris had been placed here "like an old horse put out to pasture." It wasn't a put-down. Harris had gone to work for the company as a stock boy at the end of the Depression, without even a high-school diploma. Over the decades, by dint of hard work and perseverance, he'd risen far. Briefly—and in his memory, glamorously—he'd ascended to assistant manager of the flagship Fifth Avenue shop, lording it over a staff of fifty.

Until, that is, an unspecified health problem and equally vague reorganization (with overtones of office politics behind it) had cast Harris out of his Eden: the precise reason changed almost every time O'Shea spoke, dependent upon his mood that particular day. What he never said but what was clear to me was that Harris had simply risen beyond his level of competence. He was habitual to the point of rigidity, totally unimaginative, satisfied to do as little as possible, and to take from life tiny quotidian pleasures. He possessed no skills other than an easy manner with strangers and that slightly aloof respect for books and for the written word provided by an impoverished Jewish childhood on the Lower East Side.

Unlike Harris, O'Shea knew more than authors' names and their previous titles. Jim O'Shea actually read. One benefit of our job that almost compensated for the low pay was that we could buy books at a 25 percent discount. Another was that we could borrow hardcover books as long as plastic covers were kept on them and they were returned in saleable condition.

O'Shea read current nonfiction books by the score; read them slowly, digesting them carefully. He would then discuss them with me during those long, otherwise unoccupied stretches of afternoon. Ideas and theories animated O'Shea. They intrigued him more than people did; they dug deeply into him. In another age, in other circumstances, he might have become a philosopher: he saw life clearly and he saw it whole, he questioned constantly, he spread his wings wide only in the life of his mind, taking in and cogitating say newly published accusations that the U.S. government had advance knowledge of the Japanese attack on Pearl Harbor, or theoretical problems that genetic experimentation would almost certainly entail. He'd bring up each topic unsubtly: "What would you say to the idea that we might someday make perfect copies of ourselves?" or "This guy says the earth is a billion years older than the sun. Older! What do you think of that?" Daring me to reveal my knowledge, my opinions, sometimes I now think my thought processes, watching my face as I replied for signs of something—I was never quite sure of what exactly.

My own talents in this little shop were mostly superficial. I learned fast. My eidetic memory allowed me to find any book instantly on any shelf and I kept up with what was being written and published. Also, my interests in reading filled in O'Shea's gaps: fiction, poetry, drama. And, since I was beginning to think of myself as an apprentice author, I possessed a special affinity with books neither of my older colleagues could boast.

As the holidays neared, O'Shea and I had less time to discuss Lillian Hellman's memoir or the diplomatic revelations of George F. Kennan. Women, teens, holiday shoppers began to fill the shop all the time, demanding our attention, cutting short our disquisitions. I came to know some of the "regulars," businessmen mostly who worked in the area, came to know their interests and tastes well enough to suggest titles.

A House on the Ocean, A House on the Bay

At last I was shown the "office." It turned out to be a small room
with a few folding chairs and a battered desk and was evidently
where Harris napped away afternoons, but more interesting by far
was that it was located two levels below the lower floor of the terminal, approachable only via a metal fire door and steep stairway. The
office was attached to the stockroom, located directly beneath the
other, larger, east side Grand Central bookshop in our chain, about a
block away. A fluorescently lit windowless cell, this stockroom was
a warren of shelves with one largish table for shipping and was operated by a single stock boy, Reuven, a heavy-set, good-natured Hispanic man my age with whom I soon became friendly because he
recognized me as the grass-smoking post-Hippie I'd so recently been
and hoped to once more become.

I shunned the office as far too dreary a place to spend my lunch
hours and late coffee breaks, preferring the many shops in the terminal or even getting a bite and walking around the huge railroad station and, on warmer and sunnier days, neighboring blocks. But as
we neared Christmas, I found myself downstairs rooting around the
stockroom, pulling out larger, more expensive books to sell as gifts,
and in general familiarizing myself with the not very extensive
stock.

It was Reuven who showed me what the narrow staircase continued further down into: a changing room with lockers for workers in
the nearby Oyster Bar, and beyond that, another door and another
staircase down which led even deeper into poorly lit tunnels.
Reuven introduced me to a terminal custodian who told me those
tunnels lay far below the railroad tracks on which thousands of
commuters traveled every day. The tunnels had been hollowed out
during World War II, he said, and were intended to be used in the
event that Manhattan was bombed by the Nazis. He claimed the
tunnels radiated across Midtown, north to Rockefeller Center and
west to Times Square and the Port Authority Station, and could
hold up to 100,000 people. With a huge flashlight in hand, I followed
him through the dim, spotless tunnels for fifteen minutes, and after
ascending many stairways, we emerged into the lobby of the Empire
State Building, eight blocks south.

Later on, when I became more familiar with this downstairs area and more confident about the job and myself, I'd sometimes use the changing room and tunnel (and once the huge empty stairways in the Pan Am Building directly above the terminal) for sexual encounters with men I met during my lunchtime wanderings.

Perhaps the oddest encounter I had at this time was with a handsome blond South African gentleman about thirty years old who would come into our shop regularly looking for a book about Lawrence of Arabia that purported to tell the complete truth about the famous incendiary's masochism. I'd read about the book and knew who published it. We had to order the title, and this man came into the shop almost daily asking for it. He'd talk to me about his own public school upbringing in the same institution as Thomas Edward Shaw, and as he did, he'd back me into a corner of the small shop, behind chest-high shelves. Suddenly, one day, without warning, without even changing his normal tone of voice, he began to ask if I'd ever been "flogged" and when I said no, whether I'd ever flogged anyone. Again I said no, and he asked if I would be interested in flogging someone, say an older fellow, married, well set up, like himself, who'd been flogged by boys at his school and forced to perform "unnatural acts upon their person." Half confused, half amused, I said I might consider it, at which he began to caress my pants front. I thought surely O'Shea would notice, but no, Jim was faced away from us, gabbing with some customer, and the South African went on and on, and I began to think about how to evade him, finding his attitude and fantasizing smarmily unhealthy compared even to my casual ten-minute blow jobs belowground. I managed to get away from him, but he continued to come into the shop when it was otherwise empty trying to corner me again and talk about flogging, but I learned to elude him. After he'd picked up the book he never returned, so I imagined it fed his fantasy life sufficiently.

I'd been hired as temporary help for the holidays only, and I was expecting to work until January 2 or 3, when with my salary and a small bonus, I'd be let go. But some weeks before Christmas my plans were changed for me. While down in the stockroom digging out books to fill depleted displays, I met the manager of both shops, Bob Stiles, and he asked what I was doing. I told him, and he said he was doing the same thing for the much busier East Side shop. He also said the store I was working in was showing its best final quarter ever and he added that Mr. Harris had told him I was an excellent employee. Would I consider remaining on after the holidays?

I hedged and Stiles said he would switch me to the East Side store where he was losing a clerk. He also said I'd get a raise in salary. He reiterated what O'Shea had told me: the West Side shop was a dead end. If I worked for him, Stiles could recommend me for better positions.

Bob Stiles was a tall, unusually elegant man in his late thirties or early forties, good looking in that slightly pinch-featured New England way, well spoken, intelligent, and, as I got to known him better, sharp, witty, and generous. I never found out what he was doing in that shop—a job he'd taken only recently—because, from the fine cut of his tailoring to the expanse of his knowledge he seemed like someone who should have been an Ivy League professor or at least an executive in an old-money Wall Street firm. Later on, I did discover that he was gay and lived with a man his own age not far from me in the West Village. And, though we never socialized, I came to all sorts of romantic conclusions about his past: he'd been living on a trust fund that was mysteriously stopped, or he'd resided in foreign parts until forced back to the States by the death of a parent. Natu-rally, none of this jibed with his obvious ambition and abilities, nor his shrewdness about the company and its internal politics.

A week into the new year, I received a far more substantial bonus than I'd expected and just as Jim O'Shea and I were about to start our long conversations again, I was moved to the East Side shop. Although it was scarcely the length of a football field distant, it turned out to be a huge change. This shop was located on a well-trafficked strip directly from the street into the heart of the railroad station and was busy all the time. Stiles and his assistant, Migdalia, a slender, pale-skinned young woman with a husband and two small sons, had built up the store in the year or so they'd been there. It was twice the size of the other shop and shelves and books were arranged far better. Although there was room for browsers, the books—mostly hardcovers with a smattering of best-seller paperbacks—were arranged to be instantly seen and picked up. And were they ever—customers crowded in during the three rush hours of the day and were often four deep at the cash register. Some popular books were sold out of open cartons that were sent from the main stockroom minutes before the lunch-hour rush.

Gone were long afternoon chats about the value of Zen in the modern world. My talks with my new co-workers were brief, about work, and caught on the fly between customers. And, as Stiles suspected, I filled a gap in this shop. My knowledge of literature and three months' acquaintance with more current books and authors was a godsend to Migdalia, who was not much of a reader herself. My restless nature kept me moving abut the place, improving displays, culling older titles, replacing them with new ones, trying out new sections.

By mid-April, Stiles told me I was due for another raise, and that the past quarter had been 20 percent over the previous year. He attributed this increase to my help. A month later, he asked me to join him for a drink in the Oyster Bar after work. There he confided that he was grooming me to take his job. He had his eye on the large store located in a first-floor corner of the building that housed the Lord & Taylor department store on Fifth Avenue and Thirty-ninth Street, the chain's second largest venue in Manhattan. It was being managed, Stiles said, by a young man who was a protégé of one of the company's officers. Even that shop, though, was merely a stepping stone for him. He intended to end up in that posh Fifth Avenue office where I'd been hired. If I kept up the good work, he'd make sure I followed him. I appreciated his confidence and ambitions for himself and me, but I didn't encourage him. I still wanted to quit as soon as I had enough savings: the longer I worked, the longer that future stretch would be.

The raise arrived, but June 1 came and went and Stiles still hadn't been moved to the Thirty-ninth Street shop as he wanted. Instead, Migdalia was sent to the Upper Fifth Avenue shop as assistant manager and I was promoted and told to train two new employees, one to work with me and one with Jim O'Shea. Harris was taking an early retirement, and O'Shea was being bumped up, over his murmured protests. In the middle of June, when I finally delivered his new employee to the tiny, and to my eyes, now shabby-looking shop on the west side of the terminal, O'Shea said, "Well! You're on your way!" I asked what he was talking about. "You're the one just promoted to manager!" O'Shea just laughed.

I found Stiles in the stockroom. When I asked what the hell was going on, he was brusque. He told me that beginning in one week, I'd be taking over as co-manager of the Thirty-ninth Street store. I was shocked. "Co-manager? What are you talking about? You were supposed to go there as manager."

They couldn't let him go yet, Stiles said. Then he sat down and told me the situation as well as he'd been able to piece it together. The current manager of the Thirty-ninth Street store, the one he'd said was a protégé of someone important, was barely competent, and under his management the shop had done poorly all year. Even so, he'd not been fired or demoted because of the executive's protection. Instead, he'd been warned to shape up the shop. Another bigwig at the main office thought that Sprague had risen from stock boy to manager without enough "floor experience." The two executives had argued, then had cobbled together this co-management business as a compromise.

I hated it the minute I heard it. I told Stiles I wouldn't go. Instead of agreeing with me, Stiles said, "Don't be a fool! You're exactly what's needed to show him up. Go! Let them see what you can do and Sprague should be gone in a few months."

"Then what? You'll come in?" I asked.

Stiles said no, he wanted me in charge there: he was aiming directly for the flagship manager's post. Now that he'd been passed over, nothing in between would do.

"Maybe I should quit altogether," I replied dispiritedly.

Then Stiles told me my new salary, a substantial increase. I'd be able to buy new clothing to replace what had become shabby with wear and cleaning, a second sports jacket, for example, to replace the tweed I'd brought over from London four years before. I'd now be able to go to the movies, even the theatre, which I'd not been able to afford for a while. Stiles told me how big the new store was and how many people worked there. I waffled for two days. Finally, and mostly to please Stiles, I said I'd take the job.

At my brief, tense interview at the main offices with the two executives who'd formulated the plan, I expressed my fears: How

would Sprague feel about someone coming in? They said he wel-
comed it, the work was too much for him alone. Wouldn't we be
getting in each other's way? No, they said, the shop was open 8
A.M. to 8 P.M. Sprague would be there from opening; I'd close up.
We'd be together only noon to four, and Sprague would be out on
lunch one of those hours. I remained unsure, but they were evidently pleased with their solution and couldn't see any insoluble
problem. They ganged up on me, making assurances they couldn't
possibly keep.

A week later, after working at the shop for only five days, I knew
that taking the job was a mistake. At the same time, I saw that the
store needed exactly those attentions I'd given the other shops—
new displays, innovations, a clean up. Even more, it needed a peace-
maker.

All but one of the staff complained to me about Tim Sprague's
ideas, methods of operation, impulsiveness, and personality. All but
one of the dozen employees on the main floor and all four stockroom workers already had had serious run-ins with Sprague. The
stock manager, an older man who'd worked for the company for
decades, seethed with resentment against Sprague—who'd been promoted after only a year in the same position Dorfman had held for
over a decade. By the time I arrived, the head of the small record department at the back of the Thirty-ninth Street store had developed
so complete an antipathy to Sprague, he barely tolerated any of us
"in books" near his area. Among the floor staff, turnover was unbe-
lievable. Six book clerks had each worked for less than two months.
Only the middle-aged Mrs. Schirm hadn't had a fight with Sprague.

Who was the cause of all this contention? A well-put-together as-
piring actor of about twenty-four who dressed casually, talked and
acted like most of my friends, was clearly gay, who'd gush on fifteen
minutes at a time about the latest Sondheim musical or foreign
film, and who at times could be fun. From the Midwest with only a
hint of an accent, his long legs were those of a rancher, or as it
turned out, a dancer. With regular features and all-American looks,
he might have been handsome, if it weren't for his large, protruding
brown eyes.

Alas for Tim Sprague, he'd been spoiled back home, told he was the best (which could have been true—there!), got used to being treated by teachers, family, and friends as someone special. It had gone to his head. He'd clearly come to New York expecting to take over lead parts—or at least male ingenue leads—on Broadway. When that didn't happen, he'd been more than disappointed, he'd been offended to the core. When he'd been forced to take a low-pay bookstore job, he saw it as an insult. When he'd been promoted to manager, he saw it as only fair, though still far below his talents and abilities.

He was wrong. If anyone had been promoted out of his range of competence, it was Sprague. It wasn't that he knew next to nothing about books and authors, an infinitesimal bit more about how to display, and virtually nothing about how to handle people. The problem was more serious and threefold.

First, Sprague was an actor and he possessed an actor's temperament. He flew off the handle at the least provocation; he caused drama wherever he went; he was bored unless something theatrical was going on. Fine if you're onstage or even backstage, but sheer death in the sedate world of bookselling. Second, Sprague knew he was in Dutch, knew I'd been brought in to shore him up, and being the prima donna he was, he resented it, resented me, resented anything lessening his power and position. At the same time, he'd say in front of the staff, "God, you're helping tons!" and "You're so useful!" to save what he erroneously thought he retained of face among them. Last, Sprague knew he was in the wrong job, yet was determined to perservere, come hell or high water.

I discussed all this with Bob Stiles. He clearly hadn't thought the situation would be as difficult as it had turned out and was feeling guilty about advising me to take the job. He did say one witty, if unhelpful thing. "What Sprague doesn't understand is that to be a prima donna, it's not enough to be a donna." Stiles advised me to hang in, stay cool, calm down the staff, work quietly in the background. Ditto *I Ching*, which advised me that I was "like a girl taken into the family but not as a chief wife and who must behave with special caution and reserve," and not supplant the former mistress which would lead to disorder.

My first new paycheck suggested I do the same. For the first time since I'd worked for *Graphique* a few years before, I actually had something left over after paying bills and debts. At first I contented myself with lying low and looking around. I got to know the staff: Dan Pritch, the peppery young record man who knew pop, rock, and jazz inside out and was easy to befriend: I'd simply talk about records and music. Carl Dorfman, the aging linebacker in the stockroom, was less easy, so I merely presented myself in his large, well-organized demesne not as Sprague always did—flying down there with a blown-out-of-proportion problem or impending disaster. Through subtle comparisons with stockrooms I'd been in, I let Dorfman know his was best.

Our office manager and accountant was a bibulous white-haired man who seemed apparently beyond retirement age. He appeared to have bought his clothing wholesale before the last World War and was determined to use it until it was worn through, although the vests and trousers were now far too tight for his postwar girth and buttons were constantly snapping off, eliciting form him a sound somewhat between a snicker and a sigh. Mr. Threems existed in a world of numbers and whisky labels and could only be seen at his desk, where he was surrounded by calculators of various sizes united only by their great vintage. His desk was located on the small balcony, a former display mezzanine above one edge of the shop, converted into an open-air office for himself, Sprague, and me.

Among the book clerks the only one worth cultivating was Antonia Schirm, who looked like a shorter version of Joan Crawford, a fact she must have been aware of, since she cosmeticized herself to resemble the film star, then downplayed it by wearing frilly, ultra-feminine dresses with natural shoulders. Amid all the postpubescent young women who came and went from the store during the time I was there, Mrs. Schirm was solid as the Lincoln Memorial. She'd worked there for years, knew people all over the next-door Lord & Taylor where she shopped during lunch hours, and though she talked little about her home life, I got the impression she worked not because she had to but for shopping money and to pass the time. A loyal woman, she'd only recently transferred her fealty from the semimythical previous manager, Mr. Ripton, to Sprague, so at first she was cautious and discreet around me. But she was reliable and knowledgeable, and the more we worked together the friendlier we became. Like the "superior man" of the *I Ching* that I was studying so assiduously in those days, Mrs. Schirm saw much and let many things pass. When she finally realized that Sprague—along with the shop and her job—was headed for destruction, she took my side, advising me in her quiet, contralto voice, making much use of deep green, reptilian-lidded eyes. By then it was too late for any of us.

I'd arrive at noon, in time for Sprague to barely get out a greeting before he went to lunch. He'd return at 1:00, when Mrs. Schirm left. However, he seldom took her place at the front desk, but remained on the balcony or charged around the store doing something seemingly important. In reality he was finding new ways to shore up his authority and irritate the staff. I went for lunch at 3:00 and when I returned, Sprague would have made up an entire list of things for the "staff" to do. Since by that time of day we were only one young woman, Mrs. Schirm, and myself, I ended up doing the difficult jobs. Sprague would sweep out for the day at 4 P.M. and I'd spend the next hour going around the store listening to complaints, calming troubled waters, and consoling the victim of Sprague's latest tongue-lashing.

By the time I'd arrived the next day, all had been in vain: someone had quit, someone had told Sprague off and been fired. And I'd begin the Sisyphean task again. The one time I suggested Sprague use me as an intermediary with the staff, he looked at me in surprise, then asked, "Why would I do that?"

I must have stared in shock at him for a full minute at such a complete lack of awareness before I said, "Forget it."

Somehow we all made it through as the late spring and summer settled on the city, business slackened, and I began—with Sprague's grudging approval—to change displays. His interest in theatre meant he'd ordered many oversized, higher-priced books that looked good but sold poorly. I built these into a real entertainment section, ordered other titles to fluff it, and talked Sprague into window displays whenever special film and theatre books came out. I'd discovered that our customers—unlike those at Grand Central who were mostly men and on the run and preferred nonfiction best-sellers—were women who shopped at Lord & Taylor and dropped in for novels. I beefed up our fiction, mysteries, and science fiction, and ordered classic American and European fiction and called it "summer vacation reading." I got Dan Pritch to order classical records and made him intersperse Albinoni and Handel with *Highway 61* and *Let It Bleed*. And to placate Sprague, whenever a Broadway musical was released on LP, I got Pritch to feature the album.

It required infinite patience. I ran into both overt and covert resistance at every step. Often I'd be high up on ladders washing shelves, making changes, retouching paint, and cleaning the ornate brass sconces long after the shop closed. By late August, however, when Sprague went on a weeklong vacation, I felt I'd kept revolution at bay as well as improving the shop.

That week was so very relaxing that even Mrs. Schirm was forced to admit that Sprague might not always be right—as he invariably thought. When the company officer whose protégé Sprague was dropped in unexpectedly one day, he approved of the changes. The store's profits had begun to slowly rise. I was exactly the right person for the job.

Though I didn't like or trust him, and knew that anything I'd say would be misconstrued, and even guessed what his response would be, I asked to be transferred.

He became red faced. No, it was impossible.

I told him that I'd worked months to pour oil on the waters roiling between Sprague and the staff, and the result was Sprague was turning his need for conflict on me. "He treats me like dirt in front of customers and clerks. I'm not getting paid enough for that treatment. If it doesn't change, I'm quitting."

He told me to calm down, he'd talk with Sprague as soon as he returned.

I was well aware of Sprague's combination of paranoia and arrogance. "That's the worst thing you could do. He'll just take it as an attack."

No, the executive assured me, he knew how to handle Sprague.

I was barely over this disturbing-enough visit when I found myself face to face with an equally difficult one. A man I'd been seeing the previous year came into the store. With him was a young woman. They were evidently together and were acting like lovers. Now this same man who was so cozy with this statuesque redhead had chased me for six months, phoning me and asking me out continually. I'd finally given in, mostly out of a feeling of "enough already." Although we were not really sexually compatible, he was intensely passionate whenever we were together, which couldn't help but flatter me. And although he was neurotic about having sex with men and unconsciously homophobic (as were many then), in other ways he was quite genial, even a bit charismatic, and above all intriguing. He was into Zen meditation, astrology, and Chinese language and literature—all things that intensely interested me at the time—so we hung out together. This lasted with various ups and downs until he dumped me by leaving the country for the summer and letting me know he was doing so by calling me from the airport a few minutes before his flight left. I felt I'd gone overboard for six months to adapt my physical needs as well as my true self to his requirements, and I was furiously angry with him and myself for allowing myself to be exploited by him.

At the shop, he introduced me to his woman friend and he was so open, made such a big deal out of what good friends he and I had been, that I felt he was going out of his way to use her to erase in his own mind what had happened between us, i.e., a failed love affair. It was all I could do to keep from decking him right there in the shop. Evidently I succeeded, because a few weeks later when he appeared at a party along with some guy in full leather he was obviously with, he again acted as though nothing had happened between us. He was astonished when I shoved him into a vacant bedroom, slammed him against the wall, told him he was a contemptible worm, and, poking him in the chest again and again, said New York City wasn't big enough for the two of us, did he understand? Apparently he finally got the message. He left for Los Angeles soon after and has only returned since on short visits.

*   *   *

Sprague returned from vacation tanned and loose limbed, relaxed and cheerful. He hummed under his breath one or another of the vast array of Broadway tunes in his repertoire. He didn't harass or irritate a single clerk. That lasted all of two days.

When I arrived the third morning he wasn't there. Just before she went to lunch Mrs. Schirm told me Sprague had been called to the main office by his protector. This was just after Labor Day and we were busy, mostly fending off high-school students looking for textbooks we didn't sell.

Sprague returned looking uptight—his usual expression around the shop so I thought nothing of it, not even when he dropped back down from his balcony office and began going around straightening out displays that were already quite straight and waiting on customers though he knew the stock so poorly he ended up having to refer most of them to me. When I left for lunch, he was behind the large wooden semicircular counter, despite the fact that Mrs. Schirm and two other book clerks were already on the floor. Perhaps it was the memory of my conversation with the executive, but Sprague did seem to be trying to prove something—and doing an awkward job of it.

I returned from lunch early and went up to the balcony to read. He came upstairs and kept doing things around my desk until I got the hint that he wanted to talk to me.

Although he apologized for disturbing my "free time," Sprague sat a desk away and very red-faced blurted out, "I spoke to Mr. _____ and he said you're not happy here."

I thought that was apparent and said nothing. Sprague got redder: "I don't see why you couldn't tell me first."

"It's actually none of your business," I replied.

"None of my . . . ?" he was ready to explode.

"You didn't transfer me here. Mr. _____ did. At the time of the transfer I said I didn't want to come here. In truth, I didn't want to work for the chain at all. I'm a writer. I shouldn't be wasting my time here. I should be writing!"

His face went through a series of emotions. "Well, sure," he half laughed, half snorted, "and I should be on stage, singing and dancing!"

"When I moved here," I replied, "I said I'd try it out for a few months. I have and now I want out. That's what I told Mr. _____."

"He told me you didn't like working under me," Sprague managed to get his one and only point out.

"I don't. I want to work for myself."

"Mr. _____ said you didn't like the way I'm treating you," he said. My answers that did not directly concern him meant nothing to him.

"I was told I'd be co-manager here. Once I was here, suddenly I was *assistant* manager. Evidently you and I were told different things. I don't like being lied to, or demoted before I even get in the door."

This made some impression on Sprague, who obviously could see himself in my shoes. "Yes . . . I understand." Then, ego rampant once more, "Still, you shouldn't go around saying I'm not treating you well. It reflects badly on me."

That was the only thing he cared about. I was silent.

"I know we have our differences," he tried in a less aggrieved tone of voice, "and now that I understand the source . . . I was never told you'd be co-manager here."

In fact, I believed the two executives had lied to us. "This doesn't solve the problem. I want to transfer."

"Mr. _____ said he has no positions open on your level and no one to replace you here. Maybe soon at the Wall Street shop . . ."

I'd seen that shop, a three-man shoe box. "No way!"

"Well, there's nothing open. So you'll just have to make the best of it," Sprague added in his best snooty-nine-year-old-girl tone of voice that so annoyed me.

"Or . . . I can quit."

I knew the personnel office had been after Sprague about all the staff who'd quit and been fired. Stiles told me that the attrition rate from this shop alone equaled all the tri-state area stores together. If I quit that too would reflect badly on Sprague, not to mention what my leaving would do to store profits and Sprague's position here once he was on his own again.

"How will you live?" he asked with an Actors Studio expression of "concern."

"I'll manage. I have before."

Sprague got red faced again and I thought he was about to warn me about trying to blackmail him or some such theatric, which I do believe he was actually thinking. Instead, he said rather airily, "Do whatever you want," and flounced off the balcony.

Our accountant, Mr. Threems, looked up. His desk was six feet away and he'd heard the entire conversation. What he next said made me realize that he not only listened, but he also understood the implications of what was said. This surprised me, as I'd always considered him so totally out of it all.

"Beware. That one *must* have his way!"

"So did Napoleon," I said. "And look how he ended up."

Thus began the final standoff between Sprague and me. It lasted three months. For a few days after our talk, Sprague actually seemed to turn human. He began to chat me up, drawing on whatever few common threads he believed existed between us, showing me articles in magazines, asking if I'd seen Sondheim's latest (*Follies*—I had and thought it fabulous!) and waxing enthusiastic about it. He did this all in the same awkward and slapdash manner as he did everything else in the store. He also displaced his irritation at how life was mistreating him from me back to Dan Pritch in records. One afternoon, Sprague made a big deal about leaving early, making sure I knew he was auditioning for a new Broadway show. The implication being if he got it, he'd quit—or go on leave— leaving me the store's problems: i.e., a turnaround of my own threat.

I bided my time, building up my savings account. I'd decided to leave by Thanksgiving, and when some chance errand brought me to Grand Central Station, I mentioned it to Stiles. He shook his head.

"Worst time, beginning of the Christmas season. Stay till January, collect your holiday bonus, then leave. Or," he added, hinting at some knowledge he'd picked up from his frequent contacts at the main office, "maybe by then, *he'll* be gone." Meaning Sprague.

For us the holiday season began before Thanksgiving. By mid-September we were were ordering from scores of publishers' winter list catalogues. In a nod to my greater knowledge of stock, and I suspect to make me feel more like co-manager, Sprague actually dropped catalogues on my desk after he'd gone through them and marked orders. "Go over these, will you." But he couldn't help but undercut even this, adding, "In pencil!" Meaning he'd reconsider what I'd ordered.

I never found out if he was called back to the audition. He never brought it up. He did have a boyfriend begin picking him up at the store, a colorless fellow, nondescript foil to Sprague's own flash and glitter. He even introduced me once. His now endless phone calls with this guy spelled the end—thank God!—of Sprague's stumbling efforts to befriend me.

What Sprague didn't know was that it also lost him his last ally in the store. Mrs. Schirm waited several weeks. One afternoon as Sprague and his pal left the store, chatting and laughing in what looked even to me like a painful caricature of campy homosexual behavior, Mrs. Schirm turned to me, her eyes even more hooded than usual, and said, "I don't care what people do on their own time. I *don't* think they should do it during business hours."

I'd never told her about my private life, and I know that in other circumstances I would have defended another gay, pointing out that this *was* after business hours. But I knew what she meant. Sprague was going out of his way to display this relationship and it offended her. So I kept my mouth shut. Next time Sprague's boyfriend came in to pick him up, she smirked at me and gestured a limp wrist.

Even so, she was a prudent woman and so it wasn't until mid-October that Sprague openly alienated her. Before the large Christmas book stock arrived was deemed the best time to take annual inventory. It was a horrendous, time-consuming job everyone dreaded. We had to come in all day one Sunday and tick off by price every book and record in the shop. In previous years, Mrs. Schirm had gotten the day off because she was a deaconess of her church. When she reminded Sprague of this, he hit the roof. We were short staffed, he told her. We needed all the help we could get, and she could miss one Sunday in church.

Mrs. Schirm stormed down from the balcony. It took me all day to find out what had happened. I called Bob Stiles, told him, and he managed to get both Reuven from stock and Jim O'Shea to come in and help inventory our shop in place of Mrs. Schirm. Having learned to be diplomatic, I made Stiles phone Sprague directly and say they wanted to earn the double-time pay if we needed help. Sprague told Bob he'd think about it, then dashed down from the balcony to ask me if I knew them and what help they'd be. I said they were fine, and he dashed back up and asked for them. He never knew I'd set it up. Mrs. Schirm, however, got wind of it when they came and she got the day off and she instantly let me know. Her comment was blunt: "That's what he should have done. He's a terrible manager. You ought to be . . ." She didn't finish.

October went by more or less quietly at the store. The bloom of Sprague's early love had passed and he was more annoying to us than ever. But he also seemed distracted by other matters, and the more experienced staff had by then learned to half ignore him.

Sometime in early November, I again had reason to be at the Grand Central shop and talked to Stiles. He told me at the beginning of the year he was moving to Washington, D.C., to head up the three company shops there. That decided me. The following day, I called the main office and arranged a meeting later that week with one of the two executives who'd transferred me: not Sprague's protector, but the other one.

He was curt with me, as though he already knew what I was about to say. At first he acted as devil's advocate, taking his colleague's side and pointing out how all seemed to be working out at our shop: sales were up for the two quarters I'd been there. My problems with Sprague had been discussed with him and everything was better now, wasn't it?

I told him everything stunk. I was quitting.

He offered me the managership of both Grand Central shops once Stiles left.

I told him my father had health problems, which was true, and that I might have to take over his business, which was not true. I'd try to work through the holidays, because that meant such a big deal to the company. What kind of letter of resignation did he need?

He told me to stop at the personnel desk and arrange it. I did it immediately, feeling free already. As I was leaving the personnel office, I met up with the man again. He was leaving for lunch. He told me with a half wink that he wasn't telling anyone I'd quit. Not Sprague, not Mr. _____. He hoped I would be equally discreet. He was evidently planning it to be some kind of intraoffice bombshell. Fine with me.

Sprague was determined to make this usually profitable time of year even more profitable and as we neared Thanksgiving, he became his old self again, running clerks off their feet on minuscule errands, shouting over the least error, carrying on over everyday screwups, and declaring at one point that we were all undermining him, trying to make him look bad.

After that, I was ready to quit on the spot. Only Mrs. Schirm's pleading kept me from going upstairs to tell Sprague he was a deranged queen and needed psychiatric help, fast. Two days later, after another outburst, I did: I said to his face, "You are really sick!"

He was dumbfounded. He stood rocking back and forth on his heels as though I'd struck him. I pushed past him and down to the stockroom. An hour later, he caught me on the balcony and began shouting, "How dare you speak to me like that in front of staff?"

Although there was plenty I could say, I merely replied, "My father throws fits like you all the time. That's how he got a stroke."

"I could fire you right now."

"Go ahead. I could use the unemployment." I left him steaming.

"Careful," Mrs. Schirm warned me. Later on, she added, "That kind is very dangerous when they're crossed." What kind? Actors? Homosexuals?

"I don't care," I said. That was the second warning. But I knew I'd soon be free of Sprague and I was heedless, giddy with impending freedom.

*　　*　　*

Closing the shop meant getting the customers out, then getting the staff out. The front door on Fifth Avenue had a time lock, as did the back door. Once the front was locked it wasn't to be opened till the next morning.

I would count and have someone else—usually Mrs. Schirm— check my counting of the "book register" cash, then get the "records register" and check that over with Pritch looking on. I'd remove the register rolls and compare them to what cash was actually there. Then I'd add up charges and compare them to the register tab. Often this process took a half hour because of corrections and screwups that had to be accommodated.

Once I'd more or less justified these, I'd fill out an accounting sheet, wrap the paper money in it, lock each cash drawer shut, then bring it all up to the balcony safe. If Threems was there he'd usually take it from me. Often he was gone, and I'd have to open the safe and put the drawers inside and lock it up again. Once this was done, it was another few minutes to look over the displays, shut off all but the night-lights, and leave by the back door. As a rule, I wasn't alone in the store longer than five minutes at night.

I'd been doing this task either at the Grand Central shop or at this shop since the beginning of the year, i.e., eleven months. It was habitual, rote, and the only thing that changed from night to night was the actual reconciliation of cash, which despite checking always seemed to be off a few dollars. This despite the fact that Sprague generally closed out both registers when he left at 4:00, so that there was barely $500 in the shop at night, an amount deemed so small, we'd all been advised that if anyone tried to hold us up with a weapon, we were to give them the money, and not get hurt.

That Saturday evening in late November was in no way different from any other night, except that as I got to the back door, I saw that it was raining outside. The door was already slammed shut behind me, so I had to open it and go back in to get my umbrella upstairs on the balcony.

The following Monday, when I got into work, the atmosphere seemed subtly changed. Sprague was on the phone when I went upstairs to put away my street clothing. Threems never looked up, and left the balcony when Sprague gestured for me to stay.

He was calm. "The cash from Saturday night is missing."

I turned toward the safe. It was not broken into. "What?"

"When I got in this morning," Sprague said, "I found both drawers on Mr. Threem's desk in front of the safe. The charges were there. All the cash was gone."

"That's impossible! I put it all in the safe and locked it up as I do every night."

He was very calm. "Maybe you were distracted. Got a phone call or something and forgot you left the drawers on his desk."

"No, no distraction." I was about to say that if that were so, surely when I came back in for my umbrella I would have seen the drawers on the desk. But something told me not to let Sprague know this detail. "I distinctly recall opening the safe and putting them in."

His calmness vanished. "Well they weren't there when I opened up today. The two drawers were on Threem's desk and the cash was gone."

Shocked as I was, I said, "Assuming I did leave them out, who could have taken the cash? I was the last person out of here."

As I spoke, even to me it sounded totally incriminating. To my surprise, Sprague didn't jump on this and accuse me of theft. He merely shrugged and said, "The cleaning crew came in after you."

"When?"

"It'll be on the door time-lock tape."

I thought, *now* he'll say I came back for the money.

He didn't. Which meant he hadn't seen the time-lock tape.

"Isn't it possible," Sprague began to insist, once more calm, "that you were distracted by something when you brought them up here, left them on Threem's desk, then forgot them?"

"I'd still see them when I got my coat and bag as I left."

"But wasn't it dark up here?"

Not that dark. I couldn't for the life of me think what he was after. I'd opened the safe, put the drawers in, closed it again. "How much was taken?" I asked.

"How should I know?"

"The total of the two registers was . . . four hundred and eighty," I recalled. "What about the other drawers in the safe?" I asked, meaning the ones he'd put in.

"They were fine. You *had* to have left yours out. You were distracted. Your father's sick, isn't he? Hospitalized? Maybe you got a call about him and—"

"I don't use the shop's telephone. Even for emergencies."

He lost his temper. "Well it's gone and it's your responsibility."

His phone rang and he took it and from his tone of voice I knew he was speaking to someone in the main office. Although I moved away I could hear him say, "He's no help. He's sure he put them in the safe." The rest of the call was too quiet for me to hear. Once he'd hung up, he turned to me. "This is very serious."

"I'll say. Has anyone thought to contact the cleaners?"

He shrugged. Then he said, "You're going to have to go to the main office and talk to security there."

"I'll go right now," I said, putting my coat back on.

"It can wait till after lunch."

I fully expected to be arrested at the main office. The two men who met with me simply asked me to recall what happened Saturday night, to go over it step by step. I did, as carefully as I could.

"That's all?" one asked.

"I think so. I do this six nights a week."

"You didn't do anything different that night?"

"No . . . Wait! I did. I came back to get my umbrella because it was storming out. A second after I closed the back door."

They looked at each other. "That showed up on the time-lock tape. We wondered about it."

Meaning they'd hoped to catch me in something.

"I went up to the balcony, got the umbrella, and left again. Two, three minutes at the most," I said. "I'm sure the time-lock tape will corroborate that. And that it *wasn't* enough time to open the safe, unlock the cash drawers, and relock the safe again," I added, just in case they hadn't yet gotten the point.

They asked me to wait. Sprague's protector came in, the two men left, and I apologized for all the trouble.

He seemed upset, but restraining himself. So I repeated that I had no idea how it happened. To my surprise, he took the same line Sprague had. Obviously they'd discussed it in detail before I arrived at work. Once again, I said, "No, I don't think I was so distracted that I would have passed the drawers on the desk. Even if I'd missed them before, when I returned for my umbrella I would have noticed them."

"That's what security thinks," he said, gloomily.

"You can take it out of my salary. Get someone else to close out the registers instead of me."

"The money isn't relevant. Barely five hundred dollars."

That would have been my entire remaining salary less taxes and the bonus I doubtless was not going to receive now.

He read the statement I'd written for security and frowned.

A minute later he was back to how it must have happened, asking me all over again about my father's illness, saying I might have been tired—late at night, end of the work week—on and on, until I said, sure it was possible, anything was. "None of us believe you took it," he added.

That was a relief.

"But if it was the night cleaning staff," he said, "we'll never see it again."

I didn't even know we had a night cleaning staff and said so, adding, "I sweep every night. It's no cleaner the next day."

He sighed. I was hopeless. Or the situation was hopeless.

I again offered to work off the amount missing.

"No. You'd better just collect your stuff from the shop."

Meaning I was fired.

"You'll get whatever is due you, including vacation pay."

A week was due me. Even so, I was shocked by the suddenness, the finality, and by what it said: I'd fucked up good.

"I think you'd do yourself a service by writing down what we just discussed," he said, handing me a pad of yellow foolscap.

Now I was angry and resentful. "Writing down what?"

"Your father's illness . . . possible distraction."

"I don't know what good that'll do. Unless it's intended for me to admit incompetence. I remember putting the drawers *inside* the safe."

He stood up, leaned across the desk, threatening me with further investigation, the police, all sorts of things. I was scared but I held firm.

He left the room to take a phone call. As I was writing, the other executive came into the room, picked up the report, and said, "He thinks you're being unreasonable."

I told him what Mr. _____ had asked me to write.

"He needs that for the insurance company," he explained.

"Wait a minute!" I had an idea. "Isn't there a timer on the safe, too? That would show when I opened and closed it."

"Maybe. But not whether you put the drawers inside. Let's think about this," he said. He sat down and seemed to do just that. Finally, he surprised me by saying, "Well, they've got us. For the minute."

What was he talking about? "I'll say. I'm fired."

"You were quitting anyway."

"It's different."

"Don't worry. I'll make sure you get a bonus. All this is partly my fault," he said, as though talking to himself. "If I'd let them know you were quitting, maybe . . ." He stood up to go.

"I appreciate the bonus, but he said the police—"

"No police. It's only petty larceny."

I was beginning to get a glimmer of what he was thinking. Not much, because I was still so deeply shocked and panicked, but a glimmer.

"Tell you what, write out what he wanted. *I'll* notate your personnel file so all this doesn't follow you."

The man on the white horse. But why? I didn't dare ask.

"Call me if anyone does bother you. Your final paycheck will take about a month. Sorry about that. Otherwise you're free to go."

I left and walked straight down to the Thirty-ninth Street shop, collected my gear, and left. No one said goodbye except Mrs. Schirm, whose hooded eyes glanced up at the balcony as she wished me luck.

*   *   *

Those ensuing days of unexpected freedom weren't happy. At first, I kept expecting the police to arrest me, or at least to come and question me. But when none came, I slowly moved on with my life. The final paycheck arrived after Christmas, but the bonus wasn't as large as I'd been led to expect. Still, it was something. A friend said I should apply for unemployment, which I did in January, when I knew bookstores wouldn't be hiring anyone. After weeks of waiting, I was told that my claim had been rejected: Sprague said that I'd quit. He'd sent my letter of resignation as proof. I thought of killing him. Then I thought, fuck him. If he wants to make bad karma he'll get bad karma.

I had no clue how bad that karma would be. Over a year later, I unexpectedly met Bob Stiles on lower Fifth Avenue and he said, "Have we got things to talk about."

He took me for a drink in Feathers's porched-over bar. He'd been back some months. "Were you lucky to get out when you did!"

"Lucky me!" I toasted him with my drink.

"No, really! After you left, Mr. _____ placed another assistant in the Thirty-ninth Street shop, and it was the same thing all over again."

"You expected Sprague to change?" I asked. "Especially after he'd succeeded in getting rid of me?"

"Not just his temper and acting out," Stiles said. "What Mr. _____ didn't know was that security itself sent in the assistant. And guess what?"

"Security? What do you mean?"

"They suspected him all the time," Stiles said. "And what happened to you seemed so blatant to them."

"Bob! What are you talking about?"

"The new assistant found Sprague dipping into the till!" Stiles said gleefully. "And not pennies either. Sprague was fired. The Thirty-ninth Street shop was shut down. It's a franchise of some drugstore chain now."

It was all too much for me. "How was he stealing?"

"I have an idea, but they wouldn't tell me."

"And he was caught?"

"Red-handed. You see, what security couldn't figure out was since you'd already handed in your resignation *before* the incident of the missing cash, why would you endanger your last weeks? And when you told them you returned for your umbrella, that seemed to confirm your honesty, as well as how good your memory was. That's when they began to suspect it was a frame-up."

I couldn't take it all in. "Then . . . Sprague took that cash?"

"He didn't know you were quitting. He was sure you'd replace him. He had to do something to get you out. I guess it was only later on he decided he liked having pocket money. And of course, that's what got him."

Stiles knew all this because he had moved from D.C. into the main office. In fact, he'd taken over Mr. _____'s job. That executive, quite tarnished by championing Sprague, had taken an early retirement.

We celebrated with another drink. Later on I was able to put it all together: the office politics, executives manipulating two younger men. How deeply in Sprague's protector had been forced to go for his sake. How delicately but soundly the other executive had used me. Why he'd said, "They've got us. For the minute." Realizing he'd need security to join the game. It was all that I'd feared about capitalism and company politics: it made me want to throw up.

More than a year passed before I happened to see Sprague on the Eighth Avenue subway. He was with two other obviously gay "gipsies," i.e., Broadway show dancers. He was dressed casually, with a dance bag over one shoulder. He looked good. Relaxed, almost—save for those eyes—handsome. The three men were so busy gabbing he didn't see me. They all got off together at Fiftieth Street. He must have gotten a part in a show.

I was feeling content and generous that day and thought, "Well, maybe we've both got what we want now . . ." Though Sprague had left the train and the doors had closed and I could see him walking up to the street, I still found myself saying aloud in Eva Gabor's accent, "But you're *still* an evil kveen!"

*   *   *

So there I was, without a job or much money. I appealed the Unemployment Bureau's decision, but was unable to get a copy of my resignation letter from the company's personnel office to show that it was planned to go into effect in early January, while I'd been let go in late November. My one phone call to the executive at the company who had said he would help me went unanswered. I counted up my savings and saw that I had enough for perhaps six frugal months ahead, if I could find occasional odd jobs for extra cash.

While I'd still been at the Thirty-ninth Street store planning my escape, I'd hoped to use this period to do important writing as well as a great deal of reading and thinking. Several friends whose opinion I valued suspected I was talented, or at least had great potential, but I'd so far done little to show it.

The one fallback I supposedly still had for making extra money to support myself while I was becoming a writer—astrology—was one I was quite conflicted about using. In fact, it was my decision to stop doing professional astrology that had sent me to work in the little Grand Central Terminal bookstore.

That decision had grown not merely out of questions of whether or not it was ethical to make money from doing astrology, not even from whether it was right for a young man like myself to be advising other—often older—people on their lives, when I couldn't seem to pull my own life together. More important than either of those questions was a philosophical one: whether or not I believed astrology to be just another tool for discovering people's psychological makeup and tendencies toward certain actions, or whether I believed it to be far more: a symbolic language to a completely predetermined life, past, present, and future, decipherable yet utterly unalterable.

Like most young people in the 1960s, I'd vaguely read about astrology, but it wasn't until later that it assumed any importance in my life. Among the many, many people introduced to me by Jan Rosenberry from 1968 to 1970 was a group of hip young astrologers who used to meet in a large loft in Manhattan's Flower District. Like everything Jan involved himself in, he threw himself into astrology with all-consuming, intense passion. And, like everything he involved himself in, Jan would instantly apply whatever he learned to those close to him (Arnie, Margaret, Achim, and I were all "charted" by Jan) and then Jan would attempt to involve us equally deeply. By the time this had usually happened, Jan was off on some new other fascinating tangent or entirely new trip.

When Jan read my birth chart he said, among other things, "According to this, you'd make a super astrologer. Come with me next Thursday to Wayne and Tony's."

So I joined him at the loft, met Wayne, Tony, and their friends and students, and became very interested in the new system of astrology they were using. It was invented by a German named Alfred Witte during World War I and was called Uranian astrology. Witte had devised it to try to explain and to predict battles and other such bellicose incidents he was witnessing and reading about daily. These events appeared to be unaccounted for by the standard astrological practices. One new—and controversial—aspect of Witte's system was that it posited eight "planets," or points of stellar influence, beyond the known worlds of our solar system. Each point was thought to have its own unique characteristic, which added greater depth, complexity, and sophistication to readings than was done in the usual Ptolemaic system. Witte argued that planets were being discovered all the time. Supporting his theory was the fact that Pluto was found during Witte's own lifetime, and only a few years before our meetings in the Twenty-seventh Street loft, the little planetoid Chiron was discovered orbiting between Uranus and Saturn.

Witte became so intent on the exact timing of invasions and guerilla actions, of counteroffensives and explosions, that he'd also developed a new way to time events: using "wheels" overlayed upon the traditional twelve constellations and divisions of the conventional horoscope: a 90-degree wheel that operated much like a slide rule, and another 360-degree wheel that instantly provided midpoints between the planets (where their influence supposedly combined and so was strongest). These precise points he felt were more important than old-fashioned "good" or "bad" aspects. Anyone who mastered this complicated new system, like Witte's apprentice Hans Niggeman who by then was in his eighties and living in the Bronx, could allegedly predict not only what would happen with great detail, but also when—to the minute.

Like Jan, I obtained the various tools and Ephemerides needed to learn Witte's system and studied my own chart and those of friends and family in depth. Although I never fell into the obsession with exact timing of some of the others at Wayne and Tony's, I soon began to feel comfortable enough to do fairly accurate readings. When Jan and Arnie went to California a year later never to return, someone I knew mentioned that another astrology study group was meeting on Fifty-seventh Street. Although this group didn't use the Uranian system, they did propound other "modern" ways to look at astrology, including "charting" incidents—government takeovers, airline disasters, anything really—as though they were births and using those charts to unravel details and even mysteries. In one of our classes, for example, we charted the mass murder in Los Angeles of actress Sharon Tate and her houseguests shortly after it was reported. Using our methods, we'd already determined that the crime had been done by some underground group or cult, that the assailants and the victims were not known to each other, that drugs were in use at the time, and various other details that wouldn't emerge until Manson's trial began, a year and a half later.

It was the leader of this second group of astrologers, Richard, who suggested I try it professionally and who sent me my first clients. I was surprised by how good I turned out to be at this, using both the methods I'd learned and some intuition. Surprised most of all by how unerringly accurate I sometimes was, not so much about character and personality, but about actual life situations—which is what most people really wanted to know about anyway. The first time it happened I was looking at a young stranger's chart and going around the chart section by section, and I said, quite casually, "By the way, if you're involved in anything illegal, I'd hold back for the next six months."

I moved on to something else. But a minute later, he said, "Uh, about that illegal business you mentioned? Why would I hold back?" To which I answered, "Because your birth chart shows both illegal activity and possible imprisonment, and those areas are all highlighted in the next six months." At the same time I realized he was probably doing something I didn't consider immoral like dealing grass or hallucinogens, but which was after all illegal and for which he could be busted for a long time. He'd been pretty laid back until then. Suddenly he asked about his girlfriend—what did I see there? I looked at the appropriate areas and saw something odd. "Is she planning an abortion?" To which he said, "Wow! Too much, man!"

Obviously, he recommended me to people, and with some, I again came up with remarkable discoveries, while with others, it was all more generalized. Luckily lots of my clients were young and interested in "finding theselves"—sexually, socially, and in careers—for which astrology was pretty useful at offering likely areas of interest. Even so, every once in a while someone would come along and I'd find myself really challenged about what I was doing. What I *thought* I was doing was being New Age and Aquarian, using this "tool" as anyone would use any other tool to help folks gain knowledge and live a better life. It was Jeannie Owens who threw all that in the deepest of chiaroscuro relief.

A friend and patron of Jay Weiss (she bought his paintings), Jeannie was in her early fifties at the time, but like a variety of older people who hung out with the younger crowd, hip and "together." A tall, statuesque woman, when I met her she was a beauty in ruins, heavyset, walking with the aid of a cane. During the course of the astrological reading I did, I asked if she'd been an athlete. She had been—a speed swimmer—and that was why she needed a cane. Sometime during the Olympic Games in Mexico she'd gone diving with other swimmers and had been dashed against a rock, where she'd sustained a hipbone injury. During the next decade and a half, she'd needed increasing doses of painkillers, including shots of cortisone. As a result, her hipbone had dissolved. Horrified, I went through her chart carefully, trying to find some way to alleviate her suffering.

Evidently I struck a nerve. A month later she phoned me. She had noted down from my reading that hydrotherapy was beneficial, and also that she ought to look into any radical, experimental treatments. One had arisen: a hipbone replacement with a new kind of plastic. She would have to strengthen her muscles beforehand and had already begun water therapy, which seemed to be working. Should she look into the new replacement method? Looking at her chart, I advised her to go ahead full steam. And I told her to look into foreign therapies and gave her some future dates that would be best for that. A few days later she sent me a check in the mail. Not a big one. But a check.

For the next year or so Jeannie would call and I would advise her. Most of the calls were about her health. Indeed, a new method in London turned out to be exactly right for her. Some calls were about finances: should she invest in a new fund her friend—and my acquaintance—Sam Plaia had put together? Her chart clearly showed loss through investing with friends in the near future, so I advised her not to. She did anyway and lost the money.

But while she phoned and I advised her step by step, and she sent me a check after each call, I found myself coming to dread her phone calls. The more I got to know Jeannie, the less I found I cared for her. The more I looked at her chart and learned of her life, the more it struck me that she'd been given many assets—looks, talent, athletic prowess, the ability to instill desire in others, sound sense, good luck with money—and thrown it away. She had only avoided by the tiniest margin becoming a alcohol-sodden harridan living on the streets. All this showed up in her chart not as personality defects, but as external forces arrayed against her, seemingly negating everything positive. I was relieved when she went to London for the operation and called to say it was a success. While thereafter she continued to walk with a cane, she suffered no pain, and lived long enough to contract cancer—decades of booze and tobacco use coming home to roost—and to die of that.

Jeannie also sent me clients, and if I had wanted to, I could have gone out and found more on my own. I didn't because I was now feeling that I'd be increasingly surrounded by people desperate for advice, with difficult, often insoluble problems, "bringdowns" as we called them in those days. The additional problem was how to deal with a profession in which more and more everything seemed completely predetermined, with all of the horrors—car accidents, divorces, muggings, murders—there for me to see in everyone's birth chart. Unmistakeable . . . unstoppable?

In my own birth chart, for example, the areas in deepest shadow were the fifth house of romance, creativity, and children, and the seventh house of marriage, partnership, and open enemies. According to conventional astrology, my fifth house was empty and the seventh was occupied by difficult, even death-dealing planets. Using the Uranian system, my fifth house suddenly held two planets, one signifying stoppage, heaviness, and stagnation, and the other great losses, garbage, connections with inferiors, and the influence of the past on the present. Bad as that was, in addition, the new seventh house now held a Urnaian point that represented great force and power. In conjunction with what was already there, it signified self-reliance and self-defense, but also influential enemies and severe blockage by others. It said I'd have great difficulty in any partnership: any partnership would end in death and destruction. At the very least, I'd reject and be rejected by others. And if all this wasn't bad enough, according to the new system, my career would be fueled by great idealism and high hopes, and be dashed by last-minute lack of support from those allegedly aiding me, ending in disappointment and failure. Worse, I should expect great deceptions, utter betrayals, and disappointments.

I'd come to astrology to aid me in my life, to show me a clear path, and to aid me in my alchemical transformation, *not* to discover that my future was already laid out in such a way that the two things I most desired, love and a career, were to be denied to me so totally, so spectacularly. In the past, I definitely had problems with love and romance, but I thought that was over with. I'd learned my lessons with Djanko and Bob Herron and could now sail into the future fully armed. As for my career, my first job as a social worker ended when I'd quit. The second, at *Graphique*, ended when I'd developed a debilitating (indeed a Neptunian) disease, and now this third job at the bookstore, which I'd taken for the money, had ended in a still unsolved robbery (again Neptunian) , and for me in shame and failure. All predicted by astrology.

I'd have to be blind not to see that at every point, my life seemed to be fulfilling the evil destiny Witte's Uranian system predicated. Even so, I couldn't possibly succeed if I accepted such a despairing belief. No, I must give it up, not even expose myself to it again. I had to forget astrology, push it as far away as possible, and dedicate myself to the future, to what I knew was perhaps a foolish dream, a totally baseless ideal, but not *yet* impossible.

Hoping to air my conflict, I phoned my friend Arnie at the last number I had for him in San Francisco where he and Jan and Margaret had gone to live. I was directed to call another number in Big Sur, at Nepenthe, a local restaurant. There I was given a third phone number, his home, in the same exchange area.

It had been three or four months since I'd heard from any of them, and Arnie was full of news. Jan was managing the large, successful restaurant. Arnie, along with the woman he was living with, had opened a small boutique connected to the restaurant. Everything seemed to have turned out for the best, Arnie said. "Philly, Big Sur is paradise! Life is wonderful!"

He told me of his recent travails. He'd been picked up hitchhiking outside Monterey and busted for dope by a highway patrolman. "Once in the police station, they shook out my clothing," Arnie said, laughing. "You should have seen the looks on their rural faces at what fell out! I had bennies in my pockets, acid in my underwear, Tuinals in my pants cuffs!" He told me about his month in a local prison, "half bad boys' school, half country club." Jan had remained nearby to help Arnie, and had found the job at Nepenthe by chance, become friendly with the owner and his wife, and had met Mary-Belle, the young woman who eventually helped get Arnie out of stir, and with whom he'd settled down. Arnie was living in her house. "Philly! You wouldn't believe the views from this place!" Mary-Belle had a six-year-old daughter, Tina, and, best of all, everyone at Nepenthe, in Big Sur, loved Arnie, as they ought to.

He urged me to drop everything and fly out and join them. He kept on repeating that it was paradise, that he'd never been happier, that all had worked out for the best. Tempted as I was, I said no, not yet. I had plans, ideas. I needed time. Above all, I felt I still needed to be in New York if I were to become a writer.

Almost since the day I'd been canned, I'd been fooling around in my journals, alternately trying to work out a short story set in the Village and to outline a novel, but neither were going anywhere. After a year of on-my-feet work, I was still used to being active, still restless, without the stamina or serenity to sit hours at a time writing. Instead I spent my time in what I'd excuse as preparation: mostly walking around the city, looking for hardcover notebooks in which to eventually write my masterworks; locating the proper fountain pen to accommodate my left-handedness; hunting for bargain records to listen to while I wrote; locating in some of the still extant Fourth Avenue used bookstores titles at sharply reduced prices to add to my library. Otherwise I'd get up late, read the daily papers for an hour, stroll the Village, and, on sunnier days, sit and read in the sun. I might have been seventy-six instead of twenty-six years old.

In the midst of all this, I sat down one day and began to write a children's story for Arnie's new daughter in Big Sur, whose birthday he'd said was coming up. I finished it in two sittings, then revised it another few days.

"Ivan's Peacock" was about a boy who encounters a snake that persuades the boy it's not at all a reptile, but a peacock. Not because it wants to harm the boy—it only eats pie, and lots of that—but because it's unhappy being a snake. The deception is finally cleared up, the boy goes on his way somewhat wiser, and the peacock gets as much pie as it can handle.

Lest hindsight read too much into this very little tale, I'll merely say that it was deemed a readable, indeed a superior story by the six-year-old and her parents, and when I showed him a copy, Jay Weiss was inspired enough to want to illustrate it. He only painted about six or seven pages in one of those Japanese foldout books, but they're wonderful and make it a prize possession.

Aside from this divertissement, I'd not found a subject, or the form to fully engage my attention or abilities. I was filling my journal with ideas. One was a long story about three young sisters and their willing lover (shades of "Basement Games"!) that I couldn't seem to begin to write.

Meanwhile, I could use some distraction. A night of sex with a beautiful man was just the ticket. It was that moment that Ed Armour chose to stride through my hallway and into my life.

I also remembered that during that long first study of my horoscope Wayne had mentioned that I would encounter around this time what he called a "destined connection" in my life. I pulled out my notes and read what I'd jotted down. It was to happen this year and be someone "beautiful, artistic, with important company, family, or artistic affiliations." The person would in some way be connected to a "professional revolution" in my own life, or would lead to a radical transformation—something "strongly, deeply, felt."

All this was in my mind when I phoned Ed almost a week after our first encounter. I asked how the LSD had been and how his trip had gone. Great, Ed said, and LSD was the only way to do Disneyland. Ed seemed to have so much to say that I interrupted him, "Why don't we get together and you can tell me everything?"

He suggested dinner. Thinking of my tight finances, I suggested a drink. He countered with breakfast, late the next morning at the Bagel, a tiny, easy-going hangout on West Fourth Street. I agreed.

Breakfast seems such a bland, innocent way to first get to know someone that it will probably sound overdramatic when I write that so began a relationship that even now, twenty-four years after it ended, I'm still unable to fully explain.

I'd by no means forgotten how my most recent love affair had ended and what I'd felt like then. That had been the third—count 'em, three!—love relationship that had begun well and ended disastrously. I was determined not to let it happen again.

Since then, i.e, during my year as a bookseller, I'd not seen anyone seriously. This is not to say I didn't sleep with anyone. I was living in post-Stonewall Greenwich Village. Gay men were suddenly everywhere I looked: blond, red haired, dark, Jewish, Hispanic, Italian, Greek, Irish, and Afro-American; from the Middle East and the Midwest, from Colorado, the Deep South, Venezuela and Korea, all of them converging on my neighborhood. I could walk out my hallway to get mail out of the wall boxes at the front door and return to my apartment a few minutes later with mail and a male. I'd go out fifty feet to Spyros' Deli for a loaf of bread and come back with a guy. You get the point. I was neither hard up nor horny.

I *was* determined to break a losing streak. I was still vulnerable. Although I'd come to hate working at the bookstore, and although I now prized my freedom, I thought of *how* I had left as a personal defeat. I needed to win for once.

That second meeting with Ed extended beyond breakfast to a walk in sunny warmish late autumn weather out onto the Morton Street Pier, and when it got too windy, to David's Pot Belly on Christopher Street for coffee and more talk. When we asked the time from a somewhat dizzy waiter, she said it was 5:00. So late! We'd met at 11 A.M. We'd been together all day! Ed had a dinner date uptown and I had work planned. We agreed to phone each other the next day.

"I'm having a sort of dinner tomorrow," Ed said when we spoke the next day. "Jon Peterson will be here. You come too."

Ed's apartment turned out to be one of the oddest I've been in. It was the shape of an isosceles triangle, a result of Seventh Avenue being bulldozed through the Village earlier in the century, leaving all sorts of odd lots on either side of the new road. You entered Ed's place close to the lower right angle. A slender kitchenette with windows on the avenue opened to a short corridor across which lay the bedroom, the only rectangular room in the apartment. The living room was a triangle less the apex, which had been cut off to make the bathroom. At night, sitting on the long sofa, one had the streetlighted windows ahead, a wall-to-wall carpet, solid, masculine-looking furniture, and one wall dominated by large, earth-colored abstract oils, painted by Ed a few years before.

The wall between the bedroom and the living room had been cut through chest high, covered by a little blind. But the bedroom! I'd never been in a place like it before. Lights on dimmers recessed into the wall trim. A fully mirrored ceiling above a king-sized bed with a zebra-skin cover. Pin spots with theatrical-colored gels picked out a grotesque forest of roots dangling all around the mirror, giving the room the appearance of a grotto devoted to some arcane, pagan godling.

"Wow!" I said, impressed, as I dropped my coat on his bed.

"Mandrake roots," Ed said. "Noted for sexual potency."

"Wow," I thought as he hugged me hard as a hello.

Dinner was okay. We were served drinks and Jon, having sized up the other guests as "snooty art gallery queens" by turn ignored them or good-naturedly eviscerated them. The baked potatoes took forever, and when Jon tested one he quipped, "Ed-ward! A properly baked potato," aiming it at a guest, "when hurled, should maim, but not kill!"

They finally all left and I offered to help clean up. Ed said, "I've got a dishwasher."

Ten minutes later we were kissing in his bedroom doorway. Soon after I was able to test the efficacy of all those mandrake roots.

We stayed awake afterward, talking, and we woke up late the next morning. It was chilly and we had coffee in bed. Then Ed pulled the TV over on its trolley to the living room pass-through and we sat up in bed, watching some astronaut or other walk on the moon. We showered together and when I began to towel off my back, Ed grabbed it, saying, "What do you think other people are for? Let me do that." We made love again and went to the Bagel for breakfast.

There was an easiness about the next few weeks that even then seemed idyllic. It helped that I was feeling suddenly freed, that I had a new goal in life—to become a writer in the next few months no matter what it took. It helped that Edward continually pleased me by his terrific good looks—and less expected—by his desire to teach me all that he knew.

This meant art, primarily. Although I'd taken courses in high school and college—both applied and art history—Ed's training as an artist had been intense, far more complete than mine. While I'd put together abstract mobiles and collages in school, I'd never truly appreciated what Hoffman and Kline and Albers had achieved. Worse, whatever "eye" I'd once possessed was now apparently clouded over.

Ed took me to museums. We'd stand before a seventeenth-century Dutch still life at the Metropolitan Museum and he'd ask questions: "What's the first thing you notice? The second? The third? Why did Hobbema paint the melon and fruit in those colors? No, they're not natural. Where's the light coming from? What time of day is it? What time of year? Yes, you can tell from a pile of stuff on an outdoor table!" And of a family portrait, "Why are they arranged as they are? Which do you notice first? Second? Third? Last? What does their clothing tell you about them? Nobility? Or are they wearing their best? Who are those other people? What's their precise relationship to each other? Which servant's rank is highest? What's that piece of oriental china doing there?"

Coming back from the Brooklyn Museum by subway I happened to mention a story by Tolstoy. Ed suggested we read a book together. I wasn't sure why, exactly, but I agreed. He had two copies of Poe's novel, *The Narrative of Arthur Gordon Pym of Nantucket*, and we read it and talked about it over the next few days. I found that talking to Ed about the novel sharpened my critical faculties. At one point, I thought that was his talent, to make my "reading eye" as sharp as my "painting eye."

When I asked him, Ed said, "No. In books you see far more than I do. You almost intuit their form. You have no trouble following the pattern of image and metaphor." Ed was more interested in ideas.

I pressed him on this, since whatever ideas Poe had put in *Pym* were at best transcendental and at worst nonsense.

"Let's say," Ed replied, "I want to know how you think."

What an odd thing to say, I thought. No one had ever before wanted to know what I thought, never mind *how* I thought. I was flattered in a new manner.

We listened to music together. He had a recording of the British contralto, Kathleen Ferrier, singing Brahms's *Alto Rhapsody* that he could listen to again and again. I preferred the flip side's *Four Serious Songs*, which I found less weepy, more restrained with their starker piano accompaniment. Even more, I was ravished by the two *Opus 91* songs, with their autumnal air of strange contentment and the extraordinary chromaticism of the viola part. Ed asked why I liked them so much. I spoke of their tonal approximations and piano chords, arpeggiated almost into dissonance, but I found I didn't possess the vocabulary to express myself.

I'd played clarinet in junior high and high school and had been better at aurally miming my parts than reading from the score. A visiting teacher had tested me on an upright piano and discovered I had perfect pitch. Since then, I'd taught myself more about music, forms, chords, fugues, etc.

Ed kept asking what it was I was hearing, certain it was more than he was hearing. No, I insisted. I simply heard more precisely. He argued and I finally accepted that hearing more precisely in music did mean hearing more.

That was another of Ed's talents: his power of argument. He never got angry, but he seemed to never enter a debate—no matter how innocuous—without first having arrayed all his logic and rhetoric in advance. I couldn't be in the least bit lax debating him. I often had to probe my own thinking, my own beliefs, and sometimes I had to introduce ideas and tenets into the debates that I didn't believe in to move our discussion to a place where I felt more on balance, more in my own strength.

Ed would continue these debates with such intensity that I often felt frazzled, ready to surrender. Then he'd suddenly relax, hug me, tell me I was brilliant: he'd never met anyone who'd gone this far, this long with him.

If in argument Ed was a demon, in bed, despite the mandrake roots, he was far more easygoing. From our very first contact, he'd told me that I had to loosen up a bit more, experiment more, and I learned all he had to teach. Unlike my previous affair, Ed didn't care for being either a "top" or "bottom," finding that too "gender oriented." Ed talked during sex, instructing me, telling me how he was feeling, what he was thinking, what he wanted, demanding I do the same. Neccessarily, he was sensually expert, attuned to the human body and its reaction to touch even more than I'd assumed from him being six years older, having had gay sex longer and with more partners.

I am by nature extrasensitive to pain, and after a few exploratory forays into S&M, Ed desisted. Later, recalling what Jon Peterson had told me of Ed, I apologized and offered to try again. He pulled me close and said, "You don't have to. It's not your body I want anyway."

I looked into his handsome face. In dim light, it was all angles and planes, brightened by the golden brown of his eyes. Earlier, in glaring winter daylight, I'd first noticed thin lines chevroning off the edge of each eye into the taut skin of his cheeks, noticed around his mouth other lines. Those tiny glimpses, those minor significations made me half aware he was older, not merely in years but in experience. Now, in the half-light, I asked Ed what it was he did want.

"Perhaps 'want' is the wrong word," he said, but he was neither apologizing nor waffling. "Admire. Yes, that's the word. Don't you know?" nuzzling me, "I'm terrifically turned on by your mind! Terrifically turned on!"

*　　*　　*

I'd begun to keep a journal, keep it seriously. And as I've always written, while it was mostly filled with essays, occasionally I'd simply write down occurrences that strongly affected me. Early on in those journals, these events are noted infrequently, handled in a very distanced and almost pathetically objective manner. Without the key, reading these entries is like catching stones skipping over the water at the moment they touch the surface, an enigmatic tissue laid over a life. For nearly two decades, I alone have held the key to this *parade sauvage*, and though I seldom look at those note-books, one glance at a particular sentence can bring back an entire period, a time complete with people and places.

The sentence written two and a half weeks after I'd first break-fasted with Ed reads: "At dinner last night, I suddenly found myself put in a false position." Unwritten but underlying each word was the question: why? And the bigger question: what was going on?

We'd gone to a movie that night, Jean Renoir's *Boudu Saved from Drowning*, Renoir being one of Ed's enthusiasms—at the Bleecker Street Cinema—then ended up at David's Pot Belly. We were sitting at what had become our usual table, on the left, second in from the kitchen. Ed faced the restaurant, I the kitchen. This kept my concentration on him and on whatever we were talking about.

Taking a bite, I'd evidently missed whomever had gotten Ed's at-tention, but not the immediate change it made in him. He closed up like a fist. No, more like a cactus flower that when closed is a bare rectangle, with no hint of the dramatic night bloom it can become. His eyes were cast down, not in his usual half-ironic "aw shucks" modesty I'd long ago decided I'd adored, but now for real, as though he didn't want to see something.

Someone passed our table a few minutes later (evidently return-ing from the john) and hinted at a stop. I saw the tall young man's head turn to check, and saw a sketch of recognition and puzzle-ment, perhaps indecision, across his pleasant face. Not getting the sign he'd expected, he went on.

Ed didn't relax so much as remain closed, yet opened enough of an aperture for his voice and a few rays of personality to be forced through, as he continued what he'd been saying about French film, his voice wobbly now yet with a new intensity.

I dropped my napkin as a stratagem to see what he was looking at. Behind Ed, in the booth set into the front window, was the tall young man who'd passed us. Next to him was an older man. Teacher? Mentor? Lover? When I looked up, Ed had seen that I'd looked and now was quietly urging my fullest attention. I gave it, and the young man behind Ed became unfocused background again.

They were still sitting there when we got up to leave. Ed's head was down and I was sure that he knew the tall young man and was trying to elude him. A yard from the door, Ed hitched up his denims, and to my amazement, he broke out into a smile and a bright hello. The older man was introduced. I was halfway out the door, pulled back in to meet Dennis and Professor ____, who taught music theory at Columbia University, where Dennis was a student.

Ed bantered. Neither he nor Dennis said anything important, but it seemed to me that hidden meanings all but dripped from their delivery of those clichés. I just wanted to get out of there.

"Well, I guess we could sit a minute," Ed suddenly answered. I, too, sat. Evidently Ed and Dennis clearly had a past, whether a one-night stand that hadn't quite worked out or something longer, I couldn't determine. Whatever it had been, Ed had not wanted to reencounter Dennis, yet here he was sitting and talking banalities with him. I was waiting for Ed to explain to Dennis who I was, and what our relationship was. Dennis certainly seemed curious to know. The way he kept looking at us suggested he'd like a definition. I myself wouldn't have minded one.

The conversational banalities went on. Dennis asked if I lived in the Village. How long? If I went to school? Ed glossed over every one of my answers, annotating them, no more, *explaining* me, yet never once answering Dennis's real question. Then he rapidly changed the subject to the film we'd just seen, to Renoir and Vigo and Marcel Carné, to prewar French films in general, any other topic, it seemed, but me.

Dennis asked if I'd seen Ed's artwork.

I was about to speak, but Ed said, "None of the good ones."

"Not even the big one in Ed's living room? I like that."

"None of the important ones," Ed insisted. He began to stand up, explaining to Dennis, "He's got to get up early tomorrow."

I was hustled out the door. It was dark and now wet. It had rained and was now misting. Ed charged ahead, his coat collar up. When we reached the corner of Christopher and Bleecker Streets, he turned toward his place.

"Aren't you coming?" he suddenly asked.

A hell of an invitation. I was still miffed at his behavior at the restaurant. Even more, I was curious about who Dennis was and why Ed behaved as he had. I expected an explanation.

"*Should* I come?" I asked back.

Ed was sensitive enough to pick up my problem. He said, "It's difficult to explain. Dennis . . . he . . ." Ed stopped, not so much unable, I felt, as unwilling to explain.

"Maybe you'd rather be alone," I asked, meaning: spill it or I'm out of here.

"Maybe," he answered, meaning he wasn't about to spill a thing.

Fine. I told him I had work to look over. I didn't move. Ed didn't either. We waited on the corner in mist thickening to rain, neither of us speaking for a long time. Not, in fact, until we heard voices, one of them clearly Dennis's as he came out of the restaurant.

Ed panicked. He dropped out of their view, looking, I don't know, hunted perhaps, but willing to spy too.

"I *have* been taking up a lot of your time," Ed said.

It was raining now and he obviously wanted to leave. So did I. I repeated that I had work to do, letting him go more graciously than I thought he deserved. As a rule we kissed indoors but not on the street; even so, his departure was abrupt. He didn't touch me. He turned and I watched his figure in the rain as he headed toward Seventh Avenue South. Just then Dennis and Professor ____ passed along Christopher Street. I hid, watching them, before turning north to Jane Street. Nothing at all about Dennis's attitude as he walked by said he'd just had a crucial encounter with us—or with Ed.

By three the next afternoon Ed's phone continued to ring unanswered. I dialed several times, wondering whether to go to his place. I got dressed and phoned again. He answered. He sounded terrible, ill or hung over. No, depressed, he said. In the background I heard Ferrier wailing on the stereo.

I was concerned. Ed said he'd pulled out the phone connection because he didn't want me to have to deal with him like this. I sensed he wanted company, offered it, and he said I could come by.

Nothing was changed about the apartment or Ed physically, but the minute I got in the door, it was clear something was changed. No hugged greeting, not even a handshake. He led me into the living room and sat in a canvas sling chair. He'd not been drinking. No drug paraphernalia was out. Ferrier moaned on with British restraint.

Once Ed began to speak he did so in disjointed sentences. "Nita used to say . . . Nita was my wife . . . did I ever tell you? . . . five years . . . we were married five . . . it nearly wrecked her when I came out . . . we were the ideal couple, bright and beautiful . . . she hates me now . . . her family's hate all but killed my father . . . I was the eldest . . . everything was for me . . . it was okay for my brother to be gay . . . he was summa cum laude at Harvard Business . . . okay for my brother Jim to surf and fuck around with girls . . . not me . . . I . . ."

And so on, dropping grenades of his past around us until I felt like I was in a minefield.

Ed was *so* unhappy. I'd not had a hint of this before. In truth, outside the rigidified theatrics of funerals, I'd never met anyone so utterly, hopelessly sad as he was. It hurt to see him like this. I wanted to cheer him up. Help him. Do something!

I did, after hours with him. We even put together a light supper and ate. Ed's depression returned, continuing to baffle me because there was certainly reason enough in what he said to cause past unhappiness, even grief, but still none of it explained his utter unhappiness *today*. I was still too young then to understand how a decade or more of life's events can gang up on you all at once, an unstoppable tank, crushing everything in its path.

At almost two in the morning, I could no longer stifle a yawn. Ed made me brush my teeth and half dragged me to his bed. He stayed up. I remember him explaining why, but I was already half asleep and I don't recall what exactly he said.

The next morning Ed was awake. There were signs he'd slept on the couch. He brought juice, coffee, even pancakes to me in bed. He seemed somewhat less depressed. I thought maybe he'd talked it out of his system. I left after breakfast, thinking that although Ed still looked distracted, I'd managed to avert some unknown disaster. At the door, he called me back for a kiss and hug. I felt better then, went home feeling better, and worked hard for a long time.

We talked on the phone that evening and Ed seemed shakily okay. Ditto the next morning. I was already at my desk working when he called, and ever sensitive, he said he knew he was interrupting me. Even though I said no, he was and soon rang off.

The following day I saw Ed for lunch. He seemed completely over what had so instantly, totally, brought him down. He was talking books and films again, arguing again. A few remarks he made still made me think he wanted to be left on his own. He was grateful to me, he said, for being with him during his low time.

As for me, I was outlining what was beginning to look like a large, important project, perhaps my first novel. Although I would have willingly spent all day with Ed if he needed or wanted me, since I wasn't needed, I was eager to get back to my journals where the outline had already filled up four pages and was only partly done.

Ed phoned that evening and canceled our weekend plans. His brothers were coming to town from Florida and the Caribbean. The way he spoke of them, I pictured one as a successful Cadillac dealer, the other as a beach bum. All three were going home to Westchester and sleeping over. Fine with me. My pen was hot. I'd half cracked this idea that had haunted me for the past two years. I'd try to write out the entire outline this weekend. Ed seemed content that I had something to do and wouldn't feel neglected by him.

To my surprise Ed talked more of his family. He had mixed feelings about being with them again, although because of his reveal-some hide-some manner, I couldn't exactly be sure why. I did find out the house had five bedrooms. Ed's uncle used to sleep over when the boys were younger. He and Ed's father had been in business together for decades.

"They say it's in the genes, you know," Ed said, then went on to explain: "Homosexuality. Well, I know where me and my brother got it—our uncle. He was gay. Outrageously gay for the time. He was the fashion designer for their company—one reason it was so very successful."

They had sold the company at enormous profit some years earlier, when Ed's brother, fresh out of business school, decided to get into real estate. I already knew Ed's mother was Italian-American, his father East European Jewish, and their surname an Ellis Island perversion of some name too difficult to pronounce. This mix in no way explained Ed's own looks: the Germanic/Slavic and Southern Italian had blended to produce a completely WASP youth, exotic only in the color and slight slant of his hypnotic eyes, in no way a standout among his blond, doubly surnamed in-laws in the bridal party photo of a decade before he'd shown me recently.

But this was odd: he'd said how his coming out had effectively destroyed his family. Now he was telling me how adored his gay uncle had been, how tightly bound into the family and its fortune. The two ideas seemed irreconcilable. Wouldn't a family that accepted and attributed its success to a gay uncle be eager for another gay family member?

Though I was confused by this—doodling, distractedly looking out my window at the backyard where my cat Fred was busily coralling his harem and fending off a big scarred-up old Tom—I was still listening enough to pick up place names that suddenly emerged, as though finally released from Ed as he went on talking. "Florida" became, specifically, Palm Beach. The five-bedroom house upstate was clarified as being in Scarsdale. "The Caribbean" was not some beach shack in Mayagüez, but rather "a place" in St. Thomas the family owned, indeed a compound consisting of several homes on a mountain above the city, one for each of the brothers. It became clear that properties, large ones, multiple ones, were held by various members of the family in these—and other—locations. It suddenly dawned on me why Ed didn't have a job, why he could remain at home: he didn't have to worry about money. He was rich.

Sheepishly, he admitted he lived on "an income," money from a trust fund. It wasn't that much, he said, and I never discovered how much. He never lacked cash and while he didn't flit around in a private jet and that sort of thing, later on I discovered that for tax reasons Ed was a silent partner in some family properties, including the one in Charlotte Amalie designed by a famous architect, an entire harborside project including condos, pools, sports facilities, shops, a bank, and public areas. And once or twice later on, he'd say he'd gotten "a sort of bonus," whenever he treated me to something. Meanwhile, as I was neither a snob nor a socialist, I said to him I thought having an income was great and promptly dropped the subject. Ed expressed relief at this indifference and we never brought up the subject again.

Nor—more pointedly—was anything said at this time about that night at the restaurant and how and why we had dawdled on the corner of Christopher so long, so inconclusively. I could wait, I thought, until Ed was ready to tell me what was going on. Whatever it was, I was sure I'd be able to handle it. In truth, I'd go out of my way to do so, I didn't want to lose this relationship.

*   *   *

The first thing Ed said the following Monday when we met for dinner at his place was "The family meeting wasn't as bad as I thought it would be." Then, "about a dozen times, I wished you were there with me. In fact, I called once to tell you to grab a train up, but it was late so I didn't let the phone ring."

"That was sweet," I thought. He said the family had gotten along so well, apparently for the first time since Ed's father had died a few years back, that his mother had suggested they all spend several weeks in St. Thomas together for the upcoming holidays. Because he lived closest to Scarsdale, Ed would go up and help her in the considerble task of packing. He'd probably be gone until after New Year's. He'd miss me, but it had to be done. Ed had felt out of touch with them for so long. I understood, didn't I? Until he had to go, we'd spend the days and nights together, he said.

"Aha," I thought. This must be the source of Ed's sudden depression. Perhaps that guy Dennis we'd met reminded Ed of his father's death. He now told me it had been a sudden and "devastating" death, to Ed's mother. Ed himself admitted to incredibly mixed feelings about it, partly because of an argument with his younger brother, who blamed the death on Ed's divorce and coming out. Or perhaps that professor with Dennis had reminded Ed of his father. So, I said, sure, I understood completely: I insisted he stay in St. Thomas with his family as long as it took for him to mend fences.

As promised, the next two days were a whirlwind of activity: breakfasts, lunches, dinners, walks, movies, plays: he didn't let me out of his sight. I was exhausted each night we ended up at Ed's apartment. The first night we fumbled at sex and gave up out of mutual exhaustion. The second night, I was already passed out when he finally came to bed.

The next morning Ed began telling me about a particular house in Fire Island Pines belonging to a friend. He spoke of "magic nights" he'd spent in the house—awakening to dive into the bay waters before dawn, sitting under a parasol in the midst of a yellow fog that hid everything beyond his hand. "I've always wanted to be at that house when I was with someone I really cared for," Ed told me. He invited me to join him there the coming summer. I said, sure, I'd love to go.

Then Ed was gone and I was on my own again.

My journal entry for December 14, 1970, the day after Ed Armour left for the Caribbean, mentions that I'd thrown an *I Ching*, and received hexagram #49, "Revolution," with no changing lines. When I threw it again to more fully understand it, I received hexagram #24, "Return" or "The Turning Point," again with no changing lines. Obviously something big lay ahead for me. And indeed when I looked over my birth chart I saw many signs of a major turning point in my life. "Am I ready?" I wrote in my journal. Then, even more anxiously, "Will I even know this transformation when it comes?"

Oddly, just then two people reentered my life.

The first I met on a chilly walk on the Morton Street Pier the day after Ed left town. He was riding a bicycle and suddenly swerved toward me. I'd seen him in the Village over the past few years and I'd thought he looked familiar, but couldn't exactly place him. Several weeks before, when Ed and I were walking along Christopher Street, Ed had said hello to him and I asked his name.

"Jerry Blatt. He's a composer."

"Then it *is* him," I'd said.

"You know him?" Ed asked.

"I used to. He's so built up with muscles and his haircut is different and he's got a beard now!"

I told Ed about how during my junior year of high school our family had moved to the house my parents then still resided in at Twin Ponds, a strip of New York City only three blocks wide and twelve blocks long between Laurelton on one side and Valley Stream in Nassau on the other. The spring before the move, my mother had lost her second baby in three years and she was distraught. Although my father and she had sat us all down and explained why this move was necessary to my mother's mental health, I remained pissed off. During the summer I misbehaved so badly, so often, my parents sent me to Rhode Island to spend August with my Aunt Lillian and Uncle Bert, supposedly my favorite relatives. I enjoyed their company and they mine. Even so, I returned to the brand-new split-level house on Brookville Boulevard—a nice enough place in a great setting, surrounded by all the parkland enclosing the Cross Island Expressway, including the eponymous twin ponds—in a foul mood about leaving all my friends and having to change schools. I'd attempted to get into Valley Stream High but my brother and sister were also changing schools and their credits would only be good in city high schools. Since they were seniors, about to graduate, it was crucial they be able to use all of their credits. I was forced to join them in attending Jackson High.

Jackson turned out to be a great school, better academically than my old school, Van Buren, with even more advanced classes and a terrific student body. In fact, those two years turned out to be among the happiest of my life. But I was so very grim and silent those first few weeks at Jackson, the dean called me into his office and asked me to explain my morbidity. I told him I hated the school and went into a half hour of precise detail of what exactly I hated about it. When I was done with this comprehensive listing, he seemed fairly cowed. I might be an A student, but he made it clear he thought I was headed for suicide. He and my mother spoke on the phone while I was at afternoon classes. That evening she told me of the call and how he'd decided to add a noncredit advanced English class to my program: I'd meet some new people, I'd *have* to go out for a team—of my choice—and get involved in some after-hours project. The newspaper and yearbook were already filled out, but there was always "Sing."

It was a breathtakingly grumpy fourteen-year-old me who reported to Mr. Cohen's literature class that following afternoon and who groaned aloud at the two-page "recommended reading" list; a completely irritated me who appeared in the track team's locker room, gazing with undisguised disdain at the dozen sleeker, more muscular members of the track team I was supposed to join and emulate; an impossibly grouchy student who that Friday sat in the balcony of the auditorium where a teacher met the juniors who'd be in that year's "Sing."

In later days, Jerry Blatt always insisted he invented "Sing." He scorned any competing accreditation to Midwood High in Brooklyn. And from what I understand, the two were somewhat different. Essentially both "Sings" were onstage competitions in entertainment between the three top levels of the school. The evening would be briefly introduced by a handful of freshmen, and each grade would put on a forty-five-minute-long "show" of its own devising.

What made Jackson's "Sing" different was that it used a mass of students seated on three tiers of bleachers as a chorus. Individual acts by singers and dancers were few, keyed into and often in dialogue with this chorus, which supposedly represented say every sophomore in the school, and so to be seen—like a Greek chorus—as a single character. Jealously guarded themes were developed for each grade: the sophs go to Paris, the juniors to summer camp. These themes determined not only scenery and costumes, but the music and lyrics. The concerns of each grade varied, so these differences were emphasized humorously. Given our staggered schedules for the grades, lowerclassmen often didn't arrive home in winter till quite late, so they sang "In the Still of the Night." Seniors, facing the choice of work or college, were told to "Get a Job!" Often satirically apposite lyrics were written into current rock favorites, mentioning the predelictions and foibles of certain teachers or other school personalities.

All this was explained to us newcomers by the music teacher on the auditorium balcony. I soon discovered why I'd been shoved into "Sing." In junior high I'd sung in the glee club and eventually been prodded, kicking and screaming, into a production of *H.M.S. Pinafore*, in the role of Sir Joseph K.C.B. This group of Jackson juniors was four-fifths girls. They needed male voices. But as soon as other jobs were mentioned, I put up my hand. Yes, I did want to be in audiovisual. Too late. The music teacher chose the boys who'd done it in previous years. I was selected for the art group that would make the scenery, a single painted drop across the back of the stage, with several movable pieces. I'd still have to rehearse with the chorus, but at least I'd be doing art, which was important to me at the time.

When the music teacher was done, she introduced a slender dark-haired boy who was to be our director. He began to speak. Although he was only a few years older than me—sixteen at the time?—he spoke as though he'd been in Tin Pan Alley all his life.

He'd been directing "Sing" for two years. It was "his baby," he said. He wanted this year's production to be bigger and better. He said that last year's "take" for three weekends of shows had enabled them to buy new theatrical lights with spin gels and pin spots as well as to upgrade the sound system. His audiovisual squad would be trained in a Manhattan theatre. A friend in the field would help. He played piano, wrote books and lyrics to shows, and composed music. Thus he'd help each grade with our show. He'd overlook all the artwork and costumes. The previous year he'd briefly tried rapid onstage costume changes for the chorus and thought those, with greater lighting variety, would be effective. He kept using the words "Broadway" and "professional" as well as many other words I could only guess at. He'd audition anyone with a special talent: singing, dancing, juggling, tightrope walking, and try to get them into "Sing."

His name, he remembered to tell us at the end, was Jerry Blatt.

"Sing" wasn't until early June, but we began work the second week of the autumn term and Jerry worked us hard. There were book sessions, art sessions, art and lighting sessions, and art and costume sessions. Around March, the chorus was given its parts and rehearsal began. It was excruciating, endless, especially once we were given elaborate lighting "cues."

Jerry was everywhere that year. Everywhere, I suspect, but in class. He was tirelessly inventive, solving problems as they arose, inventing new problems most of us couldn't even perceive, working them out, drilling us, pep-talking us, occasionally breaking down, then snapping back. If any of us complained that we couldn't do something, Jerry always retorted, "They do it on Broadway!"

A House on the Ocean, A House on the Bay

Clearly that was his aim, to go directly to next year's hit on the Great White Way.

To his credit, it worked. My own small contribution was helping to paint a gigantic mural piece by piece in various basements across Laurelton. Our class won that year as well as the next year, when Jerry actually returned from college to help direct "Sing" a fourth time.

Two years later, I again saw Jerry on campus at Queens College, hanging out with the hippest people there. When I became friendly with a group who hung out in the tiny old "little caf" rather than with the hoi polloi at the huge, modern new cafeteria, I saw Jerry more often, but usually from a distance. His pals included all the beatnik types from the theatre and music departments, including Paul Simon, and—visiting after class from the City College of New York—Art Garfunkel. They were already recording artists under the name of Tom and Jerry.

I was an art major, so I had little reason to be in Coleman (the music and theatre building) and so I saw Jerry rarely in class. Once he left a book under my seat in a French lit. classroom and came to retrieve it. If he remembered me from Jackson High and "Sing," he never let on.

Now, however, on the Morton Street Pier, with his bike and his brand new muscles exposed by flimsy upper garments in even the coolest weather, Jerry approached, said hello, offered and shared a joint, and told me he remembered me.

The past, however, didn't interest him at all. In an offhanded way he said, "Don't I usually see you with Ed?"

I told him Ed was out of town for the holidays.

Jerry turned out to be quite direct: "And he didn't ask you?"

"It's some sort of family powwow."

He looked unconvinced. He had the disturbing habit of constantly looking around at men walking along the pier rather than at me, and once I got to know him better of saying things like, "Doesn't that boy have the most beautiful ass you've ever seen?" in the middle of a conversation. Not knowing me well enough that first time, he withheld these thoughts, but he sure kept looking.

"I guess you know Ed from the neighborhood?" I asked.

"That too. Are you two lovers?"

As though that would decide what he said next.

"Not really," I replied. "Otherwise I'd be in on the family powwow."

"Maybe," he replied cryptically, then, "You might as well know. You'll find out anyway. Ed and I made it once." He peered at me for a reaction. When none was forthcoming, he added, "It was a disaster!" He laughed. "I thought Ed was dating someone else. I used to see them together all the time."

"Ben?" I suggested. He was the fellow who'd gone to Disneyland with Ed. "Light brown curly hair and beard? Always dressed in blue? He's just a friend."

"Not Ben. I know Ben." Jerry described someone else, looking for a name.

He was describing the young man in the restaurant. "Dennis?" I asked.

"That's it. I saw them together all the time. Before you."

I was about to ask detailed questions when Jerry suddenly said, "I've got to catch up with that guy. See him? I made a bet with myself I'd get him in bed by the end of the year."

"The blond with tattoos?" I asked.

"You're right! He's trash!" Jerry shrugged, then hopped on his bike and sped off anyway. I watched him approach the youth, slow down, and circle him. I was left thinking about Dennis and Ed. But was Jerry even right? He seemed so scattered, so distracted, so . . . I decided to put it on hold for the moment.

Different in every way was the other person who reentered my life.

I'd met Bobby Brown when he was living over a health food store on Eleventh Street off Sixth Avenue. George Sampson had brought me there to meet his brother and sister, and we'd entered in the middle of a card game called "Hell!" This was essentially four- or five-handed solitaire, played with as many decks as players. All of the cards were taken off one giant pile of cards and the participants were seated around on the floor. The object was to complete your lines first. Naturally, it aroused hostilities, because two—sometimes three—players might want a particular card, and especially on drugs (methedrine was the drug of choice here) the players could get loud, abusive, sometimes violent.

Away from the game, being host, Bobby Brown was somewhat calmer, although a wire-strung edge ran evident in him even then. He'd just met me at the apartment door, when he turned and suddenly screeched, "Bernie! Stop cheating!" I could tell he'd prefer being in the game and let him go back to it.

A few days before Christmas 1970, following two years in which I'd not seen him, Bobby Brown telephoned and said that someone wanted to turn the health food store and his apartment into a two-story health food restaurant. They were buying him out of his lease. But it had to be done quickly: January. He'd been looking for an apartment in the area and had located a long-leased one. But it didn't begin until April 1 and he'd been unable to find a sublet. He knew that George and I were good friends. He also understood—from whom, he never said and George was gone by then—that I was out of work and could use someone to share the rent with.

I was and could. Still I hemmed and hawed. I didn't really want a roommate, much as I knew it would financially help me out.

Mistaking my reluctance, Bobby suggested we meet and he'd dispel any doubts. We did meet, in my apartment, smoked a joint together and drank beer and Bobby told me he thought he and I had pretty similar lifestyles. He was very easygoing, he said. He actually seemed to be.

That established, at least in his own mind, Bobby looked over the apartment, discussing how to turn my study into his room. He worked somewhere—a head shop? A poster shop? I wasn't exactly sure—from 6:00 to midnight. So I'd be alone and free to write without anyone being there those hours, a real plus. He'd hook a curtain across the open doorway between the study and living room, Bobby said, so I could use the room even when he was in there.

He was so much calmer and more sedate than when I'd last seen him that I was tempted. The fact that he'd referred to those card games made it easier. "I don't use speed or play Hell anymore," he gravely assured me.

Again I said I'd think about it. He called two days later and *had* to have an answer. Pressured, I said, "Sure, for three months."

Thus arrived the oddest of my roommates. He came with two cats he'd forgotten to mention: "Speed" and "Skag," who were twin brothers, Bobby said, and homosexual. It only took an afternoon to appreciate their names. One was hyper and nervous. The other was so idle he might be a statue. Until, that is, they fought. Then they chased each other around the apartment an hour at a time, stopping only to hiss, screech, and claw madly at each other. These fights invariably ended with them nuzzling and making up. I would usually remain shaking for another ten minutes.

Bobby also brought with him boxes of undefined stuff with which he built a shaky wall between the living room and study. He hung dark swaths of fabric over everything. A shade was fixed onto the window so tightly no light would dream of entering. Another friend in later years called his own dark bedroom The Tomb of Ligea. Bobby Brown's was the original.

Along with all this darkness and containment, Bobby also brought a reel-to-reel tape player, tapes, books, notebooks, marijuana, and who knows what other stimulants. Of all the druggies I knew then, he was the most methodical: he even had the latest pharmacist's blue book of current prescription pills.

Bobby might have stopped using speed but he was definitely on something most of the time. He'd awaken at 2 P.M. If I didn't have earphones on, I'd hear him stirring behind the curtain, and some time afterward—often a half hour later—he'd draw open the curtain. Sometimes he reheated coffee I'd made or made his own. Neither accounted for how wired he appeared.

He remained pretty much in that room, despite repeated invitations to come out into the bright, sunny living room, until it was getting dark out and it was time for him to fix something to eat and to go to work. On weekends, he seldom strayed out of his room until dark. With his pale appearance, almost colorless blond hair, and thinness, he might have been a vampire.

Except that Bobby Brown was, in his own weird, completely individual way, touching, funny, and totally endearing. Demons definitely lurked within, but they seemed to be directed mainly at himself. His cackling laugh was harshest when he was laughing at himself or something he'd done. His quiet, intense, completely spelled-out hatreds eventually returned to lodge in his own breast. I would sometimes catch him looking at me the way a chronically ill grandmother with a fatal disease gazes on her perfectly healthy grandchild. He could admire my innocence but he simply couldn't be the same.

Bobby Brown's moving in helped solve the worst of my financial problems and didn't much intrude on my life, besides providing me with some companionship in the few hours Bobby was awake and at home. And with some distraction too. Because the holidays had come and gone, and I'd still not gotten a letter, not even a postcard from Ed, and I was beginning to wonder why.

I bumped into Jerry Blatt again, but he was in an even less attentive mood than that first reencounter, chasing after yet another man. When I asked him about Ed's past relationship with this Dennis, he simply said, "I might have gotten that wrong. It might have been someone else entirely."

Which didn't at all help.

Finally, a postcard did arrive from St. Thomas. Actually it was a photograph of a part of the family's place on the mountain outside Charlotte Amalie, but all I could make out was a steep curving path through tons of colorful flowers and off to one side, a portion of a building of weather-stained wood. Ed's handwriting was even more enigmatic and as I was unfamiliar with it, I pored over his greeting for several days before deciding he had written a "touristy" card with only the briefest mention of the trip. He signed off "Ed" with a preceding squiggle that might have meant something—or nothing at all.

That was January 4, 1971. My journal reads, "All my relationships seem static. I'm not in love with Ed, though I'd like to be. He makes it impossible."

*　　*　　*

I completed my novel outline on a late Sunday afternoon in January, sixteen handwritten pages of it, hours, days of work! I read it over that evening and I remember thinking, "Jesus! This is a novel! A book in embryo! Now if I can only write the damn thing!"

I wasn't at all sure I could. There were these . . . characters!

These . . . scenes! Sketching them was one thing, actually writing quite another.

The novel—it was written but never published and I don't think it will be in my lifetime—hadn't come from nowhere. In the late summer of 1968 when I returned to my Jane Street apartment after months of recovering from mononucleosis, I suddenly sat down one afternoon and wrote out eight introductory pages in a five- by eight-inch bound notebook that I still have in my possession. At the time, I didn't think about it and put it aside immediately. All I knew was that I wanted to get this story on paper. Short and even dry as it was, this fragment contained an encounter of three characters, a setting, a past acquaintanceship between two male characters from college days, a present relationship between one of them and an exotic young European woman, and all kinds of potential complications. Enough so that when I finally got back to it after being fired from the bookstore and said to myself, "Okay! This is it! If you're a writer, then write a book!" I found there was enough to work with.

What suggested that it could actually be done, and by me, was that in the process of working out the outline, the promising if stark eight pages had blossomed into a dozen characters, an entire background, a specific time and even more specific place, into conflicts and developing relationships I'd never suspected, but that seemed absolutely right as I sketched them in. Names, appearances, and backgrounds of each of the main characters were required—and found at my fingertips. Each few hours of work continued to expand, to draw out material exactly right for this story, of which I'd not had a previous glimmer.

All of it was exciting and at the same time quite scary. I remember much later on that final night, getting out of bed and rereading sections of the outline, almost as though it were the result of automatic handwriting: I only half believed I had anything to do with it.

The phone awakened me the next morning around 10. Ed: he'd gotten into Manhattan and slept in his apartment.

"Let's meet for breakfast in half an hour." He didn't have to say where.

I left my place feeling good. I had news for Ed I knew he'd understand the full import of: the outline I'd written, how I felt about it.

And on top of that, everything between us would be as it had been before his sudden departure.

I'll let you imagine my reaction when I got to the Bagel. It's a tiny place, so one can take in all the tables at a single glance. Sitting at our table was Ed, who was on the lookout for me, and Dennis, the young man we'd encountered and briefly talked to at David's Pot Belly.

I must have hesitated inside the doorway. Ed waved me over, and pulled a chair over to the two-seat table. He was very tanned, very handsome, relaxed, and cheerful. I sat down and he asked if I remembered Dennis. I said I did.

Coffee was brought, breakfast ordered. "My treat," Ed insisted. He seemed nervous. I became aware that he was carefully watching me, at the same time that he was trying to be blithely indifferent, the cheerful social glue of the table.

Nothing important was said, but by the time I'd finished my first cup of coffee I'd been alerted more than enough to once again pick up all sorts of underlying things happening between the two of them. Instantly, and without any real evidence, I decided that Dennis had slept over at Ed's apartment the previous night, and more importantly, he'd done so upon Ed's invitation of many weeks ago: possibly the last day we'd spoken, when I'd sensed a break in Ed's deep sadness.

The question I faced was, Why was this treachery being so blatantly thrown at me? Only one answer: so I'd have no illusions that whatever affair Ed and I had was now kaput.

It was far cruder, far crueler than I would have expected from one with Ed's sensibility. I was thinking of getting very angry, although in truth I felt rather hollow and fuddled, hardly the right attitude out of which to express wrath. Then breakfast was over. Ed stood up and said, "It's a great morning! Let's get some air."

The three of us walked out to the Morton Street Pier. It was too windy at the end and we quickly retreated back to shelter behind the Maritime Arts Vocation High School ship moored to the pier. Despite the ultrasharp clarity of the sunlight, the incredibly crisp January air, I felt as though I was sinking into a fog-shrouded fen.

Dennis checked the time and said he had to go to class. Ed

hugged and kissed him and Dennis walked off. I remained huddled out of the wind, watching a huge container ship glide past on the Hudson River. Ed hunkered down, joining me. The ship drew up parallel to the pier and for a second I couldn't tell with certainty which of the two was in motion: the pier or the ship. I'd read of this phenomenon in college physics, but I was fascinated to see—and feel—the utter precariousness of my own physical presence. So Einstein had been right!

After what seemed like forever, Ed said, "I guess you're waiting for an explanation."

He then proceeded to tell me the following: He'd met Dennis last summer and had an affair with him. Dennis, however, wouldn't commit to a one-on-one relationship, for which Ed said he couldn't blame him. He explained that Dennis was much younger—only twenty-two—and had already been dating a man his own age who'd gone off to medical school. For several weeks in September and early October, Ed tried to fit into Dennis's life. But classes and study had become too time-consuming, and Dennis spent his time off practicing music with other students at Columbia and one entire weekend with the med student when he was in town. Dennis spent all his time with him. He and Ed passed one night together after that, but Ed was too jealous and that was that—until that night at the Pot Belly.

Ed realized then that he still cared for Dennis and that Dennis was still interested in him. Ergo the source of his depression. Ed repeated something I'd said (when he repeated it, I didn't at *all* recall saying it) that had prompted him to call Dennis and agree to see him on Dennis's terms. Since the med student would not be in New York much, Ed thought he might work through his jealousy.

Everything was clear. As I'd thought, I was being dumped.

But wait! Ed quickly went on to tell me that another, equal source of depression had been his realization that in contacting Dennis again, it might mean losing me. He said he didn't want to lose me. He couldn't afford to now. He understood that while Dennis was bright and mature for his age and met some of his needs, he hardly approached me in meeting certain other essential needs Ed had. Ed hoped that—being so very intelligent, so far above most in my comprehension of psychology—I'd understand this and help find a solution.

He quickly said that naturally he wouldn't tie me down either physically or emotionally, as neither he nor Dennis were tied to each other now. Ed had already discussed our situation with Dennis, who said he was ready to try it out. What did I think?

Whatever I thought, given that kind of setup, if I said what I truly felt—that I was unhappy, wanted Ed all to myself, complete with depressions, family money, and mental instability—I'd end up sounding like a prime jerk. Admitting to being such a grasping traditionalist wouldn't be easy. And on a more practical level, if I really was going to write the novel I'd spent most of the previous week outlining, I really couldn't afford the time Ed required for hanging out. He had so much leisure! Nothing but leisure! I liked what I'd seen of Dennis. Also, it was not a completely novel idea at the time. Didn't the Jefferson Airplane have a song about such a relationship with Grace Slick begging, "Why can't we be three?" Coming out of a rather communal ambience myself only recently (with Jan and Arnie etc.), I was intrigued by Ed's scenario of this ménage à trois, curious about how exactly he intended to make it work. Lastly, if I said no, I'd probably never see Ed again. Was I ready for that?

Challenged, I thought I could be as sporting as Dennis any day of the week. I said I'd think about it and added that it didn't seem impossible.

Ed was so happy, he hugged and kissed me and went on at great length about what a liberated situation we would all find it to be, together when we wanted to be, yet never in each other's hair.

Naturally I wanted to know whether or not we'd ever make love again. But in the face of Ed's enthusiasm, I didn't know how to ask. However, he sensed this question and told me he had to be candid with me, he felt "sensually enslaved" to Dennis's body. In all honesty, he didn't feel the same with me. Thankfully, Ed said, because he didn't know how he could be as intellectually and emotionally open with me as he wanted to be if he were also in sexual bondage to me.

He made a great deal out of that. And to be truthful, I was both disappointed and flattered. All my other lovers—from Ricky Hersch on—had always made such a fuss about sex and my physicality, and here was someone who loved me for my mind. It was a brand-new sensation.

By the time we parted that afternoon, I'd gone from wavering to full acceptance of Ed's plan for our tripartite future.

At home, however, away from Ed's endless web of persuasion and his accompanying touches, I reverted to my original feelings. The journal entry for that day is terrifying to read, mostly because I knew what was really going on yet was trying to convince myself otherwise, putting the best possible face on it. Pits and obstacles abounded, and I was going out of my way to be hip, understanding, the Superior Man of the *I Ching* I studied.

Not every compromise is a concession, Lenin is reputed to have said.

*　　*　　*

It was weeks before Bobby Brown's personality truly emerged. Maybe there were hints of it all the time but I was so occupied with trying to make the three-way relationship with Ed and Dennis work that I may have been oblivious.

One afternoon a month after he'd moved in, Bobby said to me in his most querulous tone of voice, "I never get mail! Since the day I got here, I haven't gotten any mail. I put in a change of address. And yet, no mail!"

It was such an obvious accusation and so perfectly absurd that I replied quite casually, "You get it all right. I burn it."

I thought his eyes would pop out of his head. His voice became a hoarse whisper when at long last, he was able to utter, "Why would you burn my mail?"

"Why *would* I burn your mail?" I asked by way of reply.

He thought a longish time, then said in a more normal tone of voice, "I'll go to the post office and put through another change of address."

"That's a good idea," I replied casually.

But if that bit of unadulterated paranoia was one hint of Bobby's growing coke use, it was by no means the last. Whatever Bobby

Brown's own personal demon was, it had the effect of bringing out unsavory effects around him; for one thing, my Jane Street apartment poltergeist, which had been there before he arrived and had lain dormant. With Bobby in residence, it suddenly began to act up a great deal—with him as target.

Forget the special effects movies you've seen, this was the real thing. As a rule both subtle and unobtrusive, it would suddenly come to life, depending on the person in residence. A few days after I'd moved in, I was in the bedroom reading and became aware of this constant sound in the living room. Not a loud sound, but a really irritating one, and when I jumped up and went to see what it was—invisible, inexplicable. I looked out in the backyard, listened at each wall for mice, did everything. No sound. Five minutes later, I was in the bedroom again and the noise was back. Subtle at first, then definitely there. It sounded like sand falling. Irritating. Again I checked. Again nothing.

It happened a third time. Annoyed beyond restraint, I leapt up, ran into the living room, and shouted at nothing, no one, nowhere, "Shut up! Shut *up!* This is *my* apartment. *I* pay the rent! Shut up! You can make all the noise you want when I'm *out!* When I'm here you will *shut up!* Do you hear?"

When I returned to my bedroom to read, the noise did not repeat. I guess it was that apparent obedience that confirmed somewhere in my mind the idea that something was actually in the apartment, although it would be years before I found a name for it. I also thought about who had lived there before me—poor, stressed-out, hapless Joan; and I recalled the so-called curse put on her by a witch. Subsequent to this incident, the poltergeist never recurred and I forgot all about it.

Until Bobby Brown moved in. Suddenly it was reactivated. First, Bobby began complaining about strange dreams, nightmares, in which he was in this apartment, running from something shadowy and menacing.

A day or two after, the two of us were on my bed looking at a magazine and we heard footsteps from the apartment door along the short corridor to the living room. The bedroom door was mostly shut and I thought I'd left the front door open and someone had walked in. No one had. I'd hear those footsteps while I was in my bedroom, along eight feet of hallway, always in the same direction.

One day I came home to find a new shower curtain. My transparent one needed replacing, so I thanked Bobby for this bright new opaque one.

He looked balefully and said, "It makes no difference. I *still* feel like someone's watching me when I'm in the shower."

As soon as he said it, I realized so did I, even with the bathroom door closed, even when I knew I was alone in the apartment. In fact, since Bobby had moved in, more than once from the bathtub I'd hear a few footsteps, then feel someone looking at me through the closed bathroom door. Subtle but eerie. In later years, all sorts of friends would volunteer the same eldritch sensation: one guest of a friend who sublet my place for an entire summer was so terrified they never slept together there.

"What do you think it is?" I asked Bobby one afternoon.

He was sitting up in bed, smoking a joint.

"I don't know. I've seen the cats run from it."

"Didn't you go look to see if anything was there?" I asked.

"Hell no!" His eyes were huge with horror. "I just hoped it wouldn't come closer." He went on to tell me that it acted up most when I wasn't home. It never came into the study, which explained why he kept to that room.

"Yell at it," I said. "That's what I did."

Bobby was afraid his yelling would sound more fearful than furious. "It knows," he whispered as though someone were hearing what we said.

I was more amused than anything else. Finally I had to interfere.

One afternoon there was a phone call for Bobby, and the long telephone cords had become so twisted through use they didn't reach his bed, so he got up, stood, and talked as I attempted to untangle them.

The call was an upsetting one for him: he had to go to work early or stay later. After he hung up, he dropped into my bentwood rocking chair, fulminating, as I knelt down to try to untwist the phone cord. A second later, he leapt out of the chair and almost knocked me over trying to get into the study.

A House on the Ocean, A House on the Bay

"Did you see *that*? *Did* you?" he demanded. "It pulled back the chair! I almost fell out. It's after me!" he wailed.

I lied and said I was going to find a spell to get rid of it. A few days later I said I'd done it, exorcised it. Bobby clearly didn't believe me and although he didn't complain of it any more, both of us now began counting the days till April first, when he'd be moving out.

*   *   *

I'd missed Edward when he was gone over the holidays. In a sense, I was still missing him now that he was back. Yet one of the things about Ed that I'd forgotten that I missed was how much *with you* he was when he was with you. My friend Arnie used to say in praise of someone he'd met, "He was most attentive," and what the words didn't convey, Arnie's tone of voice did. In his very different way, Ed was also "most attentive."

In fact, after his return from St. Thomas and his reappearance with Dennis in tow, Ed almost seemed to be around more than before. Two weekdays, Dennis had no morning classes and the three of us breakfasted together. The rest of the week it was Ed and me alone. He always seemed to have an idea for the afternoon: a showing of some Truffaut film he'd missed that was now uptown at the Thalia Cinema or a new show at an art gallery, or an auction at Sotheby or Parke-Bernet, where friends of his worked who would take us through the place showing us and explaining everything. Even when he didn't have plans, there was a new record to listen to—he introduced me to the superb pianism of Walter Gieseking and that aristocrat of cellists, Pierre Fournier—and there were always things to talk about. On weekends, our schedule began later in the day, but was only slightly less intense. With all the brunchers out Saturday and Sunday mornings, the three of us often met later, for dinner, a movie, or a step into a local gay bar (several vaguely "western-style" ones had recently opened in the Village).

All of us were trying to make this thing work. Luckily Dennis and I enjoyed each other's company. For one so young, he would come out with the most mordantly funny lines in the most casual manner. And of course, we shared another important subject: Dennis knew classical music, played piano, was collecting all of J. S. Bach's scores, and without ever lecturing, he expanded my knowledge of music as well.

I'm not by nature jealous, but yes, there were mornings when the two of them would appear at the Bagel or at our newer spot, Elephant and Castle, looking hung over or still half asleep. That had to be because of what they'd been doing the previous night. And yes, I'd feel a twinge.

Almost by way of compensation, I sensed that their relationship was neither easy nor trouble free. Dennis would disagree with something Ed said and not let it go. He'd interpolate comments such as "That's what you'd like to believe," and "Not the way I heard it," to show his independence and to cause irritation. Arguments they had away from me were referred to in front of me.

On sunny days—and there seemed a plethora that winter—we'd walk after breakfast and watch strollers who'd stare at us in return. Jerry Blatt usually rode by on his bike and he'd stop to say hello. I'd catch him trying to not too obviously wonder. Then Dennis would kiss and hug me, kiss and hug Ed, and take off for class.

I'd be left with Ed's complete attention. About a week into this new schedule, I finally managed to find time to tell him about the novel outline I'd written while he was gone. We were alone on the pier and he prodded me lightly, probing my intentions in several technical matters, asking how the idea had developed, how I was planning to attack this character or that scene. An entire world of walkers and runners and cruising guys surrounded us, ships passed on the Hudson, an occasional helicopter flew noisily over us, heading toward the Twenty-third Street Heliport, fire engines went by on West Street, passersby greeted us, a transvestite six yards away put on an impromptu one-man version of *Hello Dolly!* But Ed managed to blank it all out: he was a giant satellite dish receiver that simply turned in a direction to capture every radio wave, pulling in everything.

Then he'd suddenly switch, and he'd be sending instead of receiving: his signal as strong, as all-encompassing as his power of reception.

He was charming me, I knew that at the time—what Bette Davis in a 1930s melodrama would call "making love" to me. When we were alone, he never stopped doing it, partly because he felt he had to work harder with me now, to keep me; partly because he charmed people naturally and was so very good at it and we all like to do what we do well; partly because I was far more receptive to it than Dennis. It wasn't lost on me that, after all, the way he'd set up our three-way relationship, Ed virtually had to reseduce me every day. And like any lover with a smidgen of power, some days I'd make him work at it.

I didn't realize yet that if someone makes love to you so constantly, even without a lot of physical contact, it's got to have an effect.

It must have been when my friend Arnie came to town that I realized exactly how much of an effect. It was a short trip for Arnie. He slept at his parents' house one night, long enough to get a car. Then for the rest of his stay he slept on my living room couch, fascinating Bobby Brown and his cats, Speed and Skag, a trio Arnie seemed totally indifferent to.

Arnie brought back his old self, with a new California redwood veneer, a polish, a new looseness, an odd new sense of contentment. Early that first night, he grabbed me by the shoulders and said, "Philly, how tight you are! You're all stressed out! What you need are sulphur baths, like the ones at Esalen. Or a good rolfing. I thought I'd die when I was rolfed, Philly. But was I glad? What you need is yoga. Get on the floor. Go on." He lightly slapped me. "What do you think I'm going to do? Jump you? I've had plenty of chances and I haven't yet, have I?" He tickled me all over. "That's it! Flat! Flat!" He pushed me down flatter. "Now, legs in the air. Come on, Grace! (This was his drag name for me, partly based on how graceless I was, partly on Grace Poole, Rochester's mad wife in *Jane Eyre*.) You know how to do that! Slowly! Slowly! We're going to teach you how to heal your body and mind through yoga."

Which he did. He even left behind his photo-illustrated Richard Hittelman book for me. I've been doing yoga in one form or another ever since.

The following night at a booth in Max's Kansas City, after he'd visited and chatted up half the tables in the big back "red room" that had been our hangout previously, Arnie said out of nowhere, "So who's this man you're in love with?"

"I never told you anything like that!" I protested.

Mock surprise. "You didn't? You mentioned someone. Ned? Ted? Mama Scorpio here simply . . . how can I put it . . . read between the lines."

I told Arnie the truth. I'd been seeing Ed. Now we were just friends.

"If you say so, Philly! Am I going to call you a liar? God forbid!"

Arnie raised an eyebrow higher than any eyebrow has ever been raised on a human forehead.

*　　*　　*

Weeks had gone by since I'd done work on the novel I'd so extensively outlined. Winter suddenly turned nasty, snowy, wet. The little bit of company Bobby Brown had provided dwindled to nothing. After work ended at midnight, he'd go out with friends, not get home till six in the morning, not wake up till shortly before he had to go to work. Most of our contact was limited to his increasingly cocaine-assisted levees. On nicer days, I'd already be outside by then, even missing those odd nonevents.

My birthday was nearing. It wasn't lost on me that it would be my twenty-seventh, and that I was in the middle of what astrology referred to as a "Saturn return"; i.e., the return of that planet to its identical place in my birth chart. In my case, this supposedly undeniably difficult period seemed to be in swing already, having begun nearly a year before, when I'd been transferred out of the relative paradise of Grand Central Terminal. I was still determined to not use astrology in any way, however, not for my life, not for Edward's, not for how our two birth charts fit or didn't fit together (called "synastry"). Whatever benefit could have accrued from its study at this time vanished.

Arnie left and I bad-naturedly wrote a poem about him, mocking his New Age spoutings, titling it "Whisperjet Prophet." I wrote another poem, out of frustration and anger, based on John Donne's "Meditations" that I titled "Indictment." Neither are very readable today. I began and wrote out a first scene to an ill-considered bed-room farce set in eighteenth-century Bavaria featuring, if you can believe it, Wolfgang Goethe and his biographer Eckermann of all people—a ghastly thing, mercifully never again touched never mind completed.

I was confiding in my journal my hopes and fears, the ambiguities and lack of clarity that surrounded me—and my apparent aimlessness.

According to the journal, by February 10, 1971, I'm hopelessly in love with Ed. The triangle with Dennis is in full swing. I ask my journal, "Isn't it hubris to demand that two people give you love? Isn't one all anyone should need?" I discreetly fail to mention names.

On February 21, I write, "My head has been spinning like a run-away carousel all week. I'm afraid that if I don't find my center, any action I take will bring me close to the death of my soul."

Later on that same outwardly uneventful, mentally turbulent day, I decide on a nobler end: to reject passion and be a friend to Ed.

That night he takes me out to a play and dinner for my birthday. We're alone. We return to my apartment and talk, talk, talk. There is a moment when he almost decides to sleep over. The moment passes. He leaves.

That possibility was enough so I begin to waver in my decision. On February 23, 1971, I write: "The memory of him astride that chair with Gieseking playing Brahms Op. 119 piano pieces as back-ground is for me enameled in fire!"

On February 25, I'm reading Sappho and quoting her; never a good sign for one in love. I'm also reading haiku with Ed at his place. Dennis calls to say he'll be at school late, don't wait for dinner. During dinner, he phones to say he's got early morning classes and he'll stay at his friend Vicky's overnight. Another moment that I feel might turn the tide. Ed does not pick up on it. After a while I go home alone.

More suffering. On February 26, my romantic disaster from a year and a half earlier drops by my apartment. He brings a copy of a play he wrote, based on Noh theatre, he tells me, inspired by me. By this time I'm apparently so gaga over Ed that even this sometimes dense guy is surprised, pleased, annoyed, but somehow satisfied by how little I care about him or our shared past. In what I assume is gratitude, he tells me to keep the LP of the Duruflé *Requiem* he left with me a year before, although it's out of print, not easy to obtain.

"Appropriately enough," is my comment in my journal, "a good time for requiems"—meaning I'll stick to my previous decision.

I begin to read Emerson's essay, "On the Conduct of Life." I'm tortured, tormented, but try to remain calm.

I'm almost glad when March 5 comes along and Ed—still not having said anything concrete about it, yet admitting he must shore up his relationship with Dennis—takes him to St. Thomas for the midsemester school break. Due to the sporadic nature of my building's heating that winter, I'm persuaded to stay in Ed's apartment while they're gone.

During my second night at Ed's, I get a phone call from a young man who won't tell me his name and who either does or does not remember whom exactly he's calling. He begins to talk dirty and he keeps reminding me of "the last time," although I've told him three times I don't live at this phone number. When he arrives, he's more than just cute: he's very hot indeed. He remembers Ed's bedroom, if not precisely who was in it the last time he was present, and he's in bed in three minutes. Among other inventions, he asks me to tie him up. He locates the required silk cloths instantly in a closet I've never even peeked in—asking me to fuck him, and in his words, "treat him like pussy."

Desperate for distraction, I do.

The next evening, one of Ed's Parke-Bernet pals drops by with an extra ticket for the opera. I'm dressed in one of Ed's sports jackets and swept out of the place to hear Birgit Nilsson sing *Salomé* at the Met, then taken to a fancy dinner on someone's charge account. I want to get work done, so in the next few days I decline a few other tasty invitations, although I do accept another drop-in visitor, a hustler by the name of Wolf, who it seems doesn't want money, just a place to stay for the night, and who doesn't seem to recall Ed at all, but rather some previous tenant.

Desperate for distraction, I . . .

The next afternoon I'm headed for the pier when I bump into Jerry Blatt. As we're catching up, the weather suddenly turns, it begins to snow, and he invites me back to his flat on Morton Street. There we smoke and after a while I begin to tell him about our ménage à trois. I'm expecting to scandalize him.

"That's light stuff compared to some of the sick scenes I've been in," Jerry brushes me aside. "Do you know what it's like going into your boyfriend's bureau drawer and finding a hypodermic needle? Especially when the week before he swore up and down he'd given up horse? Like a grade-B movie, that's what! I swear you *become* Lana Turner! You hear the cameras whirring! You check your hemline. And if you'd like to discuss how truly *hu-mil*-i-a-ting a relationship can get, in college I had this straight friend who let me blow him, right? Ignored me completely. Looked at *Playboy* or covered his eyes. Then he began giving me a certain time to get him off. If I didn't he'd kick me out!"

"Jerry! Are you saying I should let this continue?"

"I never said you should or shouldn't. I'm just saying this is the end of life as we know it. Where's that joint? Let's play 'sonnet'."

Having both been English majors, we'd developed a rather specialized way of intellectually wasting time: two-handed sonnet writing. We spent hours watching old movies on daytime TV while playing.

"Sonnet" is a rather high-toned variation of a game usually called "rumor." He'd write a first line—I recall "Crocodiles love to glide upon the flooded Nile"—and I'd have to come up with a second line (say, "They only pause to nibble mice, or sup on baby rhinos"), he with a third ("So delicate of habit, they belch but once a mile"), I with a fourth ("And to love to pose for artisans, hired by King Minos"), etc. Meter and rhyme schemes were strict, but within the poem anything could occur based on our whimsy, or more usually, our hapless attempts to get down on paper any even vaguely coherent next line. Needless to say, the final couplet made little sense except to us and then only with a stretch.

We passed much time together in this way during the next few years, Jerry and I, waiting for our lives and careers to get going. But this single, brief talk would make us friends for life. And in fact, we had dinner together that very evening, in Ed's apartment, because Ed's mother's maid had just happened to appear the previous day at the apartment with several entire meals, insisting they could not be frozen for his return but must all be eaten.

Checking the journal I note that Ed and Dennis return home and I sleep at my place again and we once again meet for breakfast. Although they are tanned and Dennis seems relaxed, Ed is on edge. He can't wait for Dennis to go uptown to get me alone.

As I suspected, he'd arranged the cute phone caller, whom he thought might amuse me. Also the friend with opera tickets. Not the hustler, who he doesn't at all know, but who he thinks might be one of his brother's from the time he stayed at Ed's place. I'm suspecting the Caribbean trip didn't go as planned, but thankfully, Ed doesn't want to discuss how it went wrong in any detail, contenting himself with saying, "Dennis may not be the person I thought he was."

Our schedule resumes: breakfasts, walks, talks, Ed taking up half my weekdays, never coming physically closer than a hug and brush of his lips on my cheek. Once, I make an attempt to break away. I have a slight cold that I exaggerate into the flu or worse, and in this way I'm able to be out of the circle of Ed's all-encompassing attention and charm for about two and a half days before he descends upon my apartment with his mother's chicken soup, baked goodies, records, magazines, and cold pills. He wants to have his family's doctor look in on me. I resist. Once again, I'm swept up into the enormous field of his wanting.

The one time I come close to verbally expressing the question I'd written in my journal, the question that tortures me daily—why should he need two lovers?—Ed begins to talk more of his childhood, telling me how he'd been primed from the very beginning to be the star child of the family. Blessed with looks, charm, and smarts early on, he became everyone's darling, received everything a child could hope to want. When he was in college, unhappy with his prelaw courses, playing with art, a noted abstract expressionist painter took Ed under his wing, declaring he had talent, and—along with Ed's "artistic" uncle—convinced Ed's father to nurture this talent. Luckily, Ed's brother was instinctively drawn to business; this removed some money-making pressure off Ed. On the other hand, he was pressured in other ways, expected to excel at everything, to graduate at the top of his class, to exhibit talents and graces far beyond the normal, to become a great painter, to marry into wealth, to make the family name famous.

"I lived the first twenty-seven years of my life for everyone but myself," Ed concluded. "I'm trying to catch up and have what I want, what I deserve."

As far as he was concerned, that settled the question.

What about what *I* deserved?

*   *   *

No particular incident was responsible.

True, Bobby Brown moved out of my apartment and into his own place two weeks early, taking with him half the rent. I didn't realize until he was gone what a small, persistent drain he had been on my attention and on my sense of well-being. Once he'd gotten all his boxes out of my study, I tore down the sheets of dark cloth he'd swathed the room in, pulled off the tape with which he'd closed out light from the window. I swept and vacuumed the little room, flung open a window to air it out.

Though March winds blew and it was by no means warm out, there were hints of spring. The few plants—acacia trees, several unexotic weeds—growing in the backyard seemed to be sending up stronger, more hopeful shoots than in years before. And the angle of sunlight was slowly altering with the season, so my north-facing living room and study were brighter.

Ed spent a few days in late March at his mother's house in Scarsdale, celebrating a birthday—his brother's or mother's, I'm not sure which. Dennis and I breakfasted together alone at Elephant and Castle. If either of us missed Ed we didn't say. Dennis had just begun buying the new *BachGeschellSchaft* edition of the instrumental works and he was filled with the wonders of J. S. Bach.

I was still adrift, unable to do anything much. I knew I had at most two months of income left, then. . . . Crisis loomed all around

me, but I seemed outwardly able to ignore it, I was already so paralyzed by Edward.

That is not to say I wasn't aware of what was happening.

My friend Susan Moldow, then living in San Francisco, sent me
as a belated birthday gift a book containing the selected letters of
Emily Dickinson, and I read it avidly, identifying with the Amherst
poet who'd suffered such restrictions and personal lacks in her life. I
copied out the following line in my journal: "The heart wants what
it wants. Or else it does not care!"

A few days later, at Jerry's apartment, I grabbed a pencil and pad
of foolscap on which we used to play sonnet and I wrote the words
"career, love, money" on the left side, and above them I marked in
each of the past five years. Then, lying across his bed, with Jerry
watching me, I showed him with pencil lines from each of the three
areas of my life, how activity in all three areas had simply petered
out, the pencil lines getting fainter and fainter till they vanished.
Jerry was so impressed, in later years, he'd often remind me of that
afternoon, and of my objective—to him horrifying—graph of my life.

On March 21, I openly wondered about my future. In my journal,
I quoted from Arthur Waley's old translation of the *Bhagavad Gita*:

> Finally, this is better, that one do
> His own task, as he may, even though he fail,
> Then take on tasks not his own, though they seem good.

I wrote, "I must find the focus of my life's work. I seem to have
to stumble through trial and error, one after another to find out
what it is." The entry concluded, "I am desperate for a sign."

Between that entry and April 24, 1971, there were no entries in
my journal. On the latter date, I again picked up the journal and reported: "Today at 5.20 P.M., New York City, I completed the handwritten draft of my first novel."

How? What happened? Nothing really, except that I sat down
one evening after dinner and began to write. And by doing so, I became convinced that I was now, for the first time in my life, a
writer: that I'd finally found my niche. It happened in the process of
writing day by day, at times quite late into the night, while Bach's
The Well-Tempered Clavier softly played on my phonograph table. I

discovered what I could at last call Joy. I didn't know what else to call it. It equaled in intensity sexual intercourse and my first LSD trips, but unlike them, it wasn't over in an hour, or even in a day, but went on giving me pleasure, a different kind of pleasure, true, intellectual yet also sensual, spiritual yet completely material. And as I kept on writing, I found that my skills themselves seemed to sharpen, abilities I didn't know I possessed revealed themselves, ideas I'd somehow or other gathered over the years that had remained in a sort of unconscious stew suddenly clarified themselves, leapt up to be dealt with. It was as though I'd suddenly developed a new pair of strong, ultracapable limbs to use, covered over until then, swaddled in heavy, tight bindings—now totally freed.

The miracle was that with the outline already written out, I didn't need it. I knew where I was going. In fact, I didn't even need those introductory eight pages I'd written two and a half years before. I simply sat down and let go and the book came out of me, as naturally as a spider spinning a web, as a silkworm making silk. For days on end I was amazed that I could continue with it, elaborate it, detail it, work out the plot despite new unexpected twists, and then complete it. I still recall the thrill that passed through me one evening when the book suddenly needed a new character, and before I could even begin to panic about it, a character I had not planned for suddenly stepped onto the scene, fully developed, with a name and a physical presence I could describe, and a history, as though she'd been lurking in some corridor just waiting for me to tap on the door for her. Mrs. Bedford she was, a housekeeper, whom the characters ended up calling "the good ship Bedford," for her size and her stability and her clarity in cutting through an ocean of complexity. Even now, I'm delighted when characters emerge out of the background and announce themselves to me, demanding their role in my work.

Miracle or not, what I couldn't get over at the same time that I couldn't deny it either, was that I was leading perhaps the strangest of double lives of anyone I'd ever known.

Every day, perhaps four or five hours at a stretch, I would be inside the world of my novel: New York City on the eve of World War I. I would attend operas with my characters at the Academy of Music on Fourteenth Street, with Louise Homer and Jan de Reszke and Olive Fremsted singing and Toscanini conducting. I'd watch other characters be jostled by policemen as they gathered for suffragette rallies in Columbus Circle. I'd join other characters as they entered questionable dives and downtown ghettos or attended glittering parties at the Vanderbilt Mansion.

In this fictional world, I wasn't merely observer. I was Prime Mover. Divine Presence. True enough, after a bit, the characters possessed enough force to make most of their own—often to me surprising—decisions. But when push came to shove, I was the one who decided all.

At the same time, in my own life, I was powerless, unable to control or direct anything. I decided nothing, moved nothing, possessed no influence upon anyone who counted: most crucially not Edward.

What had changed was me. Having written a first draft, I now had to do a typed draft of the novel, one others could read. Having begun, I desperately needed to keep writing.

*　　*　　*

I told no one but Jon Peterson of what I was doing. Because he had so many contacts, I felt I would soon have to ask him to interpose on my behalf with one or another of the literary agents he knew.

During the writing of the first draft of my novel, I'd been able to pretty much keep to the schedule that Ed and Dennis and I had established. My few concessions to the book consisted in not staying out late at night, coming home directly after our dinners, begging off their increasing excursions to local bars (to shore up their relationship, I suspected). During those quiet spring nights mostly everyone was asleep, mine the only lighted apartment facing scores of darkened ones on the Jane Street backyard, and I valued the silence for concentration, especially for going over what I'd written earlier in the day, rewriting and preparing for the following day of work.

Once I began typing up the manuscript, my hours altered. I'd expected this part of the work to be less difficult, merely a transference from my handwriting to a sheet of paper. Not so. The typewritten page looked so official, so final, compared to the more private

A House on the Ocean, A House on the Bay

self-communication of my handwriting. I found myself altering a sentence here, a paragraph there. Descriptions of characters that seemed flat, lifeless, had to be improved. Finally, entire scenes had to be rewritten. I wasn't merely copying: I was writing a second entire draft.

It was far more time consuming than I'd counted on. My four-finger typing, barely sufficient for college term papers, now proved deadly slow, as did the speed of my Royal manual, all of it complicated by my generally poor typing skills, my need to constantly erase and retype. I had set myself a goal—to complete the typed draft in a month. To meet that goal I'd sometimes be at work until three or four in the morning. That meant waking up later each morning, letting the phone ring, having to come up with excuses for why I was no longer meeting the others for breakfast.

Evidently Ed thought I was keeping away on purpose—which was only half so. One morning when I didn't answer my phone, but merely rolled over in bed and put the covers over my head, he arrived at my building, rang someone else's bell to get into the building, and stood pounding on my apartment door until I got up and let him in.

He was annoyed. "Get dressed. We're going to breakfast."

My gate-leg table in the middle of the living room was covered with my work of the night before. I hastily hid the typed manuscript under record albums and pillows on my sofa, washed my face, and dressed as Ed impatiently waited.

Once seated at Elephant and Castle he asked, "Why are you avoiding me?"

"I'm not. "

"You are. Dennis thinks . . . Well, he also thinks you are."

I weighed potential answers. What hung in the balance was our future. I could say yes, I was avoiding them, wanted out of the triad, which would be true, and which would mean losing Ed for good. Because, absurd as it seems, I believed with all the confidence of the unsatisfied lover that as long as we continued seeing each other, no matter how unsatisfactorily, something might still change our situation. So, I settled for: "Ed, I can't afford to have breakfast in a restaurant so many mornings."

"What?" This was the last response he'd expected.

I repeated what I'd said. I added up what my meal would cost, multiplied it by twenty-five, approximately the number of our monthly breakfasts. "My rent is only a little more than that per month. And I'm barely able to pay that."

He dismissed this explanation. "It must be something more."

"It's money," I insisted.

"I'll pay."

"No you won't."

Our omelets arrived—his sour cream and Russian caviar, mine cheddar cheese—and we ate in silence.

"I'm paying this time," he challenged, "as I insisted you come."

That much I would allow.

"I can't believe I won't be seeing you when I want to just because of a little thing like money," Ed said. He sounded personally affronted, as though I'd somehow arranged it to be like this.

"That's reality, Ed."

"Then we'll see each other *after* breakfast!"

"Ed," I now hauled out the big guns, "I'm working on something right now. As soon as I'm done with it, I'm going to have to find work. With Bobby Brown gone, I'm in a tight financial bind. My phone and utilities bills haven't been paid in two months."

He actually pulled out a checkbook and asked, "How much do you need?"

"I *need* a source of income. Much as I'd like to continue like this, I can't!"

Ed steamed. Ed sulked—beautifully, I must admit—then just as beautifully he smiled when I told him I would stay with him all that afternoon.

Some hours later when we were on the Morton Street Pier, our heads against the wooden barrier because of sudden gusts of wind, he asked, "What are you working on? A story?"

I lied and said yes. He began to tell me about a story he was working on.

He broke off in the middle and angrily said, "I don't understand why you have to get a nothing job just to earn money. You're a unique and remarkable person. You should get the money you need." He went on in this way for some time. At last I interrupted:

"What I am, Ed, is an unemployed twenty-seven-year-old faggot!"

He got very angry at that. He stood up, hauled me up by my windbreaker, and yelled into my face that I was wrong, wrong, wrong!

I was so surprised by this I gave in, and we made up. Even so, he continued sulking as we walked off the pier. I found myself thinking he was acting like a ten-year-old upon hearing his best friend was about to move to another city.

A week later, quite later at night, I was at work revising the novel, with Wanda Landowska discreetly tinkling a complex fugue as background music to my own sketchier keyboarding, when the phone rang: Dennis. He wanted to see me the next day. Was I available for lunch? I said no, but he could drop by for coffee.

Although I asked him several times where he was, at his own uptown apartment or at Ed's, he wouldn't answer.

"Ed's really upset," Dennis began when he arrived at my place early the following afternoon. In fact, Dennis himself looked more flustered than I'd ever seen him. As I'd thought, Dennis had been at Ed's the night before. Ed had made him phone me. "Ed thinks you're being disloyal. He thinks you're trying to break us all up. He thinks you may be seeing someone else." Dennis poured out all of the grievances he'd been getting night after night lately, making sleep unlikely and sex improbable, he said.

I couldn't help but feel a secret twinge of pleasure about having become such a huge problem in their relationship. On the other hand, I didn't particularly want to hurt Dennis.

I saw no reason to hide the by-now quite sizable manuscript of typed pages that he couldn't help but notice accumulated prominently next to the typewriter. "Truth is, Dennis, I'm writing a novel. I'm working at it very hard. I've got to finish it this month, because as soon as my money runs out, I have to get work. I know once I get work, I'll never find time to finish the novel."

Dennis was so pleased by this revelation that he both encouraged me and promised to sell Ed on the idea. However, while he now understood the cause for my distance from them, he thought it politic that I make a point of occasionally phoning Ed and arranging to see him. "You have to take a break some time," Dennis reasoned. "Arrange to see him then. Please." He all but begged. "He's driving me crazy. And I've got final exams coming up. I've already lost sleep and study time."

I promised and indeed called Ed the following morning.

He couldn't see me till later that afteroon and when we did get together, Ed told me he'd been working on a piece of writing too. He'd recently read the Australian novelist Patrick White. Did I know *The Aunt's Story*? It had completely changed his idea of what writing could be.

I knew neither the author nor the book and Ed insisted I come back to his place and borrow it.

So our rift was temporarily healed, especially when Ed told me he'd found himself so involved in his own writing that he forgot about time and had to set the alarm clock to remind himself of dates, even mealtimes. I'm pretty sure all of this was said to make me feel less isolated, now that Ed was somehow or other "sharing in" my life, by also writing.

What he never for a moment understood was that for me— unlike for him—writing the novel was an act of utter desperation: an attempt to impose order on a life filled with uncertainty, ambiguity, chaos. My book was a lifeline I'd thrown to shore to keep me from drowning in the very real professional and personal failures I'd experienced lately, culminating in the major shipwreck of his and my relationship.

The sickest irony of this entire business, naturally, was that it had all been predicted by astrology. Wayne's reading of my birth chart the year before had been right on the dot: I had met someone who'd affected my destiny in a crucial manner. Ed had turned out to be as beautiful, glamorous, and well connected as Wayne said he would be. Ed had important artistic, family, and even company connections, all as predicted. And, without knowing it, Ed had provided precisely the needed crisis to transform me into a writer. When I thought of it, I was alternately thrilled to wonder and furiously angry.

By May 20, 1971, I'd typed and revised the book. I immediately gave a copy of it to Jon Peterson to read.

As I put it into his hands, poor Jon began to explain that it was after all a first novel, and I shouldn't feel too brought down if it didn't live up to my expectations. He *was* a friend, and he *had* encouraged me to write, Jon explained, but now that I had, that didn't necessarily mean he could give the book to an agent, unless he thought it was very good. Etcetera, etcetera. Protecting his ass, which was only fair, I thought.

My friend Joseph Mathewson was about to move for the summer to Onset, a small town near Cape Cod. As he was himself a published author and I'd always respected his considerable amount of opinions on literary matters, I also gave him a copy of the manuscript, telling him to take his time reading it, as I suspected it would be some weeks before he felt settled enough there to get around to looking at it.

I was absolutely certain I was giving them both something quite special. I now know that's every hopeful writer's certainty.

Jon, bless him, read the manuscript over the weekend and called to enthuse over it for close to an hour. He was giving it to an agent friend, Charles, that next day. He was sure Charles would love it. Because of Jon's early and whole-hearted encouragement at this time, and because he actually did something toward getting me published, when a book of mine *was* published in 1975, I dedicated it to Jon.

Charles read the book the following week and told me he would handle it. He thought it was "brilliant writing." But he cautioned me that the book was unusual in both concept and execution—"hardly anyone's idea of a first novel." It might take him a while to place it with exactly the right publisher, Charles concluded.

That night I had Jon Peterson take me out to dinner to celebrate, promising to return the favor as soon as my book saw print.

I told neither Ed nor Dennis of this seeming stroke of good fortune, partly because they were busy—Dennis now in the midst of term papers and final exams, Ed with his family. His brothers were in town again, involved now in some major new business enterprise requiring Ed's presence. The next time I saw Dennis, he told me Ed was writing a screenplay.

I was astounded. Then I reflected. Ed had been a painter. What literary genre would be closer or more appropriate for an artist?

"It's about," Dennis paused, "a deaf ballerina."

I howled with laughter.

"No, really!" Dennis insisted. "I've read several pages. She has to rely on her teacher who gives her hand signals from the theatre wings."

"Stop, I'm dying." I couldn't stop laughing. Dennis also broke up.

Every word Dennis added, each new madcap stroke, provided new grounds for hilarity. I was certain this was just one of Dennis's jokes. And although in later years, he's always sworn that *The Deaf Ballerina* was an actual project, Ed never spoke of it and I never received what in court is referred to as "the ocular evidence."

*　　*　　*

Temporary relief from my monetary woes arrived in the form of a friend of a friend. Bob Chisolm was from Virginia and had just graduated from the University of Virginia, where he'd been studying fine arts. He was thinking of moving to New York and toward that end had thought to spend a summer in the city, trying it out, seeing if he liked it and if it liked him. An acquaintance had told him I was looking for a roommate. Would I mind one for only three months?

Mind? It sounded like an ideal solution. Not a complete one, mind you, as his share of rent, phone, and utilities would still leave me scrambling. But I thought I might be able to find odd jobs to help me out there.

Bob was cute. Bob was sweet. Bob was polite as only Southerners are polite and in every possible way Bob was as different a roommate from Bobby Brown as night is from day. He preferred moving into my bedroom, he said, so he could close the door and have privacy. Fine with me. I moved my bed into the study. Bob arrived the next weekend from Virginia with very little gear, barely a half closet of clothing, some portfolios, and a few bright pieces of handsome wooden furniture which went well with the rest of my apartment's so-called decor. He also brought some of his artwork—also bright and decorative—and several large hanging plants, including ferns he'd gathered and potted at the side of the road a few miles outside of Buena Vista. If Bobby Brown brought gloom, darkness, and cynicism into my life, Bob Chisolm brought life, light, and laughter.

And as I guessed, New York City did like him as much as I did. He decided to stay, to remain my roommate for another year, found himself a lover, joined a clever and talented group of young "gays and girls" in decorating and eventually opened up his own quite successful fine-art poster galleries.

Jerry Blatt also had reason to be cheerful. Someone new had come into his life, and being Jerry, he wanted to share the fun with me. During the time I'd known him, Jerry had already begun writing songs for the successful public television children's show, "Sesame Street." He'd written and produced a children's show, "Thumbelina," with future opera star Frederica Von Stade in the title role (the show was choreographed by a dancer named Rodney Griffin, who also entered my life in a sideways fashion a bit later on). Jerry and his colleague Lonnie had written a Broadway musical based on Molière's *Scapin* but were looking for a producer. None of his substantial achievements were "big time" enough for Jerry. He was still waiting for his break.

Despite all the time Jerry spent looking for sex, chasing after men, dealing with impossible, in his own words "white trash," boyfriends and lovers, Jerry usually chose women to work with, and because he was good-looking, muscular, vain, and self-absorbed, women usually liked Jerry.

So I wasn't too surprised when he phoned me suddenly shortly after I'd completed my novel and told me he was working with a new woman partner. "We're putting on a show at the Tubs of all places. She's a terrific singer, a very funny comedienne, and pure show biz. And," he added, "like me, she'll do anything, no matter how outrageous."

Anyone who has seen the black-and-white videos from the Continental Baths will agree those shows were outrageous. A few hundred gay men in white towels sitting around, or splashing in the huge pool, while this energetic little red-haired woman entertained—no one had seen anything like it. Obviously she had to be special to keep guys there when other temptations so obviously called—and she was! And could she sing! Her repertoire ranged from Cole Porter classics and current Broadway hits to torch song ballads to frenetic versions of Carmen Miranda classics—complete with huge bowls of fruit on her head. She and Jerry had worked out banter with the audience, which she cruised constantly—("See me later in the green room, big boy") and cracked jokes ("Is that a hair dryer in your towel, or are you planning to get married tonight?") No one escaped her eye. "Hands off him, he's mine!" she would say to a couple necking, then "This next song is for all you young lovers . . . Hit it, Chopin!" she would yell at her pianist—Barry Manilow on several occasions. Her name was Bette Midler.

I couldn't afford to go, which Jerry understood, so he promised to get me in "backstage" even though he admitted there wasn't much of a backstage. "We've barely got a dressing room." The following night, I appeared at the Seventy-third Street entrance of the Ansonia Hotel, only to be directed downstairs somewhere within the building's innards. There, at last, I was shooed into a back door and into a side corridor of the Continental Baths. "Good! You made it," Jerry said, seeing me as he rushed from one door to another. He was shirtless, with flip flops on his feet, his usual tight-fitting jeans, a bandana barely holding in his abundant dark curls. "Take your clothes off. You can use my locker. There's a towel in there to wrap yourself in. Make yourself comfortable. Show starts in a half hour. There are no house seats. There are no seats at all. There's barely a house," he added, sounding harassed and rushed, before I heard "Jer-rreee" shouted from somewhere nearby and he was gone.

I undressed, leaving my street clothes in his locker. I kept on my bathing suit, grabbed the towel, and went looking for Jerry to give him the locker key. Didn't find him, but I did work my way into the corridors of the Tubs: all cast-iron walkways and patterned floors through which you could look up or down two stories, little rooms with wooden doors. Someone snapped my Speedo against my body, saying "You're wearing too much!" I found the huge pool. There I dove in and hung around with a few people I knew from the Tenth Floor, a private disco in the flower district which had just opened that year and which I'd gone to thanks—again—to Jay Weiss, who knew Ray Yeates, its brilliant deejay.

A House on the Ocean, A House on the Bay

The show began—at last—and I found a seat up front. Jerry must have pointed me out to Bette because in the middle of one number, she pulled me to my feet, leaned me against the piano, and used me as a prop for a love song. She pretended to feel me up, until I was too obviously excited, at which point she stopped and said, "Sit down! You're disgusting!" to great hilarity before she continued her number.

Her attention got me sex directly after the show with one of the guys who worked at the Tenth Floor. I was in a very relaxed mood when I drifted back down to the lockers to find Jerry. I joined him and Bette in a coffee shop around the corner and we all continued to laugh and crack jokes and talk about how the show had gone. Bette was the first woman I'd met who could go from total seriousness one moment—"I was *so unhappy* in high school in Honolulu. I was the only white person . . . and I was an *ugly* white person!"—to complete camp the next: "I'll say one thing for this gig: my complexion's become totally fabulous from all the humidity!" She'd already been on Broadway in small roles in two shows: most recently as one of Tevye's daughters in *Fiddler on the Roof,* and she and Jerry had big plans: a solo album as well as a one-woman Broadway show. What really amazed me was how comfortably she seemed to be one of us. Later on Jerry would admit, "She's a gay man in a woman's body. She reminds me of myself."

We all grabbed a taxi home and the next day I spoke to Jerry, enthusing about Bette and the show. "You told me when you looked at my horoscope I could hitch my wagon to a woman's star," Jerry said. "I've got this gut feeling it's Bette and not Lonnie I should be working with from now on. What do you think?" Terrifically loyal, Jerry was very conflicted. I told him how much I'd liked Bette's personality, and as a performer, and how I thought she had "a star's charisma."

"Charisma maybe. She works like a dog," Jerry said, "and makes sure I work like a dog too!" This was not a point in favor of the new relationship. I knew how much Jerry prized his free time, his cruising afternoons, his sex in the evening, and I really wondered how, based on all these confusing possibilities, he would decide his future.

*   *   *

As the weeks went by and one publisher after another slowly declined my novel for one reason more exasperatingly arcane than the next, I found several jobs to supplement my dwindling resources. My favorite, which lasted several weeks, was cataloguing a huge private library of phonograph albums. The apartment I worked in was large and air-conditioned (by now it was a warm early summer) and I was alone there most of the time, free to play any of the thousands of records I wanted to hear while I typed out the needed data on triplicate index cards, which I then placed in several Rolodex files. Other, less pleasant jobs after this included addressing, envelope stuffing, and mailing out catalogues for several small businesses. None of these paid very well, just enough to feed me, but I had plenty of time for writing.

I was already working out new projects. I'd sketched out ideas for two novels, one based on a short story I'd written after finishing the novel. The other was based on an idea I'd had the previous year about a genius child of dubious morality and his conflict with a brilliant psychologist to secure full independence. My working title for this sketch was "Who is Christopher Darling?"

By the end of June no more odd jobs were to be found and I barely had my half of July's rent and nothing left after that was paid. When I spoke to my mother by phone, I told her of my completed novel, now out at yet another publishing house, and of my hopes to continue writing.

Instead of offering me money, she suggested I move back home. I said I'd starve in a gutter first, and she suggested I work part-time for my father.

After two phone calls negotiating half days at his produce business which would allow me writing time, I went to work for my father.

His business had grown substantially in the years since my older brother and I had worked weekends and summer weekdays as children and I had met and romanced the Taystee Bread man. Location had much to do with this change. His store was at the end of an exit ramp for a new expressway only a few miles away from booming Kennedy Airport. When we were younger, we'd hop across the low fence and stand as far down on the grass lawns as the police would allow us, watching as visiting dignitaries sped by in their limousines from the airport to Manhattan. I'd seen President Eisenhower, Fidel Castro, and Nikita Kruschev. Also my idol, John Kennedy, a half dozen times. One time, he'd been going slower and had turned to wave right at me.

In the 1960s, several foreign airlines moved into this terminal in great force. Without the corporate connections of domestic airlines and following the way they did business back home in Belgium and Munich and Stockholm, they sought out smaller businesses that would provide more personalized service. As my father was a clever entrepreneur, he accepted the extra problems entailed in dealing with finicky European managers and temperamental flight kitchen chefs in return for a good markup and increased reputation. This brought more trade from the airport, from a hotel chain when it first opened a building at the airport, and from local hospitals and delicatessens. I'd already been involved in some of this growth when I'd worked there a short while during my college days, so I was familiar with the setup.

Since that time, changes had taken place at the business, by no means all of them for the best. When in July 1971 I went to work for my father again, everything seemed slightly disordered, in need of fixing, polishing, general tightening up. Since I was traveling by subway and bus from Manhattan's West Village where I lived, it often took an hour and a half each way. I usually arrived around 10 A.M. By then some of the smaller orders had been made up and sent out by truck. But the bigger orders were still loading. It was my job to dispatch these by noon, go through the mail, sort through payments and bills, see to those smaller business customers who came into the warehouse, and hang around while my father lunched and napped until 4 P.M., when I would catch another bus and connect to another long subway ride, headed back to New York.

The first problem was that since I'd been away, my father had gotten rid of his two best truck drivers and hired in their place my older and younger brothers. The second problem was that they—and apparently everyone else working there except for Bill Trainor, aged seventy or so at the time—seemed to be on one drug or another. The third problem was that the setting for all this, the neighborhood itself, had severely declined in recent years, from middle class to near ghetto. Given the nature of such a large and neccessarily public area as our store—people constantly coming and going—there was virtually no security.

For the first few months this last didn't much bother me. In fact the job seemed ideal: I could catch up on my reading because I had an uninterrupted hour each way on the subway. I decided to read only big books, and reread *Moby Dick* for the first time since college when I'd rushed through it, as well as Dickens's *Dombey and Son*, Balzac's *Splendors and Miseries of Courtesans*, and Henry James's *The Bostonians* and *The Princess Casamassima*.

Even the dawdling bus ride though South Jamaica had its charms. Some afternoons that summer the place looked like the set of a movie location in Georgia or Alabama, say *To Kill a Mockingbird*, with folks sitting under umbrellas of huge peach trees ripe with fruit, barbecuing ribs and chicken on front-porch grills, picnicking in plastic lawn chairs amid the pervasive odors from fish-fry shops and bakeries. I'd known this neighbohood since I was a child, I'd played in its many little parks, ridden my bike through its streets and alleys, befriended children of all colors, fought with children of all colors. And since my father's business had been there since the late 1940s, everyone in the neighborhood seemed to know him—or at least know who he was. "Where you belong?" some heavyset woman in a bandana would challenge me with a broomstick, and I'd reply "Picano's Fruit Stand"—although it had long ceased to be that and was instead a warehouse and series of huge refrigerators with façade. She'd smile and say, "Well that's all right then. Come on in for some lemonade and peach cobbler. How's your pa's health?"

Though not the most tolerant man on earth, my father had been the first in the area to hire black schoolboys to work alongside white ones (including his sons) and the first to involve himself in the area's "spontaneous" demonstration and march that had followed the assassination of Martin Luther King, Jr. He'd made certain the remaining white-owned businesses had, at least, closed their doors that day and put up signs saying why. "Out of respect. He was an important man for these people," he explained, as though I—who had marched and demonstrated for civil rights with the Student Nonviolent Coordinating Committee—would not otherwise know. No wonder I felt as safe in South Jamaica as I did on Jane Street.

Another distraction was that I was very occupied in getting to learn the names and quirks of the new drivers and loaders, most of them from the neighborhood, but hired according to my father's own incomprehensible tastes and principles. I was also learning how to operate the business efficiently without stepping on too many toes. This was more easily done with everyone working there but my brothers. Even my older brother was fairly responsible. But my younger one! He seemed to live in a universe that abutted ours at only a few points. He'd vanish—"I was just out a few minutes, copping!"—when most needed. He'd take forever to make sizable deliveries so I'd get a half dozen phone calls from irate kitchen managers wondering where in hell their order was, before he'd casually arrive. Neither brother was ever there when required; they seemed to have their own mysterious agendas, which only glancingly included the way in which they supposedly earned their living. And my father seemed blissfully unaware of this, distracted perhaps by business, or more likely, by the contents of a case of Red Hackle Scotch kept hidden behind his office safe.

My supposedly simple job of dispatching became a constant battle, not only of my will against theirs, but of my will against their drug habits. I would cheer when all trucks had finally been sent out for the day and at last returned without major catastrophe and I'd sigh in relief when the drivers had all gone home for the day and my father had driven to his favorite lunch hangout and I was left alone with Bill Trainor.

But then I'd have to face the account books. An extraordinarily small, mousy CPA with whom my father must have gone to John Adams High School in the 1930s, professionally if sloppily suited but with a perpetually food-stained raincoat and a battered fedora, came by at least one afternoon per week to immure himself in the office, engaged in arcane numerical pursuits. Despite his constant presence, I was never able to make a match between our orders, the checks we got, the bills we paid, and the account books he worked on beyond a single day. Once those daily figures went into his double-column system, they began to resemble the mathematics of some fantasyland.

So, once I'd thrown my hands up over these mysteries, I'd go through the entire place, sweeping up, checking out the room-sized refrigerators filled with boxes of produce, attempting to get them in order. Their inventory had to be tallied and checked against the phoned-in orders from our larger customers that usually came in right after lunch—orders given in a variety of languages purporting to be English that I had to decipher over the phone.

A quiet time usually then: blessed midafternoon. Walk-in customers were scarce and I was often able to sit down long enough to read *The New York Times* or a magazine, eat my own midday meal, and keep phone calls away from my father, who by then was usually back from lunch, snoring away in a small side room furnished with a battered old car seat.

It was during one of those idyllic afternoons in late August that I had my first brush with mortality.

I'd seen the man come in, a tall good-looking African American in his late twenties, well-dressed in a brown leather windbreaker-style-jacket and good slacks. I'd been on the phone and I motioned to Tommy Gee, one of our loaders, to see to the man. Tommy returned a minute later saying the man didn't need or want help. Tommy meanwhile had work to do. When Tommy left, I was alone in the place, save for my father, sleeping in back.

I assumed the stranger to be the owner of some neighborhood grocery or food shop. That I didn't know him meant little. I'd not been back here long enough to know every customer. His looking around a great deal also wasn't unusual, although many owners of smaller businesses who came in wanted to be waited on immediately. I was still on the phone taking an order and I gestured somewhat hopelessly to the man that I'd be with him soon, I hoped.

It seemed forever before I was done with the particularly lengthy and detailed order. I walked up front, where orders were placed so they could be checked by my father before he left for the night. Next to this area was an old cash register, used for petty cash, because the bulk of our business was now done by monthly check.

"Can I help you?" I asked.

Close up his face looked beaded with sweat, though this room was usually kept cool by the constant opening and closing of the huge iceboxes. He mumbled something, nodding toward the cash register. I didn't catch what he'd said. He repeated it more clearly. "You going to open that? Or what?"

"What for?" I asked.

"To take the money out," he said.

"There's not much in there. We don't have much cash business here."

"I want you to open it and take the money out," he said, having difficulty in getting the words out. His words tended to slur, and I now noticed that his eyes were unnaturally yellow, as though he were jaundiced.

I still had no idea what he was talking about. "Why?"

"Because," he was fiddling with something in the inside pocket of his jacket. "Because of this!"

He showed me what looked like a large, blue-black, very fake revolver.

I thought, "Come on, you've got to be joking. That's the most bogus-looking gun ever." I'm sure this thought was readable on my face. He seemed unsure of himself.

"Open it yourself," I said and turned away.

"How?" he asked in a small voice.

"Ring up some amount!" I said, thinking, "Boy is this guy ever dense!"

"You do it," he insisted, and came closer, waving the thing at me.

I pushed it aside so the barrel wasn't facing me.

"If you want the money in there," I said, thinking this was about the stupidest joke anyone ever played on me, "ring it up."

He stood there totally baffled. I don't know if he was sick or high on drugs or what. I was waiting for him to put the stupid thing back in his jacket and admit it was a dumb stunt to pull. I heard tires screech outside, and looked away to see if there was an accident.

He might have left then, if my father hadn't for some reason awakened and come out of the little office and immediately faced this ridiculous scene.

Suddenly, from behind me, I heard my father call my name.

I turned around. He called my name again, then yelled "Get back!" in this panicky tone of voice I thought was totally inappropriate to the situation. His eyes were almost popping out of his head. His fear was so astonishingly real and so intense that for the first time I thought, "Hey, maybe it *is* a real gun." For the first time since the man had come into the building, I felt a twinge of fear.

Now, of course, I realize what was occurring: it's neccessary for people to communicate for some event, even a crime, to happen. Until that instant everything was stopped, going nowhere, because I didn't believe number one, it was a real robbery, and number two, it was a real gun.

With my father's appearance, this communication block vanished. Everything suddenly got moving, indeed it speeded up terrifically. My father pulled me behind him, and told the man not to shoot. He could take whatever he wanted. The man told my father to open the cash register. My father pushed me back more and opened the cash register. The man pulled out everything in it, including change, stuffing his pockets with the money. Finally, at last in charge of the situation, he waved the thing at us, telling us to move, move. My father kept telling him not to shoot. When we got near the office, he made us lay down on the floor. I thought this a bit much, but my father pulled me down next to him. The man went through our pockets, pulling out my father's wallet and my empty one. He told us to stay where we were for five minutes. Did we hear? Five minutes. Then he was gone.

I looked at my father's absolutely bulging eyes.

"He's gone!" I said.

"No! Wait!"

"He's gone," I said. I'd still not been infected by his fear. I got up, disgusted with the entire incident and how it had played out.

We found our wallets on the floor outside the office. When I ran to the front door, my father, already dialing the cops, told me to stay back.

I saw the thief across the street, getting on a bus. Getting on a bus!

When the cherry tops pulled up a few minutes later, I was arguing with my father. "It was a water pistol, for Chrissakes," I insisted. "If you hadn't panicked, he would have turned around and left."

No one listened to me. Not my father, not the two police officers, not the two detectives who just then arrived—we always called them Tooty and Muldoon after the characters on "Car 54, Where Are You?" the TV show—who were lunch and bar pals of my fathers and who zoomed over as soon as they'd heard our address on the crime report on their car radio.

"C'mon, what kind of cold-blooded killer could he have been?" I argued with them. "He was nervous! Sweating like a pig."

"Junkie!" Tooty insisted. "Dangerous. Shoot to kill."

"Oh, please! He took the Liberty Avenue bus as a getaway vehicle! The bus!" This last point struck me as the absolute height of absurdity.

To my astonishment, my father insisted it was only money—and not much at that—he'd deduct it off his taxes. And it had been a real gun, he insisted. He wasn't about to watch his son shot down like a dog in front of him.

Although both police cars chased after the bus, they didn't catch the guy. However, the aged clerk at the gas station across the street who'd seen the man running and shouting for the bus driver to stop had seen him put the gun inside the leather coat, and he also insisted it was real.

Tommy Gee emerged from who knew where to add to the confusion. I sat on a stool and smoked a cigarette. My father made us close up soon after and because he thought the thief might be lurking and waiting to gun me down, he actually drove me to the subway instead of making me wait for the bus.

That night I was talking to a friend on the phone and he calmly said, "It probably was a real gun."

"It looked so *fake*!" I insisted.

He told me to come to his apartment, a few blocks away, where he showed me an identical revolver to the one that the thief had waved around.

"It's my lover's thirty-eight," he told me.

I sat down and remained sitting after I'd drunk a double brandy.

An hour later I said to my friend, "I'm not getting paid enough to be shot. I'm sure as hell not going back to work there."

But in my heart, I believed that given how nervous the man was, by refusing to accept the reality of his gun, I would have ended up shaking him sufficiently for him to leave without shooting me *or* taking the money. I still believe it.

What I didn't know at the time naturally was this was but one incident of a chain putting me into contact with the close possibility of my own death. There would be more in the next few years: one even fairly spectacular, others less showy but equally designed to frighten. All I had to do was look down at the palm of my right hand where my lifeline was broken in two—a millimeter of blank skin between where one line ended and another, perilously started up again—to know more of the same was obviously was in store for me.

*   *   *

"Remember that house in Fire Island Pines I told you about last winter?"

Edward on the phone. All our contact as the summer progressed had been in the form of these increasingly rare phone calls. I told him sure, I remembered.

"The owner said I could use it a few days before Labor Day weekend. Why don't we go out there tomorrow?"

Oh sure! I was once again out of work and back in the financial lurch; yet another publisher—the sixth? the seventh?—had turned down my novel, and my agent Charles was sounding less optimistic every time we spoke; I'd just escaped a heroin addict's bullet. All I needed now was to involve myself once again in this totally unworkable and for me completely unrewarding, triangle to really complete my already severe depression.

"I don't know, Ed."

"C'mon," he urged. "When I told you about it before you said you *wanted* to go. You haven't been anywhere nice in years! And after what happened to you recently, I'd think you'd *need* a vacation."

I'd told him about the incident. I now thought I might knock the idea of Fire Island down by bringing up the topic of money—meaning my lack thereof.

Before I could even get the words out, Ed got my drift. "No excuses! I'm flush," he said. He tempered that by adding in a mumbling tone of voice, "A bonus of sorts. Some deal my brothers did came through and paid off."

I still wavered, listening with fond regret to him once again detail the many wonders of this bayside house in the Pines and all the great things we would do once we arrived there.

While I was still trying to say no, Ed said the magic words: "You know Dennis has been out west with his family for several weeks. Not that we were together all that much before he left."

I hadn't known: any of it. But did it mean . . . ? Exactly what did it mean? That without a third wheel, the van of their amour had gone through rocky roads, ending up crashed upon the embankment? And did Ed actually expect me to ditch whatever shreds of pride I still retained and take up with him now that Dennis had dumped him?

He did. And I did ditch those shreds of pride. Did it in a second. After all, this was exactly what I'd wanted: to be together, alone, with Ed. And on top of that, I'd be getting a Fire Island honeymoon!

Ed told me to pack and be ready by noon the next day. At noon, he called and said he'd be late. Maybe we ought to take the seaplane? I said fine. He called again at 3 P.M. and said he'd be at my place at four. He arrived at six, in a taxi. We didn't, however, drive to the seaplane basin on the East River, but to Penn Station instead. Even so, he'd gotten the times all wrong: we'd just missed a train and had to wait a half hour for another. It was midweek. Wednesday. The Long Island Railroad was filled with rush-hour stragglers, men in seersucker suits with ties loosened and shirts opened at the throat, women in light dresses with cotton sweaters for the air-conditioning. With our Lacoste shirts and Bermuda shorts, our sneakers and bags filled with bathing suits and frisbees, Ed and I were clearly vacationers. We sat together and he would occasionally take my thigh as he pointed to something out the window, or some item of interest in the magazine he was reading. I knew I wasn't looking my best: I was thinner than I'd been in years, exhausted by two months of summer heat and work and by being up late every night writing. I could use sun and rest. Naturally, Ed looked terrific.

Our connection at Babylon Station didn't arrive and we had to wait for the next one. By then the train ride, Ed's many little considerations, and the fresh Long Island evening air had all worked to refresh me a bit.

We arrived at the Sayville Ferry a half hour before the last boat, the midnight ferry. The terminal was dark but for a single light, a dozen people, some just pulling up to unload bags from cars, others scattered throughout the small, dimly lit, harborside cafe, where he and I sipped at overheated coffee.

We took our styrofoam cups and walked as far out as we could onto the deserted ferry dock. Across from us on Brown Creek were duckweed, and punks higher than our heads were waving in the breeze. Fireflies dappled the night, as though mimicking a million stars above. The sea salt and lightly briny air tickled my nose with promise. The distant tinkle of warning buoys at the harbor's mouth, a dog suddenly barking in a low consistent pattern, then silence. The murmur of incoming tide lapping against the rocks alongside a field of reeds. The air balmy, fragrant with sudden new odors: honeysuckle, motor oil, Ed's cologne, a toasted English muffin. I thought, yes, this is how life ought to be.

The ferry arrived—the *Fire Island Duchess*, newly in service, with its huge open-roof deck. Since there were so few passengers, we had several rows on top to ourselves. We sat in a long, back-molded pew and watched silently, almost afraid to speak as the pilot negotiated the inlet through night traffic of low, waterlined, square-roofed clamming boats, each with its single dangling lamp, heading back into port for the night. A burst of speed: we'd been released from the narrows into the huge dark emptiness of the Great South Bay.

We might have popped through the boundary of another universe at that moment, it was so silent, so still. The bay water's surface reflected the lighted white craft as if in an ebony looking glass. The prow barely caused a threaded chevron of foam wake. At the edge of the horizon, we could make out two separate chains of tiny lights: ahead, defining island villages, behind, the fading gleam of Sayville.

A House on the Ocean, A House on the Bay

On either side of the boat, faraway, like electric fish—or firefly tho-raxes—the lamps of clam diggers on a reef in the middle of the bay as they raked the sands. A light wind steadily ruffled Ed's fine chest-nut hair, flapped open the neck of his shirt. He took it off, and lay down along the seat, his legs over the side, his head in my lap. I ab-sentmindedly caressed his chest and shoulders. He closed his eyes and purred. Although in years to come I would often ride night fer-ries, no passage ever equaled that one for its perfection of calmness and beauty. Twenty minutes of potentiality; old ills healed; the past airbrushed into irrelevance.

The Pines Harbor when we glided in, was, as I'd recalled it at night, dark and vacant but for those few people arriving. The ferry lit up the area with its arrival, providing us illumination by which we located our direction—due east along Fire Island Boulevard.

It was cooler here. We had to stop, go through our bags, and find shirts to put on. We were to walk almost to the planked boulevard's end, to turn left where the boardwalk suddenly rose. The parallel walk along the bay ended that far east. I noticed names of paths fa-miliar from previous visits, names that would in later years become utterly familiar to me as I passed them several times a day: Teal, Black Duck, Floral, Shady, toward the bay; Crown, Ozone, Sky, Tar-pon, toward the ocean. We ascended a bit, trees fell away on either side and there, right in front of us, the night sky was laid out as though in an astronomical sky chart: the Pleiades just risen, below them Orion's belt.

I stopped, looked around, spotted the moon just rising, and nearby, smaller, blood-red Mars. The boardwalk was aligned to the planet's ecliptic plane, the Milky Way was well defined, thick with light, the gentle curve of land on either side of us so evident I quickly calculated: if Taurus is risen, Gemini just coming up, *my point* should be just about at midheaven, directly above us. I could never make out the Fishes, or the constellation of the Water Bearer in the sky to guide me, but wasn't that bright star Altair in the con-stellation Eagle? Formalhaut, my birth star, ought to be nearby. It had been years since I'd felt so close to the heavens. Ed asked why I was stopping and I showed him the stars, as I knew them.

He was eager to get to the house. We turned toward the bay. The house was at the end, on the right, somewhat Japanese in architectural style, Ed had told me, right on the water. Here a narrow staircase dropped at the end of the walk where dories had been beached upside down among dried bladderwort. But this couldn't be the place! This house was lighted! We heard voices inside! We were supposed to be alone.

Ed walked right in, dropped his bag. A head turned from a bar, brown hair plastered across a face I later described as "Bambi with a Leer."

"Dahl-ling! Expecting company?" he/she/it half drawled, half slurred, in question to someone out of sight.

A close-clipped gray head with startled blue eyes within a parboiled red face peeked out of the kitchen. "Oh! You must be Ed!"

He was Bernard. That was Antony. No *h* please, just An-to-ny, and where was Payter? There he was, fortyish, overweight, lots of blond hair, wearing something cut like, though far too sheer to be, a jumpsuit.

"Bernard! I told you they'd arrive," Peter called in his bet. He had one of those indistinguishable northern European accents: Danish? Finnish?

"We're not officially here," Bernard apologized.

"But we are here," Peter said. "At least for the night."

"I'm not," Antony drawled. "Having a cocktail doesn't count."

"The way you have them, it does too count," Bernard warned.

"Don't I know you?" Peter said to Ed. "Weren't you at ____'s?" He began to enumerate a list of social functions, several of which Ed had indeed been present at: among what Dennis and I called to his face, Ed's "uptown people," and behind his back, "snooty uptown queens."

"Could we put these bags somewhere?" Ed asked. Under his breath he whispered to me, "I didn't know they'd be here."

I hushed him. Ed introduced me to Peter who appeared initially alarmed to meet me, then made a point of ignoring me. He left us alone in the master suite, a separate wing of the house with ceiling fans, louvered windows, two tiny decks: one off the bathroom almost hidden in jungly foliage, the other off the bedroom facing the bay, the waters now moonlit with yellow streaks.

A House on the Ocean, A House on the Bay

"Just like it promised in the brochure," I joshed.

"Except for . . ." Ed nodded toward the main house. "They'll leave tomorrow. Meanwhile . . ."

"Forget about tomorrow, dahl-ling!" I imitated Antony.

Ed was sort of surprised when I put my hands around his neck and kissed him. I was more surprised when he regained his poise so quickly and kissed me back so much more intensely. Behind us, somewhere, we heard three separate strands of more or less male laughter. When Ed finally let go of me, he said with an edge to his voice, "We finally made it."

I tried not to read too much into that. A few mimutes later he dragged me out to sit in the main room in an oversized chair and to sip at a cassis, while Bernard and Peter talked and talked, occasionally stopped by a quip from Antony, or an answer from Ed, who looked like he was on "Twenty Questions," but who, after all, was equal to any social encounter ever devised. Naturally, within ten minutes, he'd charmed them all.

As always with new people, I kept my mouth shut. At one point, Bernard dragged Ed off to another room to look at someone's framed photos, and Peter turned all of his blond focus upon me. "So tell me, Feliz, how long have you been in our country?"

Now I somewhat understood his earlier look of alarm seeing me. He'd thought I was familiar, someone he knew and perhaps didn't expect to see in the Pines of all places. Who . . . ? He'd pronunced my name as though it were Spanish. Aha!

"Oh," I replied in a thick Hispanic accent, " 'bout two three yeaaahs."

"And do you have a job?"

Meaning was I a hustler.

"Really! Payter," Antony drawled in mock indignation.

"Not righ' now," I replied. "I'm lookin'."

"I see. And how is it you know our Ed?" Peter asked, using a possessive that would have astonished and annoyed Ed more than he had any idea.

"You know, 'round the Village an' all."

"I do know. But haven't I seen you at night there? Where is that place I mean, Antony?"

"Dahl-ling," Antony said, "your boredom quotient is rising dangerously!"

"The meat rack, I think it's called," Peter said. "Washington Square?"

"Got my own spots. Ed and me, we like to spen' afternoons near da river."

"In daylight?" Peter's mouth fell open.

"Sure. Any time."

Bernard and Ed came into the living room. "Did Felice tell you Charles is representing his new novel? You know Charles, Peter?"

Bafflement on Peter's face. "But he . . . he—"

"Dahl-ling!" Antony the slush got it first. "You've been had!"

Peter looked at me, "Then you're not—?"

"Not who?" Ed pushed a place for himself next to me on the huge easy chair.

"Not a Puerto Rican hustler," Antony explained. "Not that I personally have a thing against Puerto Rican hustlers mind you. Corky Maldonado, for one, is divinity fudge."

Ed still wasn't sure what was going on. Bernard warned, "Pay-ter?!"

"I've been gauche," Peter admitted in exaggerated horror.

"Dished herself with Sevrés," Antony summed it up, then laughed in his whiskey voice for the longest time.

The dining room connecting two wings of the house was completely glassed in, surrounded by a garden on one side, the bay's glories on the other. Constellations sedately whirled above, visible through the glass ceiling. Ed and I were served a good late supper that guilty Bernard "just threw together," while Antony watched and slugged down more margaritas. Of the three, I liked him best. Ed meanwhile socialized, catching up on all sorts of gossip about mutual acquaintances. Peter, unfortunately, attempted to cover up his previous gaucherie by talking to me on a topic he figured we had in common.

"Bernard and I know a writer," he said and named a middle-aged woman who wrote suspense romances for secretaries to read on the subway.

I said I didn't know her or her work.

"Bernard has all her books. Signed!" Peter dug himself in deeper.

"Pay-ter, dahl-ling!" Antony warned, having caught the sneer in my voice.

"I just loved her last one," Peter went on. "What's it called?"

"*Hot Fog!*" Antony replied for my sake.

"No. I know: *The Nymph in the Maze!*"

"I like *Hot Fog* better," I said to Antony. "'It was a warm and steamy night . . .'" I paused. "For some reason I'm reminded of 'Nimrod.' You know, from Elgar's *Variations*?"

"I always want to ejaculate when it reaches that part," Antony agreed.

"It was not titled *Hot Fog!*" Peter, lost, insisted.

"I've got it!" Antony said, "*Hot Fog*'s opening line: 'Every inch of her naked torso was permeated with perspiration . . . .'"

I knew this game from playing sonnet with Jerry so often. "'Only April,' she moaned, and flung another white rat to her pet boa constrictor!'"

Antony picked it up: "'Fata Morgana uncoiled herself lazily, ignoring the frightened rodent for the longest time. Then flung itself, a diamond-quilted lariat. The rodent whimpered—'"

"'. . . its girded windpipe shut, it died. The maid chose that moment to enter."

Antony added, "'Horrified. As usual.'"

"What *are* you two talking about?" Peter demanded, nonplussed.

An hour later, a pouting Peter convinced Bernard that they had to go to bed. Antony was led to the front door. "Dahl-lings! Pour me a taxi!"

Ed and I offered to walk Antony to where he was staying so he wouldn't fall off the boardwalk and in his own words "be ravished by one of those allegedly straight telephone linemen who are always dawdling about long after they should have already gone home to Nowhere, Long Island."

It wasn't far, and he kissed us chastely on our cheeks as we led him indoors. "Don't mind Payter," he told me. "You're young, good looking, smart. It's only natural he'd hate you."

The house was almost completely dark when Ed and I returned. He insisted we go out to the back deck that commanded a 180-

degree view of the Great South Bay. A swimming pool lay embedded in the decking. We stripped off our clothing and dove in and swam to the far edge, where from within the water, we could look out at more, even darker water: the bay itself.

Ed nuzzled me. "Let's go into the bay."

We pulled ourselves out of the pool and knelt over the deck's edge. Below us we saw about five feet of wooden pilings. Then the black bay waters.

"Is it deep enough?" I asked.

"High tide," Ed said. "Look at the wood. No high-water mark."

We stood there and side by side dove into the bay. It was colder than the pool, but smooth and as black within it as it had looked. We swam until it seemed we were so far away from the house we could no longer make out which one it was. Ed urged me on, just a bit more. I dogpaddled in the water, while he took little dives, searching for what? Clams? Pearls?

"Here!" he resurfaced. He'd found us a little sandbar to stand on. We seemed to be equidistant between two strands of dimly lighted shorelines, but here the water rose only to our hips. We stood holding each other, looking around, pointing out things. It was—as he'd promised months ago in his triangular apartment in Manhattan—quite strange and wonderful.

We returned at last to the house and remained outdoors on adjoining chaise lounges. Slowly, almost desultorily, we began to make love, until suddenly I was coming, and Ed was saying through his teeth, "Yeah! Yeah! Yeah." He led me inside to bed where we all but passed out.

Antony was at his spot—the bar—when we arose late the following morning, a perfect, hot, cloudless day. He was drinking a citrus juice confection, alcoholic content unknown but presumed. Peter and Bernard were nowhere to be seen.

"They're gone," Antony assured us. "I'm a lot harder to get rid of."

Bernard had fixed us an elaborate breakfast that only needed reheating. Antony pushed the idea of food far away, then allowed himself to be persuaded to pick at strips of bacon and a cantaloupe slice. By daylight he was far younger than I'd thought—about my age. How much of his sophistication was an act?

A House on the Ocean, A House on the Bay

After breakfast, we sunned on the back deck. Antony was in a big white straw hat, his surprisingly tanned and muscular legs all but hidden in long linen shorts, either a cigarette or a glass rim constantly at his lips.

Ed and I dove into the pool, cooling off. He remained in longer, swimming laps. I was seated next to Antony when Ed drew himself out at the far end and shook himself dry.

"One might eat champagne sorbet out of a navel like that," Antony commented with what I took to be rare admiration. "And to think, he's all yours."

"Hardly," I replied.

"But dahl-ling! Last night! The hijinks I heard about. Yes, they were awake. If only he didn't slouch like a gorilla," Antony added. "Is he a gorilla in the sack?"

"Orangutan."

"I've never done it with an orangutan. Head back!" Antony shouted to Ed, who'd been too far to hear us but was now approaching. "Chest out. Tummy in!" Antony concluded as Ed followed his directions good-naturedly, ending up with a salute. "I can't stand it!" Antony groaned and fled indoors to the bar.

"Staggered by your bearing," I explained casually, adding "I owe you one."

"One what? Oh, you mean from last night?"

"I know you didn't get off. How about now?" I suggested. "Blow job in the semi-enclosed outdoor shower. Scandalize the neighbors!"

"They've seen it before!" he replied. Then, "Not me, of course! Maybe later on, after the beach."

It turned out to be after the beach, two spontaneous parties at houses we visited, a trip to the grocery store—Antony said he was cooking!—and drinks on the back deck, that I finally maneuvered Ed into the outdoor shower.

Antony wasn't a bad cook. After coffee and dessert, I was ready to pass out. Ed wanted to go out dancing.

"You'll have to go to the Grove," Antony told us. "Nothing's open here in the Pines on Thursday night."

It took all of Ed's prodding and a good deal of Antony's espresso coffee to get me up, dressed, and out the door. We walked to the harbor and phoned for a water taxi, since the dune-hugging cabs of the past had been outlawed shortly after one had killed the poet Frank O'Hara. We sat at the end of the tiny motorboat as the driver—who couldn't have been fourteen—swerved and swirled through the bay, enjoying it most when he could send curls of water high enough into the air to spray us and to make Antony go into near shrieks of "Dahl-ling, don't splash the Chanel!" I found it delicious, invigorating.

The beachfront dance place I'd recalled from my last visit to Cherry Grove in 1966 with my straight social worker pals was still there, with, apparently, the same clientele as before, though perhaps older, blonder, and more cosmeticized. Antony settled at the bar as though he'd never left. Ed and I looked around at a mostly empty dance floor, the aging queens primping for our benefit then quietly dishing us when we ignored them. The Discaire alone had changed. The music was no longer rhythm and blues but show tunes and fox-trots.

Knowing it had been a bad idea and wishing to compensate somehow, Ed waited for the first halfway decent slow number, then drew me out onto the dance floor. I wasn't used to dancing like this, or being led, but he did it with his usual authority. In minutes, we were like kids at a high-school prom. The Discaire obliged, luring one other couple onto the dance floor. We returned to the bar to receive scattered applause from onlookers and thanks for "bringing back romance" in the form of two rounds of drinks. Even Antony was included in the freebies.

As usual, Ed made friends quickly and I kept quiet. When we left an hour later, he suggested a walk along the beach. The gibbous moon lighted the sands more brightly than it had the bay water. The tide was out, the strand wide and white, starkly shadowed, creased here and there by the tread marks of the infrequent beach patrol vehicles. We walked to the end of the Grove, then collapsed against towering high dunes between the two communities. Ed pulled out some grass and we smoked. He was still restless and had a new idea: "I bet no one will be there, but you ought to see the local meat rack," Ed said. "How's your night vision?"

It was okay, I thought. Ed led me up a long boardwalk back into

A House on the Ocean, A House on the Bay

the easternmost end of Cherry Grove and a short distance back to the bay side. He made me follow him closely, jumping off the edge of the wooden planking and directly in a thick heavy wood.

Nel mezzo del cammin di nostra vita
Mi ritrovai per una selva oscura

I chanted, quoting the opening lines of Dante's "Inferno."

"It's pretty dark," Ed agreed. "But look!" He pointed to where someone had painted white slashes along certain trees: a path. He held my hand, led me deeper into the woods. We passed solitary figures against trees, other figures entwined. One group of five seemed involved watching two men. Hands reached out for us as we went past and Ed suddenly stopped and propelled me into the group.

In seconds, I was surrounded. Hands were caressing me, lifting my shirt, tugging at my denim buttons, pulling down my pants, lifting and wrapping my T-shirt around my neck. I tried to look for Ed. Then someone was kissing my neck, someone else kissing my nipples, someone else kneeling in front of me taking my cock in his mouth, someone else kneeling behind me doing something nice between my buttocks as other hands came form nowhere to touch my arms, legs, chest, flanks. It was an extraordinary sensation, series of sensations, wonderful. But where was Ed?

A gap opened before me. And there, not two feet away, as undressed as I was, as surrounded by men, as at the center of his own ministrants of pleasure, was Ed. He reached a hand out to brush my face, then managed to get closer, so we could kiss, thereby becoming the central focal point of maybe eight other men bent on giving us pleasure. Shortly after that, first I, then Ed reached orgasm, our lips still brushing, tongues in each other's mouths.

A minute later we were alone. The others vanished, as though they'd been sylvan deities with the ability to transform themselves into leaves and branches of trees. Only mosquitoes remained, buzzing hungrily. We dressed and stumbled through increasingly tortuous paths until we made it out of the wood and onto the boardwalk. We reached the beach, where we fell down on our backs on the sand.

"Welcome to Fire Island." Ed laughed.

"Is it always like that in there?" I had to ask.

"So long as you be young and I fair."

The sex had completely exhausted me and even with a rest, brought back all of my earlier exhaustion. It was all I could do to manage to slog the long way back through beach sand to our crosswalk, and stagger, unwashed, into bed.

"The cities of the dunes. That's what I call the Grove and the Pines," Antony said next morning when Ed and I finally awakened and left our room. Clouds covered the sky this morning, and the air felt heavy, rain filled. "After M. Proust's *petit tôme*," Antony explained his allusion.

Ed and I were tired and lazy. It took forever to get breakfast made and eaten.

We asked how Antony had gotten home.

"A park ranger gave me a lift in his jeep. I offered to blow him in thanks, but . . ." Antony waved a hand. "I've always depended upon the kindness of strangers. Usually the stranger the kinder. By the way, you two were quite the thing at *le bâl*, last night. I'm certain that after your performance, dozens of old fairies went straight home and trashed their corsages."

He went on complimenting us, digging for information about what else we'd done, which neither of us would say, until Ed dove into the pool.

"Everything hunky?" Antony asked me.

"Okay."

"Do we post the banns or what?"

I laughed.

"Really. Three nights and it's a real romance," Antony assured me. "Tonight will be the kicker!"

The rain threatening all morning arrived at noon, a sweeping, brief electrical storm followed by a torrential downpour. Antony had left not a minute before, taking with him the house's only umbrella. Ed and I remained in the living room reading, occasionally looking out. The phone rang and he got up to answer it. It was the house's owner, calling to say he'd come out on Saturday. We could stay if we moved to another suite. Ed seemed unsure. The man was Ed's friend, so I told Ed it was entirely up to him.

The rain seemed to put him in a far less relaxed mood and I wondered if he thought the elements were conspiring to ruin our stay. I loved the rain: the way it beat on the roof and deck, its patterns on the pool water's surface, its varieties and changes. It all seemed so authentic out here where everything was so open to the sky and air, so unmediated.

While I read, or let my book drop to watch the rain, Ed paced. Looking out upon the falling rain, he seemed to be so uninspired. He went into the bedroom at last, leaving me alone, and I heard him talking on the phone. I found myself wishing he'd leave, go for a walk. Unaccountably, I wanted nothing more than to be alone, in all the elements, safe inside the house, yet exposed via all that glass to spectacular sheets of lightning and ominous thunder, to be alone as the rain slowly ended, and water slowly dribbled down onto the decking.

A decade later, I'd rent a house on Midway Walk on the west side of Fire Island Pines and live there May through October, years in a row. And while in it I didn't directly face the bay as in this house, it was in many ways the fulfillment of the covenant that seemed to have been made during this brief stay on the bay side, an experience quite different from the ocean side.

What distinguished the two most clearly, and connected them so closely, was intensity of sound. On the ocean side, the constant susurration of the surf seemed to blanket all in an undertone of white noise. But here, the waves' constant onrolling was muted, distant, only really clear late at night, so it was the island itself and its life that filled my awakenings and my dreams, its multiplex birdsong: house doves cooing, blue jays screeching as though strangled, cardinals mocking, secretary birds cackling, and the gulls' high cries, cutting through it all as they dove for minnows—screams like fire alarms falling from the sky—or alighted erect on a post pier, and then, at night, the frail, solitary moan of an owl ominous with midnight.

Sounds first, then sight, that was the bay side's manner. At three in the morning, a sudden mechanical sputtering upon the stillness of the bay waters, then minutes later, the telltale, barely visible glimmering of white and red lights of a yacht would become apparent. Or the high flutter of thousands of feathers beating the early September afternoon air, and only minutes afterward, the onrush of a thousand swallows, flying two by two across the treetops, around chimneys in a do-si-do as they migrated west and south. Or, the metal jangle of a chainsaw slashing two by fours, its pitch rising higher, unbearably higher, only to drop an octave as the pieces of cedar split. Or, the soft, regular, undulating thump of deckwood, soft, inexorable, rumbling portentously as someone approached from forty yards off, crescendoed to thunder at arrival, or continued to softly thrum and hum and softly buzz into nothing.

In this concatenation of sound, human voices held almost no place, coming to you not in definable words or phrases, but partial, distorted: the harsh constricted vowels of a construction worker shouting an order, or the voice of a single woman among men, wavering and overmodulated, uncertain she is being listened to; or a single call of a name, Paul, that would stretch seemingly forever, before snapping too suddenly for the labial to be obvious, the tone the only clue to what kind of animal was making the sound. And all of it through a constant smattering of leaves and boughs. Sound and resonance: the air-soaked drone of an airplane, or a whippoorwill whistling overheard, all of it heard as though you were living within some gigantic carpet.

I must have dozed off. The skies cleared by seven in the evening and we were treated to a dramatic, posed-for-the-camera sunset over the bay. Ed hadn't touched me all day. Now he held me, began speaking in a low voice about sunsets he'd experienced in St. Thomas, in Puerto Vallarta, in Ireland, wherever the sun set over water. Every word he uttered sounded to my sleepy ears like a promise.

Perhaps, I thought, we would after all make it three nights in a row, as Antony predicted. Why did I suddenly seem so unexcited by the prospect? Why did I suddenly want the house, the island itself, to myself—even without him?

The phone rang again and when Ed returned he said, "We're invited to three houses here for dinner."

He explained who the three hosts were, and who, most likely, the other guests would be. He reminded me it was social time—Friday night, the weekend's start. As he described them, I sensed him subtly putting them all down, so I said, "We don't have to go. We can stay here tonight."

But no, that wasn't at all what Ed wanted. He was restless again. He *wanted* to see all these people, to be seen by them.

"Here's my plan." Ed outlined it: we'd stop at one house for before-dinner cocktails, go to the second for dinner itself, and to the third for after-dinner drinks. Then we'd go dancing.

It seemed an exhausting program. I wondered if I'd be able to do it all. Ed had been nervous, edgy all day, eager for anything! But I'd been content to sit, read, watch the rain. Naturally, Ed didn't merely present his agenda: he urged it on me with all the power of his logic and charm. Eventually, I gave in.

Cocktails were taken on the second-story balcony of a house not far away. Nine or ten others were present, including a middle-aged woman who looked like the actress Terry Moore (but wasn't) and seven men named Michael (nowadays it would be David). They were aged forty to fifty-three, carefully groomed, and carefully "beach-casual." None had a clue what to make of a silent young man like me. Ed they clearly adored and made much of. He tried to get me to talk and I did, to the woman, who said she was the madam of a Washington, D.C., cathouse (her word). Her escort popped out of nowhere, a tall blond fellow Ed's age with a face right out of a Lucas Cranach painting, a muscular, long torsoed body but plump cheeks and merry blue eyes. He was already in his cups, and obviously—and to Ed's obvious embarrassment—knew Ed from some previous carnal encounter.

Dinner at the second place was more intimate, if no friendlier. Only three Michaels present, with a Robert and an Arnold. They were more laid back and a smidgen less alcoholic, although of the same age and social set as the previous group, whom they knew well enough to dish. Dinner was in a screened-in gazebo on the bay sands, served by the youngest Michael, who, it turned out, was the houseboy. Ed got into an argument with Robert about a piece at auction. Ed argued with usual full intensity, till he had all our attention, then he backed off gracefully.

Arnold and one Michael—not the houseboy—joined us at the

third house. Here the crowd was much larger and a bit younger. The house was huge, built by a well-known residential architect I'd never heard of. I was taken on a tour. Evidently the owner was a noted collector of Polynesian art. Ghastly masks, giant figurines with elongated limbs and huge quivers of overdecorated arrows the size of spears filled the rooms. Our hostess, the "ineffable Joffy," stood so close to me for so long I almost swooned from her perfume. She was pretty and large featured but her makeup couldn't hide her bad complexion nor could her Oxbridge accent cover her Cockney origins. Arnold rescued me from her, then put a not too subtle make on me himself, only deterred when his Michael came looking for him.

I returned to the partying people. I felt sated, a little drunk, and very tired. The clock read 1 A.M. I'd been up till three the night before. I wanted to go back to the house, dip in the pool, make love with Ed—and above all, sleep.

He was nearby, and—was I hearing right?—having the same argument he'd had with Robert at dinner. Except Ed was taking the opposite side of the argument, defending as staunchly as he'd defended the other side an hour ago.

A line came into my mind and would not go away. A month before I'd picked up Proust's *Sodome et Gomorrhe* looking for a particular description of a place that I'd recalled and wanted to reread. I hadn't found it. Instead I'd read entire sections of the book and had found myself especially struck and I'd copied out into my journals a description of someone at the Duchesse de Guermantes's hundred-page-long afternoon party:

> . . . his nature was just like a sheet of paper that has been folded so often in every direction that it is impossible to straighten it out.

Why this came to mind, I didn't at first understand. Then I did. The quote summed up Ed. He could argue two sides of any question an hour apart. He could claim to love two men differently yet equally, at the same time. He could be a Greenwich Village street cruiser and S&M master in the Chelsea leather bars, and at the same time fit right into the Upper Fifth Avenue moneyed museum crowd. And it wasn't because he was so protean, so adept, it was because he didn't know *who* he was and looked to others to tell him. We were mirrors in which he saw himself. The steadier the mirror, the stronger, and better the reflection. It wasn't Dennis's body or my mind Ed loved: it was the strength, the purity of our power to reflect him back to himself.

Once I'd grasped this, I began to understand this trip. An idea that Ed had last summer and that he'd thrown at me when we'd met. Probably at others too. But I'd accepted it more, reflected it better, strongly enough in fact for Ed to work out all the details and see me in it. When the opportunity arose for him to come out to that house, I wasn't merely the best companion, I was the only companion. Had I been anyone else, the hustler Antony had mentioned—and also had reflected back the idea—Ed probably would have asked Corky Maldonado out and not me.

Ergo: this trip didn't *mean* anything, or nothing beyond itself, to Ed. The minute it was over, our relationship would be back as before: in abeyance.

That's what Ed had been subtly but surely telling me all the time we'd been here. His honesty had broken the surface at crucial points over the past days and nights. Those points had been significantly sexual, as though he could lie to himself and me, but couldn't get his body to do so. The first night, I'd come, Ed had assisted. The second day was a classic "scene" out of some West Hollywood porno flick, "blow job in the deck shower," also strongly defined and limited. Later, yesterday, had been an alfresco encounter involving eight other men. Not once since we'd gotten out here had our lovemaking been equal, shared one-on-one intimacy. Intimacy was not in the scenario for us here. Never had been.

Ed might argue that this in no way meant he did not love me. I didn't even know what love meant anymore—after Djanko and Bob Herron, and last year's failed romance, how could I? But I was sure this was not it. Not my own carefully restrained obsession over the past ten months, not Ed's corresponding fantasy projection. Never was, never would be.

Grasping this, at the after-dinner party, I was appalled. My heart felt green and hollow like a cactus tree. It wasn't as if I hated, or even fully blamed Ed for it. I did want to get away from him, fast!

Unfortunately, he chose my moment of realization to sit next to me.

"What's wrong?" he interrupted something he was saying. Mr. Congeniality, I found myself thinking. To me, he looked as though he were wearing an Ed mask. "You look white as that napkin," he said. "Are you nauseous?"

Nauseated, I mentally corrected, and thought, "Yes, but you wouldn't understand the nature of my nausea." The mask he wore was perfect, right down to the hints of crow's feet along his angled eyes.

"I may be . . . food so rich . . . and the drinks!"

Arnold and Michael joined us, concerned. Clearly I looked awful.

Ed said he'd take me home. The thought of being alone with him was more than I could bear. I also knew he'd probably go out of his way to be nice to me, making it all the more appalling. I also knew that at some point I would try to rip off that mask he wore so well and find . . . who knew what, if anything at all, I would find.

"No! You go on. I'll go home and lie down. Maybe I'll join you later."

"I can't do that," Ed said.

At least his mask said that he couldn't do it with all these people he knew and socialized with watching us so closely.

Arnold and Michael stepped in. They were not going dancing. They'd walk me home, make sure I was okay.

I latched onto that. Even so, Ed walked halfway before he let Arnold shoo him away. Especially, as he explained (although how he could tell in the darkness I'd never know) that some of my "color was back." Back at the house, Arnold fixed me a bicarb of soda and recommended sleep. I went to bed and dropped off in minutes.

Two hours later I woke up. No sounds in the house. Nothing. But the wind had changed direction. Even with the ceiling fan on, the room had become unbearably stuffy and hot. After taking off all my remaining clothes and the sheets and trying all sorts of positions, I gave up, got up, and went onto the back deck. It was incredibly still, warm, only a bit of a breeze. I lay on the chaise and found a large bath towel to wrap myself in. The moonlight bothered me. I shoved the chaise along the deck until it fit in an indentation between the

A House on the Ocean, A House on the Bay

kitchen and outdoor service area. I wrapped the towel tighter, turned over, and slept.

This time I was awakened by voices: someone going "Shh!"

The moon had set. It was considerably later. I saw Ed come out of the darkened living room onto the deck and go to the window of the bedroom we slept in. He peered in but couldn't see anything through the blinds and shrugged.

I was about to say, "Here! I'm right here!" but another figure stepped out.

"He's sleeping!" Ed explained. "He felt sick before."

"He your lover?" the guy asked.

Ed shook his head no.

"Boyfriend?"

Ed again shook his head no.

"Then what? Friend?"

"It's complicated . . ." Ed began, but didn't finish the thought.

I now realized that in the niche I was hidden from their view.

Suddenly Ed said, "Here's the pool!"

They stripped down and slid into the pool, I guess to avoid waking me with a dive splash. They ended up at the far side where I could see their heads close together. Ed said something I couldn't make out and they lifted themselves out, knelt at the edge of the deck over the bay, talking quietly. Without hearing their words, I had a good idea of what they were saying. I felt as though I were watching a rerun of my own life. A minute later, they dove into the bay.

When I could no longer hear Ed's voice in the distance urging his companion on, just a little bit further, I went into the house. I knew they were standing on a sandbar, possibly that same one we'd stood on two nights ago, holding each other, Ed pointing out the same sights he'd pointed out to me. To my surprise, I didn't care. I slept easily, deeply.

"We're going back to the city today," Ed told Antony the next morning. "Felice still isn't feeling too well."

Antony waited till Ed was out of the room before looking at me with a quizzical expression. "You get third-night jitters, Dahl-ling?"

"Would you blame me if I did?"

Antony looked deep into the heart of his Bloody Mary.

"Let's just say," I began, "that last night I had what you would call a *horrible surprise!*"

"Prince Charming became a frog?"

"Something like that," I admitted.

Antony twirled the contents of his drink in front of his eyes. "I'm not too surprised. I thought a smart lad like yourself would catch on soon enough."

"Meaning what, exactly?"

"Meaning no one can make head or tail of him."

"Oh! He works at that," I said.

"He does, true. Even so . . . who was it, could it have been Thomas Mann who said after meeting Einstein, 'He's a very nice fellow, but he exists at a slight angle to the universe'?"

"Ed's no Einstein, but I see what you mean."

Antony was remaining at the house to greet our host. When we were packed and ready to go he kissed me lightly on the cheek. I said, sincerely, that I hoped to meet him again.

"You'll land on your feet, Dahl-ling! Next leap will take you even higher."

"Cra-a-ash!"

Once Ed and I were walking toward the ferry deck, I began to dread the return trip. Ed knew something had gone wrong between us, but he didn't know what. The last thing I wanted was two and a half hours alone with him on the boat, train, and taxi. He was certain to ask and when I couldn't reply, to begin to grill me. What could I possibly say?

Mercifully, at the harbor, I met an acquaintance with a car going back to town. He was dying for company.

Ed rode in the front seat with the driver and they talked most of the way into Manhattan. I slept fitfully and got out first. When Ed offered to join me, I said he shouldn't. He was getting along well with my acquaintance and thought they might have a late lunch together. I encouraged them but told them to count me out. I was still feeling queasy. Ed made some sort of awkward move toward me, thinking to, I don't know, maybe hug me or something. He must have seen the look on my face because he rethought the move midway and said we'd talk later.

Over the next few days I had my roommate answer the phone whenever he was in the apartment. I didn't answer at all when I was there alone. It took about two weeks for Ed to get the hint.

*   *   *

I'd returned home to a letter from my agent telling me that although he'd tried all the editors he knew for my novel, he'd not been able to place it. He partly blamed himself, and partly them; he was nice enough not to blame me. He added that he was returning the manuscript by separate mail. It arrived the following Monday. In the same mail was a breathless missive from my pal Joseph Mathewson up near the Cape. He'd loved my novel, he wrote, and he was surprised to find himself writing that I was a "genuine new talent." He sincerely hoped I'd have the book published in the fashion it deserved. I reread the letter saying to myself, "You're wrong, Joe." I read sections of the book at random and it did seem as good as he and Charles and Jon said. Why then wouldn't anyone publish it? Was it not the book's fault, but mine? Was I, because of astrological patterns, doomed to literary ignominy? I tried to recall what Wayne and Richard, professionals who had looked over my birth chart, said about me as a writer. They'd not really addressed the issue, despite my asking them, because of their own concerns. When I looked at my chart, it looked distinctively like that of a writer. I didn't get any of it!

That week I applied for several jobs, none of which was interesting or promising. I felt like a complete failure in every single area of my life.

Dennis returned from his visit to his family and he said he'd ask if they needed help where he'd worked part-time during the late spring and summer and where he would return for fall and winter. It was a midtown international bookstore located on Fifth Avenue, "between the Plaza and St. Regis Hotels" Dennis added with a twinkle in his voice to signify it was frequented by the rich and was somewhat pretentious. However, he said the night staff was manned by young artists and musicians. He liked them. So would I. Naturally I was hesitant: one experience with bookstores was enough to last a lifetime. On the other hand, he worked in the record department and thought they might be able to use me in the gallery where my education and experience in art would be of use. I was so broke that I told Dennis to ask the manager if he had a job for me.

The week ended, the next began, and though I knew Dennis had returned to work, I still hadn't heard from him. My money was gone. Girding my loins, I applied for welfare. At first, I was sure I would feel some distinct and newly terrible humiliation. I didn't. I wondered how the caseworker would respond when he or she saw among my past work the very job she now held. If the young black woman who accepted my case had any comment on this, she kept it to herself. She did say I'd have to get a job soon and added that they'd pay the current—i.e., overdue—rent and utilities bill but not my telephone bill. I was to report to their employment bureau the following Tuesday. I was given a check to cover food expenses for the weekend. It came to $28.

Walking home from the welfare department offices along West Thirteenth Street, I thought, "Well, that wasn't too ghastly." I wondered what kind of jobs they'd come up with for me. Unless the city's bureaucracy had miraculously changed since I'd worked there, it wouldn't be much. Still and all, and given how I'd been living recently, I could make twenty-eight bucks stretch a week. I'd have to cash the check at my local bank where I still had $1.12 in my account, then spend half at the supermarket. God, my life was a toilet!

On the corner of Jackson Square I ran into Dennis.

"I was on my way to see you," he said. "Mr. _____," he added, naming the manager, "wants to meet you. Can you put on a jacket and tie and come uptown with me?"

I joined Dennis an hour later and met the manager. He managed more than the bookstore. The entire operation consisted of the building on Fifth Avenue housing the shop, as well as upper floors in which worked reporters and others connected with several foreign magazines and newspapers also owned by the company.

He was a remarkably tall, dignified man whose bearing and face reminded me of those Renaissance bronzes on every piazza in Italy.

He'd been a concert pianist, and he still had ties with the international music scene.

He was interested in my bookstore experience and asked how long I worked at which shop of the chain. He was pleased with what I told him. He said something vague about needing someone with knowledge of American books and publishers. Dennis had told him I'd left my last job to write a novel, to head off inquiries to that other company's personnel files, because I wasn't sure what they'd say about me. The manager now asked what I knew about point of purchase, advertising, and display, and I told him what I'd done for the Thirty-ninth Street shop. He wanted to compete with that chain's flagship store. Did I think it possible? "Sure," I replied. I was hesitant because he wasn't talking about the gallery. "But you'll have to do it not by copying, but by stressing the books, records, and art that are your strength." He concluded our meeting then by asking, "When can you begin?"

I thought fast. I could start right now. But I did want a few days to get my life in order, to get myself into a fully employed mode again, and I didn't want to seem overanxious. "Next week, some day?"

"This coming Monday evening at five o'clock!" he commanded, settling that. "Dennis, take him to the third floor to sign on. And, Mr. Picano . . . ?"

"Yes."

"Shave off your beard," he commanded.

I had the rare pleasure that Monday morning of calling the welfare caseworker and telling her I'd found a job.

"That was the quickest case I ever had," she commented. But she added that she'd keep me on for another two weeks, until my first paycheck came in. She'd issue another check that included two weeks of carfare allowance.

"They said I can borrow against my paycheck." I wanted out.

"Be sensible," she insisted. Having had her job, I knew that as soon as she'd officially closed my case, another would drop on her desk. Doubtless *not* an open-and-shut one like mine. I listened as she said how she planned to "service" me to return to work. I'd have money not only for carfare and to buy dinner at work, but also probably enough to give my roommate, who was now single-handedly paying the phone bill. So I said, sure, okay, fine, thanks.

I began work Monday night and within a week agreed with Dennis that it was a most pleasant place. The staff was unique. Everyone on night shift had another career: musician, painter, dancer, writer. Though there were seldom more than six of us present, we never felt overworked. The customers who came in were not only rich, they were famous, and many really glamorous. Abba Eban, S. J. Perelman, Senator Eugene McCarthy, Dali, and the Kennedys were all regulars and one night I returned from my dinner break to find John Lennon and Mai Lee, Gregory Peck and his wife, and Maria Callas (in a pale violet evening gown, tiara, and silver heels) and her escort present in different parts of the shop. By then I'd learned the clerks' *sangfroid*. And though many businesses claim to be a family, this group was. Our father was the not very paternal Spanish super-realist painter Antonio Ximenez, who threw temper tantrums we didn't get because his accent became too thick to comprehend. On other nights he would have fits of giggles that infected all of us. He gossiped on the telephone forever, and periodically stormed off mumbling that we were *"terriblé pretentiosos"* for some offense or another against art or nature or himself, but he would defend us with the tenacity of a mother bear should any customer impugn our ability or integrity. We all socialized outside of work, and I made friends there who I still see and correspond with a quarter century later and now that we are continents apart.

The manager wanted to elevate business significantly and with my experience, I was to be a key player in his plan. I was to teach him those trade secrets and practices used by my former employers, who he saw as the competition, and to instill American sales practices into the general *far niente* attitudes of the Europeans. By then I'd come to like that very serenity, and I moved slowly, building up sections of the English-language stock and foreign titles in translation, and working with the excellent classical record department and art gallery in cooperative ventures. In three months, I was assistant night manager, a year later assistant day manager. A few months after that, I was ordering all but foreign-language books and art books, which Carolyn Markowitz was infinitely more knowledge-

A House on the Ocean, A House on the Bay

able about. Several art book specialities fell into our hands at the time. We bought up the first two printings of Dali's madcap "cookbook," *Diners de Gala*, which became a best-seller despite its high price and being in French. We did co-op book and art gallery tie-ins, including the first American edition and show of the works of the Art Deco artist Erté, also of the Art Nouveau Czech, Jiri Mucha. These were glittering star-filled events in the store. Josephine Baker flew over from Paris for her friend Erté's first exhibit since the 1930s, and when she ascended the marble stairway trailing twenty feet of white ermine to be greeted by cohostesses Jackie Onassis and Bianca Jagger, Dennis and I, at the bottom of the stairs in rented tuxedos, greeting guests, looked at each other with our mouths open. We couldn't believe what we'd managed to pull off.

Many of the staff were involved in these successes and the store's morale, reputation, and profits rose accordingly.

There were setbacks, annoyances, and hassles. But I wasn't ambitious for advancement at all: I continued to do my writing by day and always felt among friends. I don't know how this experience could have been any more different than that in the previous bookstore, with its constant animosities and betrayals, political maneuverings, and jockeying for another tiny step up another minuscule rung of a ladder to nowhere very important.

The manager began to confide plans to me: shops in Chicago, Los Angeles, San Francisco, all over the country. In a few years he would open a publishing branch for art books. I was slated for an important company position, he said.

But I'd heard that before. My response was always the same: I thanked him, told him I was glad he liked my work, told him I was a writer and as soon as I got a book contract, I would leave. His response was equally always the same too: I was being unrealistic. And at times in the three and a half years I worked there, I often couldn't help but feel he was right, and I was deluding myself. Sometimes I'd look at the dozens of novels that rose from out of the stockroom and I'd think, "Why isn't one of them mine?" I'd get depressed, desperate.

My first break came as a result of the good offices of a co-worker, Alex Mehdevi, originally from Majorca, whose delightful book of children's folktales had been published a year earlier. In the fall of 1973 Alex and I were talking during our dinner break and I mentioned that I too was a writer, and had a finished novel. He promised to show it to his agent. Dutifully, expecting nothing (I'd already had several nibbles from agents before which had turned into nothing), I brought in a copy of the manuscript and gave it to Alex. To my surprise, Jane phoned me a few days later. She'd not even finished reading the book when she signed me on, and although she eventually had no better luck selling that first novel than Charles had, she did get me a publishing contract for another, only partly written novel— my five-year-old Christopher Darling concept—which became my first published book, *Smart as the Devil*.

Sad as I was to leave the shop and those friends I'd made in the stockroom and upstairs offices, among the day and night staffs in books, records, and art, and whose friendship and good wishes had sustained me so well through my period of waiting, I felt that by doing this I'd worked off all the bad karma that had accumulated from the first bookstore experience and was now ready to move on. I was eager for the unknown.

*   *   *

And Ed? A few years after that Fire Island Pines weekend, I was in a local gay bar, the Roadhouse on Hudson Street, talking to another writer I'd met through Jon Peterson, when Ed came in the door. He nodded hello but stayed at the other end of the place. I was prepared to allow that to be our fullest contact. However, this acquaintance said to me, "I've been wanting to meet Ed for the longest time. Would you introduce me?"

I hesitated, not knowing how Ed would react. I'd heard from mutual friends that losing Dennis and me in the same month—that August in 1971—had been very hard on him, and Ed had considered it a major betrayal on our part that we'd continued on as friends after in effect dumping him.

Even so, when I approached him, Ed was friendly enough and he'd heard of my acquaintance through Jon and others, though he'd not read the man's book. I introduced them and after a few minutes, they seemed to be hitting it off, so I moved away to other people. Shortly thereafter I left the place.

"Been playing Cupid?" Jon asked a week later on the phone. He seemed amused as he told me that Ed and the writer I'd introduced him to had become, in Jon's words "a major—if quite curious—item around town." Jon went on to say that the two were now to be seen everywhere. He thought this especially odd as the writer, while admittedly very bright and funny and completely unique, was by no means handsome, and Ed had a reputation for only dating good-looking men. But I was reminded of my own relationship with him. Despite appearances, it had been based so much on thought, on argument, on stretching the mind, on—if you will, "head fucking"—and I thought perhaps that's what Ed was going for again. Jon, on the other hand, thought it was more a class thing: Ed purposely "slumming." He either never intended to bring his new pal to those uptown museum parties, or else he intended to shock them all by flaunting this new relationship.

Whatever it was, they lasted several years. By then I was traveling and living most of the time outside of New York City, and I never found out what they were really like together, nor why they broke up.

During the later 1970s, I began bumping into Ed at various places: discos, bars, parties. He was now living in what must have been the most open gay marriage in the city, with, surprise, surprise, that same Lucas Cranach blond I'd met escorting the madam at that predinner cocktail party during Ed's and my last night in the Pines together. Ed had moved from lower Seventh Avenue to a huge loft in the teens off Fifth Avenue, which suggested that even more money was coming in than before. He seemed to be socializing more with the ritzy uptown art and auction gallery crowd, according to pals of mine who worked or hung out at the D & D Building. But guys I knew came across Ed in more louche circumstances: they reported seeing him in the Mineshaft, at the Hellfire Club, and especially at a private S&M club held weekly in someone's NoHo loft.

In the autumn of 1983, over a decade since we'd last spoken, Ed called me up out of nowhere. With his usual charm and forthrightness he said, "I want to pick your brain about small press publishing." It turned out he wanted to know about printing a limited edition of an art book, and had heard of my own limited success as a small press publisher. Someone was interested in putting out a book about a painting Ed had done. Would I come up to the loft and talk about this?

I was intrigued. It was years since Ed had done any painting. I was curious what this new work could be that had excited him and galvanized someone else into doing a book.

The painting dominated an entire large wall of his loft: maybe ten feet high by twenty-six feet long. It was in false perspective, a view of the entire Morton Street Pier, seen from three-quarters above, as though you, the viewer, were swooping in from above on a glider. The Maritime Arts High School ship was moored behind, forming most of the background, though other piers, the river, and the opposite side of New Jersey Palisades was visible. On the pier itself were scores of small, yet immediately recognizable figures, rendered in an illustrative style I could only compare to the work of the Japanese master Hokusai: not quite cartoon, yet not completely realistic.

All of the figures were doing what they might have been seen doing on the pier any afternoon that we'd been out there together, Ed and I, years ago. Here was Rollarena zipping through a crowd of leathermen on her skates, using her star-burst wand to make magic. Here was Jerry Blatt, shirtless and muscular, stopped astride his ten-speed bike, attempting to pick up a blond sunbather. There was Bambi, the homeless alcoholic transvestite with one very limp wrist extended, and Ruth Truth in her Statue of Liberty outfit. Here was a group of Hispanic kids dancing to the music from a tiny, perfectly rendered boom box. People on their stomachs across towels sunned and read paperbacks. Others sat in twos, out of the wind, smoking grass, while others chatted as they walked their dogs. The dogs—also individually rendered, from schnauzer to great dane—were sniffing and fighting with other dogs, straining at their leashes, barking. Two men and a child were flying Asian fighting kites. Some office workers from nearby businesses, their ties flapping in the breeze, jackets held over one shoulder, were pointing toward the viewer, or rather toward the Verrazano–Narrows behind the viewer. I looked at it for an hour. It was wonderful.

Ed pulled out a camera and insisted he had to take a photo of me walking and waving from various angles. He showed me where my figure would go.

"I'm in it twice," Ed told me, pointing out one characteristic figure of himself, madly painting away at an easel, and another, bald figure sitting in a foldout chair.

"What's that? The future you?" I asked.

"No. Recent past. That's when I first began chemotherapy," he said. "My hair's grown back since."

Which was how I learned two stunning facts: first that Ed had Karposi's sarcoma, and second that he'd finally made a fine piece of art.

He was planning another painting, of equal size, in the same style of, he said with a mischievous grin, the Fire Island Meat Rack.

"I'm not letting you take photos of me for that," I commented.

We spent the rest of the evening talking about how to publish the book. It was to contain a color foldout of the painting, photos of details, and a preface by someone au courant he knew in the art world. In addition to practical advice, I gave Ed all the praise and encouragement his achievement and illness called for. The roommate appeared briefly. It seemed their two lofts adjoined but were quite separate. He was pleasant, slightly tipsy, funny.

I kept going back to the painting, drawn to it by a childlike sense of delight in the small and excellent. The painting was, I knew, the sole yet absolutely appropriate accomplishment, monument, of a man who'd required all his life to find himself. I wondered if he'd done so too late.

As I was leaving, I touched Ed's arm, simply to make contact. He flinched, then explained, "the lesions," meaning the Karposi's sarcoma had returned despite the chemo. I settled for a light kiss on his papery cheek.

I noticed then that Ed was smaller than me. Ed had never been smaller. We'd been the same height. We'd looked directly into each other's eyes. Then I realized that two years of illness had literally shrunken him, contracted him. We promised to keep in touch.

I did phone him every few weeks thereafter. Most of the time there was no answer or he was sleeping when I called and I quickly said I'd call back later, though I seldom did. In January 1984, when he answered my call, Ed sounded sleepy again, but he said I shouldn't hang up, he wanted to talk to me. He told me he was going to "rest" at the family place in St. Thomas. He'd been feeling poorly lately, cold all the time, and he thought the warm air and familiarity of the resort would help. He would call me when he got back, he said.

The next morning, I wrote in my journal, "Ed said good-bye yesterday. He's flying down to Charlotte Amalie to die."

*　　*　　*

If there was a book published of the painting, I never saw it. I would love to see it. There was a memorial held at Ed's loft. I heard about it, but I wasn't invited. I have no idea where the painting is now. Somewhere people can look at it all they want I hope, and wonder about the bald man in the foldout chair, and the crazy boy with glasses and a dress on roller skates, and the furiously engaged painter. And perhaps even the dark, bearded, sad young man waving directly up at them from a pier that is now chained off, no longer open to strollers, but taken over by homeless squatters, the high-school ship long taken away. Waving from a past located somewhere after the start of a disaster that was somehow still in his future.

BOOK TWO

The "Class" of '75

To have reached thirty . . . is to have failed in life.

H. H. MUNRO (SAKI)

February 22, 1975. My thirty-first birthday. Lunchtime. Midtown Manhattan. The Brasserie, a French-American café set in a ground-floor side of the Seagram Building off Park Avenue and Fifty-third Street. I'm eating lunch during the one o'clock crowd. To my right, my agent, Jane. To my left, my publisher, Don Fine. Across from me, Andrea, the young woman responsible for book editing and overlooking general design. The reason for the gathering: a celebration. Not of my birthday, but of the publication of my first novel, *Smart as the Devil*, by Fine's company, Arbor House Publishing, on this very day.

We're discussing possible future reviews that might piggyback on the little bit of success the book had already achieved through early reviews in trade weeklies like *Publishers Weekly*, *Kirkus Review*, and *Library Journal*. The book is set in New England—Darien, Connecticut, and Boston, Massachusetts—so Fine believes *The Boston Globe*, the *Hartford Courant*, and possibly even the *Providence Sun-Journal* will review the book. Likewise the local paper that serves Greenwich and Darien. Further publicity planned for the book includes a morning Amtrak trip for me to that area next week to be interviewed by the paper and to sign some books at a Darien bookstore. The editor is also working on an appearance for me the following week on a morning radio show out of Hartford, as well as a possible interview with someone from the paper there.

In retrospect, and even at the time, it's all pretty small stuff, local stuff, from the inexpensive, not very glamorous, celebratory lunch onward. But as Jane and Don Fine make clear to me, it's an awfully good start for a writer's first book. Many authors they've represented and published never got the chance to go out and meet the public in any fashion with their first novels.

Anyway, what should I be expecting? I only received a $3,500 advance on the novel. It will just earn out that amount, selling some 4,000 hardcover copies at $8.95. On the other hand, the book has been picked up by Doubleday Book Club's "Mystery Guild" and more importantly, Dell Books, the biggest paperback publisher of the day, has made a substantial offer for softcover rights, $15,000, which I will split with the publisher.

So, while I'm quite calm during this lunch and the discussion, still I sense the amount of potential growing beneath me. Aren't I about to sign a second contract with Fine for a second novel, based on an incident in my own life, which Jane thinks will prove even more of a literary and commercial success, and for more money too, $8,500? Fine and his editor have just received and "looked over" the two opening chapters and fairly detailed chapter-by-chapter plot and character outline of *Eyes* that I've spent most of the past two months preparing.

Once, that is, I was finally able to get away from the international bookstore. I'd done exactly what I'd told the manager I would do from the day he hired me and often in between: I quit my job as manager of daily operations the very week I'd received that check from Arbor House for an advance against royalties.

The problem with my quitting wasn't only that my boss did not believe me and would not accept my resignation. No, the real problem was that I'd succeeded in doing what every good and sensible employee is supposed to do: I'd made myself horribly indispensable. And even though I gave months of warning, the fellow I was finally given to train to take over my job was clearly not going to make it. I could tell, and everyone else on the staff could too.

Unlike the night staff or part-time Christmas help, the day staff of the bookstore was professional. Selling books (or records or art) was their career, their life. They took it seriously enough so that every managerial incursion (and I made some) into their tiny fiefdoms was met with resistance, any alteration (and I made some of those too) of the shop, its layout, and the areas of importance was met with sulking, backtalk, and sometimes outright refusal. Sometime in the early fall of 1973, however, it became clear to all of them, the Italian, the French, the German, the records, art gallery, and magazine departments, the stockroom, the accountancy office, that I'd been left pretty much in charge, and the previous manager, now hardly ever to be seen in the building, was quite busy with other projects and would simply refer any problems that did reach him right back to me. I called the staff together one morning before we opened the store and said, "I'm not happy about this either. I'm not getting paid enough and I'm planning to quit as soon as I sell my novel to a publisher. In the meantime, however, I'll let you know how I've been told to run the store: the higher your department's sales, the more space, help, stock, publicity, and ordering you'll get." I then listed the highest departments in sales over the past year in decreasing order: art books, English-language nonart books, the art gallery, records, and periodicals. "Italian books was next to last," I explained, to everyone's shock. "Which is why American books have moved to the front of the store and Italian books to the back. I didn't make these rules. But, clearly, they're making the store more profitable and giving it a higher profile. I'll personally help anyone who wants to overhaul or increase the sales in their area. Just ask me."

"Ooh, Pschoo!" the head of the French book department said. And many of the rest of them murmured rebelliously. But as a result of that little speech, not only did the flame-haired madame come to me later in the week, on some excuse or other, and ask what exactly what I'd meant by helping, but so did a few of the others. So I was able to form one-on-one relationships—often personal ones forged over lunches in nearby restaurants—with many of the staff who'd previously ignored me before as irrelevant to their suzerainties.

Profits rose, publishers—especially large foreign ones launching specialty titles—now requested our art gallery space for publication parties, with concomitant outlays that led to an even higher profile and more profits.

Little wonder the general manager, busy starting a downtown shop and a mail-order division out of Long Island City, was irritated when in the spring of 1974 I called in my chips and told him I was leaving.

"This is impossible!" he said dismissively.

"I've signed a contract," I replied. "By September thirty-first I've got to give Arbor House a hundred-thousand-word novel. Period!"

He stared at me. One eye half closed. "How much money have they given you?"

"None of your business."

"I'm just trying to help."

I told him.

His reaction, as I guessed, was "Pah! This is nothing."

I pointed out that I was taking home from the store, after taxes, something like $150 per week. The money I'd been given by the publisher equaled six months at that rate. I fully intended to quit.

"Then what? How will you live?" Before I could reply, he went on, "Listen to this idea. Take off from April through September. Write your book. Then come back. It's quiet in summer. Mrs. Markowitz and maybe Señor Ximenez also will agree to take over your work. But for Christmas holidays you'll be back here."

I didn't like the idea, but after discussions with Carolyn and Antonio, to see if they'd agree to co-manage (at higher pay, natch) and with Dennis and my friend Ruth Oesch in the record department, I agreed. As the latter two pointed out, perhaps Carolyn and Antonio would work out so well as a duo, our boss would forget all about me, not need me in the autumn.

Well, that didn't quite work out as planned. Not only didn't Carolyn's and Antonio's personalities fit as well as mine had fit with each of theirs (she was cool, dispassionate, rational, he was, well, madly Antonio!), but both began to be more creative themselves during this time. Antonio started a new series of paintings taking Old Master's themes—St. Sebastian, St. Agatha, Salome with the head of John, *Noli Me Tangere*, eventually even a huge Last Supper—all larger, bolder and more exciting than what he'd done before; and Carolyn, a jeweler and goldsmith, had a breakthrough in alloy and wanted to begin a new line. Luckily it was summer and relatively slow. But even our boss saw the problem and so he had hired this fellow to work under me when I returned. I was to train him for eventually taking over my job.

Only thing was, I loved spending six paid months off writing every day. That middle of the year 1974 convinced me that it was precisely the life I wanted. I wrote when and how I wanted to, getting done just the amount of work I required of myself to fulfill my contract, pacing myself almost naturally, finishing a handwritten draft of the novel in a notebook in two months. I would then take another two months to type a second draft, get it read and commented on by my agent, then either rework those criticisms into the book or not as I chose. Several years before, I'd quoted in my journals an Indian scripture that spoke of doing the precisely correct work for oneself. What I was doing now felt the right way for me to be living and working. It felt exactly right. I didn't want to go back to the bookstore, which I now knew was not the right work.

Financially, I didn't think I would have to. Even on my small salary, I'd lived frugally and saved up enough to live on another five months. Of course, it meant no California vacation like the two-week one I'd given myself the September before: a week visiting my friends Arnie and Margaret and Jan in Big Sur, then back up to San Francisco for another few days to stay with my and Jay Weiss's pal Zeb Freedman and his new crowd. So, these next months might be financially tight. But to counterbalance that, I would be *free*. Free to try out ideas for new short stories, new novels, new plays, anything I chose to write.

If writing my first novel had been a desperate, a necessary act, one that had ended up saving me mentally and emotionally by first distancing then liberating me from the relationship with Edward, writing this second novel, for a publisher, had provided another kind of liberation: it allowed me to feel that I could now begin to release all those ideas, all those characters, scenes, people and places, all those *stories* that seemed to have accumulated inside me. I found I needed that in my life more than money, possibly more than food. But how to explain this rather arcane desire to someone who did not share it?

Meanwhile, checking my journals, I see that my few visits with Dennis during these months I'm free bring word of troubles at the store, and during the one dinner I have at this time with Ruth she talks about "dissension in the ranks, possible mutiny!" if I don't return. I approach my agent about this problem. She lays out how she believes the next six months or so will work out in my brand-new literary career. Given the glacial pace of book publishing, even in the speeded-up scenario, Fine will read and make suggestions on my finished novel in August. As she thinks the book is strong and tight and in need of but minor revisions, I'll probably have September to myself. The book will come out in February. Terrific as she thinks my idea for the next novel is, she doubts that I'll get a new contract on it before mid-March of 1975. In other words, I *can* actually spare the time to go back to the bookstore.

This is not what I wanted to hear.

I take off for Labor Day weekend with Jay Weiss to share a room with him at the Fire Island Pines Boulevard house of Ray Yeates, his German-born lover Horst, and their twin housemates. I immediately dub the two "Heckle and Jeckle" for their sharp high voices and how often they use them in their very public quarrels about virtually every topic under the sun, from how to arrange the flowers we'd brought as a house gift, to how much egg to add into the food bowl for Jay's cat to improve his fur, to how much Vaseline to use during anal intercourse. On the first day of our holiday in the Pines, however, at Tea Dance, I meet a stalwart young man who sweeps me off to his house for much of the remainder of that weekend and invites me out for the next weekend and the rest of that week to the place he's sharing and where he plans to be alone. He's from somewhere distant—Billings, Montana, or Helena, Wyoming—and he makes it clear that he is otherwise committed and this is merely a late-summer romance with lots of good sex. Relieved that's all he wants, I accept his invitation.

Relaxed by sun, surf, beach fun, and the nonstop physical attentions of this man, I at last return to my Jane Street apartment, which looks awfully small and dirty and dark by comparison. It's been a fabulous time. I've met a few interesting people he knew, as well as all those others who remembered me from Ray and Horst's house. I'm beginning to sense how much Fire Island Pines has changed from the way it used to be when I went out to visit Sam Plaia or even from a few years ago when I went out with Edward.

For one, the people are younger, my age, and whereas I seldom knew anyone who summered out here, I now know many from the

Manhattan bars I sometimes go to—the Roadhouse, Ty's, and Boots and Saddles (which we call Bras and Girdles). Some I know from the bathhouses and especially from the private clubs I've been going to at least once a month: the Tenth Floor, and when that closed down, the more racially mixed Loft, and—just recently opened down on Reade Street in what is not yet called Tribeca but merely "downtown"—Michael Fesco's new place for music and dancing, art, and film display, catering mostly to gay men, modeled on a famous club in pre-Castro Havana, and like it called Flamingo.

More gay men are coming out every day in New York City, so there are more of them out at Fire Island Pines, which—rather than Cherry Grove—the new gays have decided to concentrate on and settle into. This is possible partly because living arrangements are different: where the Grove has always had tiny little cottages, Pines residences were larger "family" homes with two, three, even four bedrooms. But families aren't often seen much in the Pines anymore. And instead of one wealthy gay man or couple renting a house and having guests as they used to in the Pines, those older, more moneyed gays are going to the Hamptons, while new kinds of gay "families" of anywhere from three to eight people come to the Pines, rent a house, divide it by room, sometimes by time. The result is a Pines population that is professional and fairly successful, if less wealthy, but also younger, hipper, better looking, dance-and-recreational-drug using rather than cocktail party and alcohol imbibing. Also, they are a lot more "out" about being homosexual than the previous generation. They kiss in public, they neck on the beach, they wrap their arms around each other at Tea Dance, they dance close together at night at the disco Gene Brown has set up at his harborside restaurant, the Sandpiper, they walk hand in hand along the boardwalks. Not only are they in the Pines in larger numbers, they've also invited their young friends or even a potential boyfriend for a weekend. It's summed up in the city's first gay newspaper, the *New York City News*: "What's left of the gin-and-Judy (i.e., Garland) set has hunkered down in the Grove. In the Pines it's all Speedos and Drugs and Disco."

To accommodate these changes, gay and straight home owners in the Pines have not only given up their own places to renters, they've begun building rental houses on other properties they own: large houses, with conveniences young gays who grew up in the suburbs require: dishwashers, washers and dryers, large sometimes multileveled decks, hot tubs, outdoor showers, pools, sometimes roof decks. Already prominent decorators and architects have chosen the Pines as the place to build their experiments, what will be called their "signature" houses.

With the influx of designers and architects, younger residents, and more building, the Pine's architecture gets wild, whimsical, and wonderful. Themes such as Swiss Chalet and Cape Cod are replaced by structures based on motifs like the Gothic Cathedral, the Romanesque Donjon, the Shakespearean Theatre, the Hansel-and-Gretel Cottage Gone Berserk. Every new, larger, more expensive house that goes up is instantly dubbed by its resemblance to something else: the TV House, the Solar House, the Kodak Pavilion, the Ramada Inn, Camp Tommy, Lincoln Center! They're written up in *Architectural Digest* and *Better Homes and Gardens*, and even the Sunday *Times*. Owners who've been sitting on tiny fishing-season cottages on the beach or the bayfront sell them to people like Angelo Donghia, Halston, and Calvin Klein, who tear them down and have large lavish new showplaces put up.

And since they need a place to show off themselves, their chic friends, and their fashions, they adopt the little "tea dance" held on Saturday and Sunday afternoons at John White's Boatel as the place to see and be seen by day, and at the Sandpiper at night. No new Pines residents will step foot in the Grove, unless on a day tour for giggles at its tackiness. By Labor Day of 1974, my friend (Zeb Freedman's ex), artist David Watts, uses a 180-degree Hasselblad camera lens to take photos of holiday Tea Dance that shows a crowd of 200 handsome men (and a few women), each wearing at most a pair of jeans and a tank top, splayed across the decking, terrace, front boardwalk, and accompanying Boatel property. Fire Island Pines has arrived.

When I return to Manhattan in late September, tanned, fucked out, sunstruck, and not a little starstruck too, it is to find a message wedged in my mailbox from Dennis asking me to phone him at work as soon as I get in. I do so, and he tells me that Carolyn Markowitz has fallen ill, needs some kind of operation, and, naturally, has taken a leave of absence, its length unknown, but effective immediately. There's no day manager starting next Monday.

Thus am I dragged, kicking and screaming, back to the bookstore, feeling not dissimilar to Jacob in the Old Testament who, having worked seven years for Laban, must labor seven more years for what he thought he'd already earned.

"Only through Christmas," my boss says, so unguently I almost slip on the steady stream of oil he exudes. "I've got a new man for you to train. He's older. More steady. I think he'll stick!"

The new trainee shows up at the bookstore the following day. He is a short, thick-bodied, middle-aged, Italian-American man in a good suit with a bald head and an obvious outer-boroughs accent, whom I know will #1) immediately be dubbed by the staff "Mussolini" whom he slightly resembles, #2) be hated by the staff for not being young and suave and terrifically overeducated like the rest of us, and #3) not fit in. However, I'm conflicted. I *want* him to work out as manager: if he doesn't, I'm stuck here. On the other hand, I also want my friends to be in a good management situation, to be happy at work. What do I do?

What I attempt to do is to get through the holidays, which turn out to be the busiest season by far, and at the same time train this man and try to convince him and the staff to accept each other. He's no fool, and it's clear within a week that, as I predicted, the others sneer at him. He brings this up to me one afternoon, calling it "lack of respect" and I don't know how to respond except to say the same thing happened to me: one has to earn, gain, their trust. When he says he doesn't understand their attitude, I point to pretty, pouty Barbara who works in the travel section and helps with Italian-language books and magazines. "Her parents are both American, in the diplomatic corps," I say, "so she was born in Katmandu, went to private school in Saigon, finishing school in Rome, then the Sorbonne. She speaks French, Italian, Vietnamese, and English fluently, with a little Nepalese and Mandarin Chinese. She's working until she marries a diplomat. She doesn't need this job. She is very knowledgeable, very good at what she does here, and I like her," I conclude.

For a few days all goes better and I'm a bit more hopeful.

A House on the Ocean, A House on the Bay

One late, relatively quiet afternoon, little red-haired Rose Kennedy, matriarch of the most famous family in America and active as hell despite being in her early eighties, bustles into the shop. I've met her once or twice here and we've had pleasant if abbreviated chats. I know she flies down to New York to see the publisher of her autobiography, which is coming out next year. The publisher's office is up the street. This afternoon Rose has an even more commodious than usual handbag, which she opens up. She takes out something wrapped in a silk kerchief and proceeds to unwrap it over a flat book display as she says, "My editor wants photos for the book that no one's seen before. So I went through old albums and drawers in Hyannisport and found these. But they're so many and I don't know which to choose. I don't really trust her taste. Will you help me select?"

Flattered by her request and thrilled to be seeing Kennedy family photos not seen for years and never seen by anyone outside the immediate family, I say, "Sure." And we spread them out and go through them while she makes comments: "Jack first had his back problems, here. You can see him wincing. My, he was thin!" Or "That was so-and-so, a neighbor girl, we all called her Teddy's girlfriend. But he wouldn't even talk to her! He was eight!" And so on for the next ten minutes. I'm about to suggest that we either go up to the art gallery, where we can sit and be more comfortable or to my office, when Rose looks up and says, "Isn't that Blanchette Rockefeller?" I look up, and indeed it's the tall, imposing, regal figure of Mrs. John D. Rockefeller III, who comes into the shop monthly for books on one of her interests: old Chinese porcelain, or nineteenth-century majolica. "I met her a long time ago," Rose Kennedy says, "but I'm sure she won't remember me. Would you mind reintroducing us?"

I wonder how anyone could not remember Rose, but she seems so shy suddenly that I say of course I'll reintroduce them. Rose gathers up her photos, putting those we'd selected in a manila envelope that I supply, sweeps them all back into her huge bag, and I introduce the two women. A minute later, I return to where I left them and tell them they're welcome to go to the gallery. Stella has just brewed fresh coffee. They thank me but leave for some place—

Schrafft's? Le Grenouille?—who knows, somewhere where the Ladies Who Lunch go.

As they're stepping out, the management trainee comes onto the floor from his afternoon break and he says "What's up?" I tell him what I've just done, and as I speak, I see beads of sweat break out on his forehead. "The president's mother?" he keeps asking, unbelieving. Then, when it does get through his noggin, he speaks of her as though she were the Virgin Mary incarnate, and so finally, I let him go about his business and I'm left wondering how he would have handled a situation I found I've done with casual poise and which made him sweat to even consider. Looking at him, I finally conclude he wouldn't have: Rose Kennedy would never have talked with him long enough to have formed trust for him to look at her family photos. In other words, without someone like me or Carolyn in charge here, the soul of this place—which we all love so much, value because of how special it is—shall change. Our boss doesn't care about its soul. And if it doesn't change when I leave, it will the next time management shifts. But it *will* change, there's no stopping it, nothing I can do.

That confirms it. By January 10, 1975, with a sizable bonus and my boss's statement that I'll be welcome back, I leave and launch myself into the world of freelance writing. I've never looked back, and never again worked for another.

*   *   *

Don Fine and Andrea have left the Brasserie but Jane and I linger over another cup of coffee. She tells me she's spoken to the Dell editor who purchased the paperback rights to *Smart as the Devil*; they lunched recently and Jane told her about the proposal for my second book. Linda said if Don Fine didn't take it, she'd be interested in looking at it. She'd already told Jane my book is on the fast track at the book club, and Dell is planning a first printing of 50,000 copies next March. I should be thinking ahead to the possibility of a third book. Do I have any ideas?

I do, one idea in particular, but I merely mention it, don't describe it yet. One thing I've noticed is that my first novel, the one I worked on so long, the one that brought Jane and me together, is no longer even mentioned. There are two reasons. First, it's not been sold to those editors Jane knows and works with, and second, it's quite different from what I seem to be getting published. It's a big, complex novel, set in a specific historical era, concentrating on scene and character. What seems to be sold are compact, contemporary novels of psychological suspense, dealing with issues pertinent to the day.

In the twenty years since it was published, I've met people who still find *Smart as the Devil* to be their favorite work of mine. Where the book came from in me, how it was merchandised, and how it has been perceived—including by many who never read it—is all so contrary and twisted, it bears discussion.

While Jane still had my first novel going the round of publishers, she asked what else I had in my desk drawer and I pulled out the outline I'd put together for what I had thought might be a second or third novel, then titled *Who Is Christopher Darling?* I'd come across that name in an anthology, *The Elizabethan Journals*, which I'd bought as "background" for a college English course in 1962 and which I'd not gotten around to reading until 1971. Most intriguing to me of the journals had been those of Shakespeare-era magicians and astrologers, like John Dee, who secretly worked for Elizabeth and James I's Star Chambers, as well as other, less exalted purveyors of the supernatural of the time. Stories of witches and possessed children which we believe to be endemic to Salem, Massachusetts, turned out to have been an export, common in sixteenth-century England, as attested to by town criers and reported by various early precursors of the news media.

Shortly after finishing my first novel, and perhaps unconsciously seeing how it was not going anywhere for me, I became interested in the Greek myth of Phaëton, who steals his father's—the sun god's—chariot one morning and attempting to emulate his father's power, manifested in his daily ride, nearly burns up the earth and the heavens, until he's destroyed by a thunderbolt from Zeus, king of the gods. I thought this tale of the overambitious but untrained youth might be a "universal" human myth. To me, at least, it was a fascinating one and I wanted to update it. The modern gods and even priestly caste, I thought, were today's psychologists and psychiatrists. The area of the mind, and especially aberrations of the mind, from schizophrenia to manifestations of the supernatural, seemed to be the field upon which the younger and older main characters in my story should play out their power game. But I wanted the "son" in my tale not to fail like Phaëton but to succeed, and to do so through what was supposed to be his mentor-adversary's supposedly greater strength, i.e., deep knowledge of human psychology. To that end, the child's extraordinarily odd behavior, which first brings him to the attention of the grown man, must be of a spectacular as well as a precisely realized nature. Thus the alleged possession of twelve-year-old, upper-class Darien resident Nicholas De Luca by the spirit of a seventeenth-century Salem boy named Christopher Darling, a "possession" induced by the child putting himself into a trance by eating slightly toxic boxwood hedge leaves, and by "automatically" speaking and writing in the perfectly imitated voice of the alleged seventeenth-century child.

In addition to solving a purely creative, intellectual problem, I guessed that this story would address a more personal issue—yes, I believe a good book, fiction or nonfiction, must operate on at least these two levels, the abstract and the personal, to be intensely communicative. The problem was the same that Nicholas De Luca, others, and indeed I myself had once faced: of being a child with an obviously superior intellect and intuition in a world that not only doesn't value that quality in children, but punishes it. "Wait a minute!" you'll say. Or course we value superior minds in children. We reward them with higher grades, school prizes, etc. That's not what I mean. I mean the truly superior child who operates outside all norms, all conventions: for want of a better word, the genius. Someone who thinks so beyond the common mold at an early age that he's seen as strange, teased, bullied, and taunted for how much he frightens people by the quality of his thinking, it's sheer oddness.

I didn't have to think hard to recall how badly I'd been treated as soon as I'd revealed a superior talent as a child. My junior high school short story had been branded a fake, a plagiarism, taken out of competition with the other pieces to which it was obviously superior. Even though I'd been in a class for accelerated learning, among others with high IQ's and with teachers and guidance counselors supposedly hired and trained to deal with the possibility of genius children, they'd all fallen on old standards. Unable to deal with the truly new, they'd all failed me, every one of them. This book, *Smart as the Devil*, would be my way of explaining this experience, and at the same time of at last getting revenge on those who'd crossed me. As the old Italian proverb has it, revenge is a dish that tastes best when it's served cold.

Naturally, that was not at all how the book was sold, not by my agent, who didn't know my life story; not by Arbor House, who first published it; not by Dell, who published it in paperback. They didn't give a rap about universal myths, about power games between generations, about misunderstood child geniuses. The novel was marketed specifically to fit in a bracket set up by *The Exorcist*, where the child was a mere tool of some outside force: neither intellectual, nor much of a child either, never mind a superior one.

The same year my novel was published, another first novel by a new author came out treating the same idea—and was about as successful at first as mine—Stephen King's *Carrie*. Both books had original cover art playing up the alleged *Exorcist* similarity. Like my novel, King's had a more interesting theme: how a child who is an outsider, living with a repressive, ultrareligious mother, hated by her peers for being different, comes into her own in an act of violent revenge. Both books were originally published, reviewed, and sold because they appeared to fit into a popular niche. There were several others at the time which have fallen into obscurity. King's and my book went on because readers found them different, unique, and word of mouth found them a readership beyond the primarily targeted one. The book club edition of *Smart as the Devil* sold about 10,000 copies, the paperback, in three editions, would eventually sell 225,000 copies. It also sold well in England, in both paper and hardcover, and in Germany, translated as *Klug Wie der Teufel*.

How many of the third of a million or so readers of the book read it as I'd intended I cannot say. I'm always astounded what people do and don't read in my work. For many, who only saw the book's garish paperback cover on an airport newsstand counter carousel, it must have seemed another rip-off, sensational trash. Naturally this bothered me, even though I couldn't control any of it.

Although the book never got much national coverage, I did end up on a morning TV show in Washington, D.C. as well as the Hartford, Connecticut morning radio program, and the book was spottily if well reviewed in various newspapers around the country. I suppose the combination of an ingenious plot, well-drawn characters, a suspenseful psychological duel, chapters written in imitation seventeenth-century English, good reviews, and some word of mouth helped. To my great surprise (and doubtless because of Don Fine's politicking) the book became one of five finalists for the just-instituted Ernest Hemingway Award for best first books. Although it didn't win—Michael Sharra's *The Killer Angels*, about the Battle of Gettysburg (his only book), got the award—and although I would have preferred my first written novel to have been my publishing debut, *Smart as the Devil* turned out to be more typical of how my career would play itself out. It was both commercial yet literate—only really scorned by the avant-garde. As for the ultimate test, the last time I picked up *Smart as the Devil* looking for something, I was sucked into its world, and read for the next hour and a half.

*   *   *

As Jane and I left the Brasserie, said good-bye, and split up on the street, she to go to her office nearby, I home downtown, I couldn't help but think how different this birthday was from others. The last good one was two winters before, and had been memorable thanks to a surprise arranged by Dennis.

Although he continued to work part-time nights in the record department, Dennis was taking graduate courses in music performance and musicology at Columbia University, a great deal of work, even for someone as bright and energetic as he was. Once I moved to the day staff at the bookstore, I saw him a great deal less than before. No more shared work breaks; even Sunday brunch meetings were difficult when his young doctor came to town for the weekend. We had to schedule a week in advance to see each other. Thus, one lunch meeting, postponed at least four times by one or the other of us for a month, occurred on my twenty-ninth birthday. I'd decided to take a day off work to get much needed errands done. Dennis would be in class all day, so we agreed to meet at his school, then go to lunch at an off-campus café.

I wasn't really feeling sorry for myself, but it was clear that no one around me had remembered my birthday, and I was a little depressed. Despite his other faults, at least Edward made certain to celebrate the day by a dinner, play, or gift, and I found myself missing that. When I arrived at the music department building, at the room where I was to meet Dennis, it was not yet noon, and he was at the piano, noodling, trying out Beethoven themes with a woman cellist. They greeted me, and Dennis said to take a seat and he'd be with me shortly. A few minutes later a tall young man entered and took out a violin, and began tuning up, as the others continued to practice chords and figures. A silence fell; then Dennis said, "Oh! By the way, happy birthday!"

The three of them then played a familiar, bold, Beethovenish prelude. And I thought, "Oh, they must be practicing the 'Archduke Trio'!" They went on from the prelude into the first theme's exposition, its modulation into a second theme, and the alternating development of the two. I blushed with realization and pleasure: they weren't going to stop, they were going to play it through to the end, the entire trio, one of the greatest and most difficult in the chamber music repertoire. Here was my birthday present. My only present, but Dennis had succeeded in making me feel special—archducally special. It was a thrilling performance. Dennis also took me for lunch at the goulash restaurant across the street, and I was humming the music all the rest of the day.

At the time, both of us were quite poor, despite work, with no future looking likely for me but continued book clerking. Only two years later, I seemed to be moving ahead as a writer, while Dennis had finished his studies and gotten his master's degree. He'd left the bookstore but hadn't yet found a job that would utilize his musical talents. At least not fully. Only a few weeks before my novel was published he'd told me about a documentary film he expected to be helping with. Dennis would help score the film, or find appropriate music for it: he'd not been that clear. Since then, he'd gone to work on a three-day-a-week basis at some studio across the Fifty-ninth Street Bridge. He was assistant to the set director, a man named

Roger, whom it turned out I also knew, having met him during my stint at the graphics art magazine, when he'd been an up-and-coming TV commercial and prize-winning industrial filmmaker. Always difficult, something of a perfectionist, Roger had quit one high-paying job after another in the creative departments of the trendiest advertising agencies in New York.

I saw Dennis the night of my thirty-first birthday and was able to give him a copy of my first published book. Dennis was excited for several reasons and quite voluble about the documentary film, on which preshooting preparation was about to be completed. As far as I could figure, Dennis's excitement was attributable to several people: first, Charles Gaines, the author of the book upon which the movie was based and who'd adapted his previous novel about bodybuilders, *Stay Hungry*, for a film still to be released, starring Sally Fields and Jeff Bridges; second, the man producing and codirecting the film (with Roger, the cameraman-director), George Butler; third, the stars of the film, two huge bodybuilders, one from Europe and one from Brooklyn; and fourth, a guy named Bob Lowe, a nonprofessional bodybuilder, who was assistant set director and stage manager.

It was difficult to sort out the new names and the personalities attached to the names, but Dennis's usually cool demeanor and blasé attitude were utterly changed, and I wasn't sure if it was because he found himself in the midst of an actual, fully financed movie (Dennis said Charles and George were "rich kids" who had gotten other "rich kids" to invest in the movie), or because Dennis was surrounded every day by men with huge muscular bodies wearing little but posing straps, or because he was infatuated by this guy on the set, Bob, about whom he couldn't stop talking. So I sat back and listened. Dennis said bodybuilding was always considered a homosexual interest, or worse, a lower-class American subsport/subart. Now this Austrian fellow, this Mr. Universe three years in a row, Arnold something or other, was determined to bring it out of its class closet and to the public. Dennis talked of how smart and ambitious and well-spoken Arnold was, how sweet and attractive the other bodybuilding star of the film, Lou Ferrigno—who'd been Mr. Universe previously and was Mr. America several years in a row—

always was. He also spoke of how visionary and canny the producer-director George was, and how, despite so many daily screwups, Roger (himself a bodybuilder, I'd not failed to notice during our two business lunches together) seemed to be enjoying himself, not throwing fits or giving off any attitude. Dennis made it sound as though the main reason for all this general harmony was Bob, who, according to Dennis, besides being physically gorgeous with a whiz-kid mind, was "almost naturally" nice with people, as well as experienced. He recently had been assistant stage manager of the Royal Ballet, working with choreographers like Antony Tudor and the ballet stars Rudolf Nureyev, Dame Margot Fonteyn, Anthony Dowell, and Antoinette Sibley.

Nearly a month would pass before I would get the opportunity to judge for myself exactly how fabulous and interesting the people he enthused about were. Not that I was doing nothing, although to many it might seem that way. I was waiting for Arbor House's go-ahead on my next novel, and I was beginning to research what I thought might become the third. Because if it is true that I didn't really know where that first novel, written in 1971, came from, and while I knew very well that my first published novel came from deep within myself, the new book to be contracted came out of a much more recent and odder experience.

On the other hand, what I thought might become my third publishable book arose directly out of the headlines of *The New York Journal*, dated March 17, St. Patrick's Day, 1901. This curiosity was given to me several years before by Joseph Mathewson's previous boyfriend, my antique-hunting pal, Nunzio James D'Anarumo. That day's paper had a sixty-four-point headline reading "Nebraska Prosecutor Shoots Defendant!" accompanied by a drawing of two well-dressed turn-of-the-century gentlemen facing off in a crowd, one determinedly pointing a revolver at the other, who falls backward, clutching his shoulder. Among the aghast onlookers is a richly dressed, very attractive woman, her widow's veil partly lifted by an ebony gloved hand.

When I'd first gotten the newspaper it was merely a curiosity, like the New England pine pencil box or somewhat bent pewter candlestick Nunzio had also given me. One day, however, lacking reading material during breakfast, I'd taken up the old newspaper and gone through it, really looking at the remarkable old woodcut advertisements, scanning each news story and even the "house and kitchen" secrets of Mrs. Beeton, published as a column. Even so, the most wonderful and astonishing thing of all in that issue turned out to be the lead story, what was being called the strangest trial in the history of the young midwestern state, indeed, of the whole Nebraska Territory. The immediate day's report was about how the trial's well-known prosecutor, who as attorney general originally charged the defendant and brought him to trial, had on this twelfth day of the trial awaited his adversary outside the courtroom. After a particularly frustrating and difficult day of testimony that ended up with the defendant himself on the witness stand, the prosecutor shot and wounded the man. The widow illustrated was evidently the one who'd previously testified that she'd fallen under the defendant's hypnotic spell: her husband, a recent suicide, had been his main victim. The defendant himself was described as an "itinerant dentist and purveyor of various elixirs of uncertain effect," but was also "a favourite [sic] of the Ladies for his politeness, an Apollo in looks, and of remarkably charming eyes."

It was all so odd, with so much left unsaid, so many apparent relationships among all of these participants hidden between the lines, that I needed to know more. It helped that I felt I somewhat knew this era already: it was only a decade or so before the time I'd written about in my first novel. Yet in that decade several important inventions we've come to think of as defining the twentieth century had taken hold in America: the electric bulb, the telephone, the automobile, the airplane. There were intellectual advances, above all Freud's first papers on hysteria, dreams, and his theory of the divided mind, as well as Einstein's first published articles on relativity. I needed more information, not only on this specific Midwestern drama and its players, but on the period, a crucial one in American history, overlooked by writers and historians.

My first stop was the New York Public Library. The Forty-second Street reading room had *The New York Journal* and other papers on file for the dates surrounding that of my newspaper, and I spent a week of afternoons reading, soaking up the material for this Nebraska story, soaking up the life of the time, the styles of clothing and furnishings, the politics of the day, the personalities of the time, how people spoke and read and wrote, how much money they had, and how they spent it. I took out books on the period about territories that became states in the last decade of the nineteenth century. I read up on the letters and documents of the era, thinking somehow that this knowledge, this "authenticity" was the element missing in my first novel—and what had kept it from being published. Ultimately, I met with a historian specializing in territory law to have him explain legal niceties of the case that had escaped me.

What I had in mind was a nonfiction novel. I'd been tremendously impressed by Truman Capote's *In Cold Blood*, as I later would be by Norman Mailer's *The Executioner's Song*. I felt certain that my topic would be equally amenable to that kind of handling, though I was neither a contemporary of the events as Mailer was, nor a day-by-day reporter at the trial and witness to the execution as Capote had been. But as I delved further into original sources, I ran into a brick wall. I'd written to the city in Nebraska for information about the trial. I'd hoped to visit it in person later on in the summer. But someone wrote back to tell me the records of the trial—the most famous in the state's history, he admitted—had been destroyed in what the writer called a "suspicious" courthouse fire sometime in the 1920s. I then phoned him and asked if any of the family of the participants in the trial were still alive. He said he knew of two and gave me their addresses. When I wrote asking to interview them, I came up empty: one very elderly woman claimed she knew nothing as no one in the family had ever spoken of the matter. Another very old man point-blank refused to meet with me and open up "old wounds." Hoping to find more information on the trial—or rather "mistrial" as it had become after that infamous shooting—I wrote to Nebraska newspapers. The only one extant at the time of the crime unfortunately had used the exact same reporter and printed the same articles I'd already read in *The New York Journal*.

*   *   *

It was in the midst of this frustration that my agent called with good news. Arbor House was taking my next book. Don Fine and Andrea both thought the idea I'd proposed intriguing, exactly right to follow up *Smart as the Devil* because it was also a psychological study, yet of a different, more everyday kind, with as strong a concept, yet fresh, set in the "singles scene" of young urban professionals. They also hoped it would attract a female readership (it was a large readership) because the novel was written from the point of view of both a young man in Manhattan and a young woman voyeur with whom he ends up having a strange double relationship. The contract was for $8,500 for hardcover rights, and a fifty-fifty split of paperback and book club rights, more than double my first book. I was to receive half the money on signing the contract, half on acceptance of the complete manuscript. A hand-in date of September 31 was set up. And, as with the first book contract, they wanted the right to read and be the first to decline my next novel.

Two things became immediately obvious. First, even if I hadn't run into so many dead ends with the book project I'd been researching the past month, I had to put it aside and get back to work on this. Second, what had been for years a Great Wall of China of unceasing obstacles blocking me from being published—without a chink for me to catch a glimpse of a possible literary future through—had been pulled down overnight, the debris instantly cleared away, and what I faced instead was an unquestionably well-paved, smooth road, leading up and away.

Why had this happened? *How* had it happened? I couldn't for the life of me understand. True, I'd followed the advice of *I Ching*, even though it had consistently given negative hexagrams to my queries. Following hexagram #26—which with my year or so of self-taught Chinese and my big Yenching Institute dictionary I translated as "Great Power Held in Restraint"—I'd "practiced chariot driving daily" since 1968, writing something every single day, even if it were only a short journal entry. In 1971, when Charles had returned the manuscript of my first novel saying he couldn't find a publisher and all leads seemed completely blocked, I'd received hexagram #29, "Water Swirls Through a Dangerous Gorge," and I'd "emulated the example of water and gone around the most immediate and obviously dangerous obstacles" to wit, the relationship with Edward and Dennis and working at my father's business. Following hexagram #39, "Obstacles All Around," I'd remained steady and determined when all seemed darkest: I'd not let backward moves and oppression keep me from losing my determination and confidence, but had kept on writing any time I could. I'd then followed the advice of accurate, nasty, hexagram #47, "Adversity," and looked for people to help me: "beginners" like myself, Dennis and others at the international bookstore, with whom I could share hopes and troubles, with whom I might align myself to present a stronger, more united force. Receiving hexagram #36, "Censorship: Darkening of the Light," I'd taken "the most indirect route, one that seemingly leads away from the goal" as it had told me to do, going back to work at the bookstore when it proved financially necessary and keeping quiet about my abilities and talents though it galled me to do so. Once settled there, I'd again received Great Power Held in Restraint and gained greater determination to succeed, using the new limitations "as a halter is put on young oxen so they constantly push against it and in this way become stronger." After a year of forging friendships, I had stumbled onto a new path into the literary business.

The most challenging and trying time was not, oddly, when there was no hope, no chance of getting published, no agent, no publisher interested in my work, but after I'd met Jane and she'd taken on my first novel and was trying to sell it: because it *was* so hopeful, yet so intimidating, waiting for something more concrete to happen, the other shoe to drop. Jane and I arranged our first meeting by phone: I was to go to her office after I'd finished work at the bookstore and we would go out for drinks and "talk about the future."

She worked for an agent named Kurt Hellmer, though in a year she'd strike out and open her own agency. Hellmer was Swiss-born and had come to the United States in the late 1940s. He represented the work of many foreign authors in this country: Frederich Duerrematt, Max Frisch, Eugene Ionesco, Albert Camus, Uwe Jacob, and Siegfried Lenz. An impressive literary lineup, which might be duplicated on the reading list of a graduate seminar in contemporary European literature.

Hellmer's agency was located in a small suite in the labyrinth of offices in one of those almost invisibly tall, granite-brick buildings on Vanderbilt Avenue, that three-block street along the east side of Grand Central Station, unknown except to its denizens and immediate neighbors.

It had been a remarkably warm, ringingly clear early November day, one of those secret joys of New Yorkers. I'd walked around most of my lunch hour to enjoy what might be the last warmth of the year, and it still wasn't cold as I strolled Fifth Avenue, playing peek a boo block by block with a rubicund sunset over the Hudson River. By the time I'd followed this jocular twilight's most attenuated red-gold glimmers upon skyscraper walls, I was in the dim fastness of an area that seemed to belong not to midtown today, but to downtown in an earlier, more crowded, less imperial New York City than what I had just walked through.

Hellmer was a small, unprepossessing looking middle-aged man with a creased forehead and wire-frame glasses, dressed as if he were in Zurich in dull herringbone slacks, matching vest over an off-color shirt, and featureless tie a bit too wide. His office was anal-retentive neat, oak shelves lining three walls around his desk, dropping below the two windows that looked across a few yards of sooted darkness into other office windows of the same building. A tiny foyer between his and Jane's office was barely roomy enough for a captain's chair and a miniature receptionist desk, clearly a fiction as I never saw anyone at it, and never heard anyone other than Jane or Kurt answer the phone whenever I called.

Jane's office was as much of a contrast to his as she was to Kurt personally, being bright, young, attractive, elegantly dressed, and altogether vivid and colorful to his general dullness. Different-sized, oddly colored, ill-matched bookshelves held, not the nearly uniform colors and sizes of author's collected works in various languages editions as in his demesne, but instead one shelf of what looked to be a quirky bunch of college-lit titles: Hoelderlin's *Hyperion*, Kierkegaard's *Diary of a Seducer*, Hamsun's *Hunger*, Dostoyevsky's *The Gambler*, Ibsen's *Peer Gynt*, Radiguet's *Le Bal de Comte D'Orgel*, Unamuno, Kazantzakis, and Henry Green. But far more numerous were shelves that held brightly bound and covered novels and paperbacks: contemporary romances, adventures, and thrillers I assumed she'd been instrumental in getting published. More shelves held gray and brown and tan and cream-colored boxes, bundles, and loose-paged gatherings of manuscripts in multicolored rubber bands. I guessed these scores of manuscripts were the work of her authors, in process of becoming what Jane called "finished books."

This was just one of many terms I heard in that ten-minute visit; there was an entire argot of the publishing business I'd never guessed at which fell trippingly off her tongue as she spoke about what for her was the only business, the only career to have—unless of course one were an author.

Kurt said good night, Jane vanished to check her makeup, and I looked at all those competing manuscripts and wondered what I was doing here. It seemed too much, the lingo, the competition. She returned brightly, however, and we breezed out of the dreary offices, into and through the terminal, up escalators into the Pan Am Building, up more escalators to another lobby, into elevators that floated us to a rooftop restaurant with huge surrounding windows. I couldn't help but be struck by the literalness of the difference of a few years. Not too long ago, I'd toiled in the stockrooms of a bookstore located in the depths of this very terminal, while I now ascended to the very roof!

As we sat in a leather booth and nibbled nuts and sipped at drinks, Jane told me she'd joined the Hellmer agency a few years ago, and was already billing most of the agency's income. Kurt had good authors, she admitted, but he was old-fashioned, too much inclined to the old-school gentleman's way of doing business, insufficiently direct or aggressive at seeking out new contacts. She, on the other hand, had no problem being assertive. She'd made contact with many new editors she believed were headed to the top of the industry and she wanted to represent not established writers, but bright new authors, people whose writing she could directly relate to, whose careers she could help shape. She mentioned three authors I'd not heard of, then said she hoped I'd be part of her "stable."

We spoke of my book and where it was at the moment, but she almost dismissed it; even if no one published it right away, I should be getting other works ready to be sold, or even presold before being written. She laid out how this was to be done, with several chapters and a detailed outline. I ought to learn how to write outlines of all my books bcause they could be used not only to sell books but also for possible film adaptations.

A second round of drinks arrived, the nut dish was refilled. More well-dressed people drifted in. Around us building offices dimmed as the city put on its sleekest nocturnal midtown garb. We watched streetlights go on directly below us, then street by street, all the way up Park Avenue until they were hidden in the general glow of the Upper East Side.

I felt as I hadn't felt in years, not since I'd stepped into Walt Whitman Hall, the English department at my college, in early May 1964, where the senior class standings were posted before graduation. I certainly hadn't intended to go there, but Barry Bialik, one of my pals, thought he'd scored high on the comprehensive exams we'd taken a month before. These exams tested our knowledge of English and American literature which, with our course grades, would constitute our departmental standing. I'd gotten A's in many electives, but I wasn't competitive and hadn't given standings a thought, so I was casually looking for my name on the list of 150 students and getting nervous not finding it, then really nervous when it wasn't at the bottom. I thought my exam score was lost, I'd never graduate. Suddenly a young woman who'd been in my eighteenth-century literature class asked, "Are you Felice Picano?" and when I said yes, she said, "I'm Barbara Garson. We're on top." She pointed and sure enough, there were our names, side by side, set off by a few lines from the others, at the very top of the list, given top honors in the English department. Barry didn't believe it. He had to see for himself and shoved me aside to look. Students had begun to gather in the corridor to check their standings, while a dozen faculty members were exiting the department office where some staff meeting had just ended. The word circulated that Barbara and I were there, and they began to applaud, stood there in that packed corridor and applauded for the longest time, and I couldn't move it was so jammed, but had to stand and listen to it and I'd felt exhilarated and embarrassed as hell and exhilarated all over again.

Now it was March of 1975, a year and a half after that drinks date of so much promise with Jane and things appeared to be coming true as she'd predicted while the city lay at our feet, lighting itself up like a big present, just there for the taking. I still wondered if I'd succeeded in doing what I'd set out to do in the late 1960s, i.e., to change myself, to become another person. Most of the time I felt I had only partly succeeded. I'd not yet let go of the past entirely, which I suspected I needed to do. I was closer to my mother than in many years. She was unhappy and I wasn't sure what to say to her, whether or not to confirm what I thought she already suspected, that my father had a mistress.

I was seeing more of my younger brother, too, but that could hardly be construed as "family." Jerry had left my father's business and was now either unemployed or working part-time for an art-framing shop in Manhattan, living at various people's apartments, especially those of a group who hung around Andy Warhol's Factory: people with names like Jimmy Name, Girl Ondine, Rotten Rita, the Won Ton, and Norman Billiards; and among those closer to the Warhol scene, Boy Ondine and Nico, two "stars" of Andy Warhol's (actually Paul Morrissey's) film *The Chelsea Girls*, as well as Brigitte Polk and Richie Berlin. I had come across some or all of these people when Jan and Arnie and Margaret were still in town. We'd all met at art show openings or in the Red Room at Max's Kansas City, sometimes upstairs where Eric Emerson and his group or Nico and her group, The Velvet Underground, performed on weekends.

One unexpected familiar face for me in Warhol's world turned out to be his cameraman and director, Paul Morrissey himself. Paul had worked in the same room, next unit to mine, when I was a social worker in East Harlem from 1964 to 1966, just before I moved to Europe. Since my desk faced his desk, I got to see Morrissey's daily routine. He would come into work late, skeletally thin and looking insomniac, carrying a film can, a newspaper, and a huge styrofoam cup of black coffee. After mumbled greetings to whichever of his co-workers were in the unit, he'd spend a few minutes going through notes attached to clients' cases on top of his desk, being generally surprised at what he was reading. Then he'd spend the next hour looking at huge spools of film by the light of the tall windows (it had formerly been a school building). At the time I had no idea who

Morrissey was, or that these same films were being shown at galleries and even museums: films like *Empire State*, *Sleep*, and *Blow Job* which first made Warhol's name, films I'd seen (or seen parts of). Morrissey would sigh loudly, turn to his *Times*, read a while, spend at least another hour on the phone, then leave for the day. The others in his unit—Debbie Applegate, Katie, Don Shorter (the jazz trombonist's brother), and even his unit supervisor—would cover Paul's cases.

One time I was down in "intake," the meeting area between social workers and their clients, when I noticed a young woman with a baby in her arms at the elevator. Every time a male worker came or went, she'd ask in a thick Spanish accent, "Meester Moratee?" I spoke to her and it turned out she'd been Paul's case for two years and had never laid eyes on him. I said I'd find him for her, but when I got upstairs and mentioned her to Paul, he stared at me completely aghast. "Who?" he kept asking, and as I repeated her name, he began rifling through his cases, clearly without a clue to who she was, until Katie got off the phone and said, "I'll see her!" before she jumped up and rushed downstairs. Paul subsided in relief back to his paper-strewn desk.

Katie told me later on that Paul had "better things to do" than serve his clients, which at the time struck me as somewhat elitist. "He's an artist," she explained, to which I huffily replied, "Who isn't?" Even so, Paul never remained alone in his unit as emergency worker one afternoon a week, as required. Someone from his unit, occasionally even his supervisor, covered for him. And when, years later I mentioned to him where I knew him from, Paul didn't remember me and ran a hand across his eyes, as though wiping away those social worker years as a bad dream.

Many in that Factory crowd, including members of the bands, would end up sooner or later visiting my little Jane Street apartment. Accompanying my brother Jerry, they'd sit on the big red sofa in my living room smoking hashish, talking, drawing "daisy chains" of men having sex across the entire length of a foldout Japanese art book, fighting with each other, making phone calls and reversing the charges or charging them to bogus numbers, and laughing outrageously when they hung up. Some would discretely excuse themselves to go shoot up in my poltergeist-ridden bathroom, then leave behind little gifts on the mantle of my long inoperable fireplace: baggies with a hit of crystal methedrine, a chunk of opium, or some grass. Still others, like Boy Ondine, visited on their own, bringing LPs of Maria Callas—whom he worshipped—shooting up in the john, coming out to listen to her sing, going "Aaah! Ooh! Aaah!" as we sipped tea.

Some, having heard I was a published writer, would come by to read me the lyrics to new songs they were planning to record and we'd talk about this word or that. A month before I moved out of my Jane Street apartment in late 1977, a now noted songwriter-performer from this madcap group rang my bell and stepped in for a visit, just like old times. We were sitting drinking coffee, I in my big chair, he opposite on the sofa, when he suddenly reached below the sofa arm, grappled around, then came up with a roll of papers in a rubber band. "Am I in luck!" he said. And when I asked what they were, he said, "Songs. Last time I was here, I was speeding like a demon, high, and totally paranoic I'd be ripped off. So I hid the songs while no one was looking." He's since recorded them.

Others, with less obvious talents, like Mr. Clean, the reputedly straight scion of a Brazilian diplomat to the United Nations who often chauffered the others around in his huge Fleetwood, would come by late at night looking for a place to crash and try to get into the sack with me.

Although most of those closest to Jerry were gay, and in some cases, wilder queens than any I'd ever hung around with, my brother was not. What connected them was drugs, mostly amphetamines, increasingly heroin. They'd all pile into Kenny's station wagon and go to Riis Park's gay beach for the day or to the baths all night; Jerry, who went with them everywhere, seemed to think nothing of it. In fact, he appeared to have a girlfriend, a blond woman named Lynn, older than himself, older than I was at the time, with whom he sometimes lived and who came and went among his crowd.

Hosting this crew, I felt I'd come a way from the naive young man I'd been when I'd graduated from college, for that matter, the naive young man who'd been a social worker, the naive young man who'd gone to Europe, the one who'd come back, who'd begun work in that tiny bookshop in Grand Central Station, or—most crucially—the naive young man who'd written a novel people with taste admired. To me it felt like an entire lifetime, not merely eleven years (one transit of Neptune in a sign, I couldn't help but recall from my astrology studies) since I'd last been honored, last had a promise fulfilled.

*   *   *

This very night at dinner, I planned to tell Dennis the good news about the new book contract. He'd arranged to have me come in the afternoon to the studio in Astoria, originally built in the mid-1920s by United Artists' founders Charlie Chaplin, Mary Pickford, and Douglas Fairbanks, Sr. Dennis's group was in the middle of filming the documentary film now officially titled *Pumping Iron*.

I arrived too late that day to see any actual shooting, but I'd missed it by seconds and the excitement of filming "good takes" was still in the air. The few indoor sets they were using were still up, and people in the film were either present or had just stepped into dressing rooms. I'd met a few of them previously at a small predinner party that Dennis had taken me to in the huge TriBeCa loft that belonged to Charles and his wife. The party was memorable for the generous amounts of cocaine and the two long black limousines parked across the street at all times, available to guests, the drivers' faces hidden behind newspapers they'd put up as they napped.

In addition to this trendy, attractive couple was the film's coproducer/director, George Butler, who, the minute I was reintroduced to him as a writer began telling me about his dream to turn William Gaddis's experimental novel, *The Recognitions*, into a film. Had I read it? (I had: 40 of its 600 pages.) What did I think about the kind of film it would make? ("A long, totally inscrutable one," I thought, but didn't say.) The more I listened to George, the more familiar he seemed. I had the feeling we'd met before, half a lifetime ago, but couldn't remember where. I managed to extricate myself and Dennis from these three and more just-arriving heterosexual guests, and allowed one of the limo drivers to drop us off at David's

Pot Belly in the Village—our glamorous arrival there a "scene" on Christopher Street. I'd felt, without saying so, there would be other parties at that loft with more cocaine and strange discourse before the film was put before the public, and my intuition was working overtime: I was right. The film wasn't completed for almost another nine months and not released until 1977.

This, however, wasn't a producer's chic loft, but a film studio, the actual workplace! Here I would remeet Roger (who had lost more hair but compensating had grown a pirate's large moustachio curving like a scimitar, and who was nice enough to remember me). I'd also very briefly meet the stars Arnold Schwarzenegger and Lou Ferrigno (he'd go on to fame in the TV series "The Hulk"), be shown all the accoutrements of a film set, have all the objects explained to me, and meet Dennis's new heartthrob, Bob, who had not been at the earlier party.

In the years since, I've tried to remember that meeting, but what I can recall is like tuning in a TV program where the aerial is partly connected, and unlike the sharp, high-definition precise memories of my meeting with Jane, for example, which I knew in advance would be important in my life, for which I was geared in advance. I recall Bob was dressed in a close-fitting T-shirt and denims. I remember that when we left the studio after my "tour," Bob was carrying a gym bag, because all three of us took the IND line subway into Manhattan and he was on his way to work out at the Mid-City Gym and he got off at the Fiftieth Street stop while Dennis and I went further to the Village. I recall being relieved Bob had a "normal" body compared to what was the unattractively overbulked Arnold and Lou—i.e., he didn't look too worked out, just really healthy. I didn't find Bob to be particularly handsome, at least he didn't fit into any of my types of male beauty. Despite his name, which I immediately (and it turned out correctly) assumed to be the Americanization of some eastern European, probably Jewish name, Bob looked much more southern Italian-American, Calabrian or Sicilian, with blunted Taurine features and jet-black hair, large dark eyes, prominent nose, a good complexion, and olive skin. I'm certain it is later knowledge that makes me picture Bob standing in what later would become a familiar pose, posture perfect, torso tilted a bit forward in greeting, head even more forward in anticipation of meeting, open and honest as always, a look upon his face I'd characterize as half sincere interest in meeting you and half concern for you, with just a hint of puzzlement brushed over it all, a bewilderment that vanished as he made your acquaintance, heard your first words, replied in his smooth, unaccented baritone voice, joked with you. He straightened up, his head aligned with his body, and he was "with you" from then on, as almost no one ever is; not with the intense nervy onslaught Edward utilized but with his own quiet, calm, lovely presence.

This, of course, is retrospective. Because while Dennis had talked Bob up, he'd made it clear he was very interested in Bob. I wasn't planning another three-way relationship, nor what used to be picturesquely called in gay life "bird dogging," so I thought Bob was Dennis's boyfriend, and left it at that. Who knew, given this meeting, that in a few years Dennis would fall away and we'd end up being the important people in each other's lives for a decade and a half? None of us had a clue at the time. Anyway, it wouldn't be until some months had passed that I'd see Bob again.

*   *   *

Which brings up the question of Dennis's romantic life. It's almost a truism that no matter how well you know two people, once they're in a relationship, you have no idea what's going on. Nothing typified this better than Dennis's relationship with Ed, about which I had as much knowledge as anyone in the world, but about which I truly knew nothing, including how or why they'd broken up. Actually "why" was clear, given the situation, their diametrically opposed personalities, lifestyles, and ways of going about things, and the general emotional messiness of the three of us together. But because I left the triad first, then was working and otherwise unavailable, neither told me what happened to precipitate the breakup, and out of a combination of *schadenfreude* and misplaced delicacy, I quashed my curiosity to ask Dennis when we began meeting again, two friends, occasionally for lunch or dinner.

I had known one impediment to Ed and Dennis was Dennis's relationship with Larry, the Columbia student who had moved to Washington, D.C. to attend med school. During the years when I was at the international bookstore, Dennis dated Larry whenever he was in New York and I met Larry twice and could confirm that he was attractive in a "white bread" manner I didn't care for. Dennis assured me this belied Larry's considerable sexual appetites and experience, his wild erotic imagination, his considerable horniness.

Like Dennis, Larry came from a very poor family, had done well in high school, and had won a scholarship to an Ivy League college. But once at Columbia, he needed to supplement his income and had done so as he'd done since he was a preteen back in the Midwest, by hustling; only now he hustled not Greyhound bus stations but the better Fifty-third Street and Third Avenue gay bars, places like the Round-Up and the Caravan. In one, Larry had encountered a well-to-do middle-aged gay couple who bought him for the night, then, taken by his personality and intelligence, decided to keep him and pay his way through Columbia as well as through med school. All Larry had to do was stay in the guest bedroom at their posh Upper East Side apartment when he was in town and be their "son." According to Dennis, this wasn't even sexual, leaving Larry eager to spend the time he was away from them in New York with Dennis.

From the way Dennis spoke of their time together, I got the impression this was and had been by far the most important male-male relationship in Dennis's life. That might have been the reason why he and Edward had broken up. According to Dennis, when Larry was finished with his residency in D.C., he planned to come to New York City to open a practice. This is what he did do in the early 1980s, after a longer-than-anticipated stay in Washington. Larry became partners with Larry Lavorgna in a large, successful, gay practice in Chelsea, where he utilized his specialization in infectious and tropical diseases to try out new treatments and drugs against intestinal paramecia and amoebae, as well as to study control groups in the ever-widening spread among gay men of the several types of hepatitis. Indeed, Larry treated me for one illness, but though I saw him a half dozen times, he never recalled we'd met through Dennis. And I never discovered why he and Dennis didn't get together once he'd come to the city, as they'd planned for so long. Perhaps by then Dennis was living with another man, older than himself. Larry—or "Doctor Larry" as he became known in our Pines-Flamingo set—dated around and for a few months was Michael Fesco's steady, but they never settled down.

In the mid-1970s, since Larry wasn't in town often, Dennis also was dating on the side, which made sense. I never found out whether that was how he met John or whether they'd known each other before. I tend to think the latter, because John was from the West, Carlsbad, New Mexico, not far from El Paso, where Dennis grew up. They must have met each other on the gay scene there. John was a rising young executive in a big bank, Chase or Manufacturers Hanover. He and Dennis shared an apartment in Brooklyn, spacious, well-kept, but—located at the Brooklyn-Queens line—a long subway ride, too expensive by taxi.

It was there, at Dennis's birthday party, that John began talking about his summer plans—and how I again got to Fire Island.

John was sharing a house on the eastern ocean side of the Pines with two men he'd met through the gym. Both were professionals. Both were, according to John, "very hot" and they knew not only "the scene" in the city, but also the scene out in the Pines. The only trouble was that John had just met Randy—he was at the birthday party, a dark, cute, curly-headed guy—and now John wasn't all that interested in the Pines scene. Randy had planned a vacation in the Pacific Ocean, Samoa, Fiji, someplace like that, for several weeks in summer and John was thinking he'd like to go. John wanted to sell the second half of his Pines share house: August 1 through mid-September. Was I interested?

I was interested. I felt this was going to be a hot summer, and I didn't want to remain in my Jane Street apartment with window fans cooling me the entire season. Also, I had work to do. I was in the middle of writing my novel, and I thought I'd finish a first draft, then bring the work out to Fire Island and live out there for a month and a half and finish a second, typed draft. Best of all, I could now afford to go to the Pines. Thanks to my new advance, I had enough money to pay both my relatively low rent in town and rent on his room.

Even so, I hesitated. Who were these guys? Would I get along with them? And if they were so cool would they even talk to a stranger?

A House on the Ocean, A House on the Bay

John solved the problem. I could go out for a weekend, stay at the house where Randy had a share (he slept in John's room anyway, barely using his except to store clothing), and I could come to their house, meet the men, hang out, and we could see if we got along.

A free weekend at the Pines sounded fine to me. It was before the enormous Fourth of July holiday weekend, and the oceanside house Randy had a room in was already full when he and John and I arrived at the Pines. I was dropped off at Randy's house at Crown and Ocean boulevards and in the most casual way possible introduced around. Present were five other guys, including one I'd met at the Roadhouse and slept with a year ago, and another two I used to see at dance clubs. They were a step above what Dennis called "ribbon counter queens at Bloomies," a derogatory, if not inaccurate description of the shallowness of their interests and mentality, and like Randy before me, I wasn't nuts about them. Even so, I was forced to spend that first Friday night dinner with them, as the men in John's house—where I hoped to stay for the rest of the summer—planned to discuss the future, i.e., me.

What might have been a totally superficial Pines evening was enlivened when the fellow I'd previously had sex with invaded my room while the others were at Friday Tea Dance and initiated a repeat performance. Shallow as they might have been, the others were socially acute enough to recognize I wasn't a stranger, but through their housemate, "one of them." So it was easier, and they claimed to be disappointed that I "couldn't play with them" the rest of the weekend.

Randy brought me to the house on Ozone Walk between Fire Island and Ocean boulevards the following morning. The first thing I noticed even before I'd gotten inside was that although it was at the bottom of the hill, the place was surrounded by decks. It even possessed a small roof deck, what might have been called a widow's walk, overlooking the foliage and other houses, where one could sun, watch sunsets over the Great South Bay, turn and see the ocean. On a ground-level deck outside two connected bedrooms that I assumed belonged to Jack and Frank, I couldn't help but notice worn-looking leather mats, a half dozen gradated hand weights, a barbell, and loose black discs of weights.

What would turn out to be my first home in Fire Island was as unextraordinary as it turned out to be beachily practical. These guys were not in *Design and Decoration* or *Better Homes and Gardens*, and the place reflected that. Externally, it was two slanted-roof wings attached to a central living-dining area in ginger-colored cedar planking. Inside, the same planking though in a lighter, unweathered shade. Above the large refectory table, a good-sized skylight opened to abet circulation from opposing floor-to-ceiling-glass-door walls. The bedrooms were rectangles just large enough to hold a double bed, with closets. John's had its own bathroom with tall shower and was next to the kitchen and was thus a bit more private. Jack's and Frank's rooms were in a wing across the spacious center and shared a bathroom. The kitchen was in dark greens and reds. Functional. Two pieces of art decorated the barely furnished—couch, two rattan chairs, a few lamp tables—living area: a brightly colored parrotlike papier-mâché sculpture off one wall, and a pop-art painting of a part of an American flag and the right half of someone's face. I later discovered these pieces had been brought out by Jack, their creator. One deck had wooden chairs and another table. It all looked simple and masculine and I said as much to Frank and Jack. They'd evidently been out late Friday night and looked not totally awake when I arrived and they unhelpfully grunted in response.

It was the oddest meeting of future housemates. John and Randy vanished into John's room to fuck, while Jack and Frank ate breakfast, made plans succinctly for the rest of the weekend, and occasionally would ask a question and then barely listen to my answer. I found both dauntingly handsome and butch. Jack, with his sculptured head and close-cut curling hair and his prizefighter's face—large soft eyes, broken nose, and sensuous mouth—took the breakfast dishes and began washing them. He wore tight-fitting shorts and a loose T-shirt that couldn't help but show off his lithe compact body and catlike movements, his heavily muscled arms. Frank, meanwhile, brooded darkly over a third cup of coffee, brushing crumbs out of his luxuriant black beard. He was more muscular than Jack, with a "Draw Me and You Too Will Become an Artist" conventionally dark-eyed beautiful faces that defied precise ethnicity. A few years later, Frank's tattoo of a black hawk swooping along his huge forearm would become famous via Robert Mapplethorpe's photo and an iconographic postcard. Frank's head and torso would be photographed and later drawn by David Martin, as Zeus, king of the gods, in the book version of my own novella retelling the Ganymede legend, *An Asian Minor*.

For the moment, however, Frank Diaz was the number three person, under Kitty Carlisle Hart, in the tonily successful New York Endowment for the Arts. Jack Brusca's art had become so successful that he'd been commissioned by the government to go to Brasília and put up a 100-foot-tall sculpture. Though they didn't say a word at the time, later on both privately told me that I fit their idea of a housemate better than John had: in the arts, as they were, and masculine in appearance and attitude. They also separately, later on, told me that despite being fairly hung over that first meeting, they'd both found me attractive enough so that after I'd gone to the beach with Randy and John, they'd said, "Neither of us gets to fuck him until after the summer share is over with. Agreed? Agreed!"

In Jack's case that turned out to be that fall. It took Frank a few years longer. In both cases I was astonished by their interest in me when they did come on. And if I'd overheard their compact at the time it was made, I doubt I would have believed it. Although only a few years older than me, both seemed so completely "arrived" not only in their careers, their looks, and bodies, but in their attitude and demeanor, their totally assumed manliness, that I felt not only completely out of the sexual running with them, but like a child next to them, determined to carefully, not too obviously, watch and learn.

Jack laughed when I told him that some years afterward. He told me how he and Frank teased me that summer, recounting ever wilder tales of their sexual activities, sometimes going out to indulge in crazy scenes with questionable partners the night before just to be able to relate the tales at the breakfast we shared over our refectory table the following morning. And how whenever I was alone with one of them in the house, he and Frank would go out of their way to cock-tease me by wearing the least amount of clothing: the shortest shorts, the smallest Speedos, the tiniest possible posing straps for their workouts, a face cloth barely covering their crotches whenever they'd step out of the shower and come looking for something they suddenly required where I might be working or sitting and reading. He reminded me how each had ended up in my bed once that summer, though they'd not broken their agreement; they hadn't had sex with me. Frank stumbled into my room naked, bedsheet trailing, early one morning when he knew Jack was sleeping out. Mumbling "Damn blue jay is yelling into my window," he flopped into my bed, wrapping himself and his sheet around my astonished self. For *his* foray into my bed, Jack pretended to be too stoned to know he was in the wrong room when he fumbled his way in from being out all night, and once in bed next to me, had done his best to excite me as he undressed himself, till I'd half panicked, unsure what in the hell he was doing, and had got up to go to the bathroom, at which he'd relented and left. Yes, they'd had their fun with me.

And while we all got along pretty well that summer, beginning two weeks earlier than planned, because John had taken off with Randy for the South Pacific and let me move into his room, Frank and Jack went out together, without me, at night, or infrequently to "tea." Frank and Jack seemed to prefer a bar, the newly opened Monster in Cherry Grove, rather than what they called the "twinkie" spots such as the Sandpiper or the Boatel I frequented. They were the first men I knew who dressed in leather: leather vests over bare torsos or over a tight-fitting black T-shirt, sometimes skin-tight black leather pants and crotch-and-ass revealing chaps over tight denims. And while I had to assume that they each scored a man anytime they wanted, they never brought one home, or if they did, didn't let him sleep over: we were never more than three for breakfast.

It wasn't just the black leather, wasn't the ultrarestrained low-keyed approach to everything, or their closeness to each other that kept me from feeling close to them. What really stopped me was that when we were just sitting around relaxed, listening to music, passing a joint, and they began to open up, an all-pervading darkness seemed to rise and hover around the room. Negativism, a fascination with pain not as something aesthetic but something deserved, with humiliation and degradation not as an act, theatre, but as something so familiar it must be embraced and accepted, all of

A House on the Ocean, A House on the Bay

which I couldn't help but shudder at once I was alone again and which I secretly felt beneath me.

The two had many friends, but the group they seemed to enjoy most, in a big new house on Beach Hill on the west ocean side of the Pines, while also handsome, muscular, and masculine, seemed even more attracted to darkness and creepy shit than they. I recall visiting that house one evening with Frank and Jack. A large, new volume of the gruesome, oozing-cloaca paintings of Dutch artist R. Giger (who later designed the movie *Alien*) and another book of sickly mordant sexually perverted "cartoons" of Tomi Ungerer were passed around, discussed in detail, and highly praised. The rest of the conversation was of suicide among acquaintances: two successful ones about which they spoke in great, shivering detail, and an unsuccessful one—which they mocked. Later on, in a picture book on gay life, I'd come across a double-page photo spread depicting a dozen men from that house or friends of theirs I'd met there. They looked as beautiful as I recalled them, as they nakedly played at tug-of-war. But even before AIDS came along, eight of those twelve were dead, either by their own hand, through overdosing drugs, or, in one case, by homicide.

I was never able to ascertain how much Jack Brusca subscribed to these morbid and thanatological interests. I know that he did go through spasms of depression and uncertainty, but his art seemed to carry him through the darker patches of life, as later on did a loving companion named Raoul, a stunning and sweet Brazilian man. One time while we were waiting in the coat-check line of some club Jack said, "I didn't know your father and mine were competitors." It turned out that his father and uncle owned a large wholesale produce company similar to my father's not far away on Horace Harding Boulevard in Queens and they and my dad often vied for new customers. Like me, Jack had to fight his family's wishes and plans in order to become an artist. That lack of parental support continued to breed uncertainty. It galled him, remaining internalized for years, making every little defeat more bitter, every step forward more gratifying. Even so, Jack always met me filled with future plans and recent successes—he was doing murals for a ministry in São Paolo, had a museum show in Mexico City, and he'd just designed the costumes and sets of Roland Petit's ballet corps—filled with optimism, which is how I remember him now that he's gone.

I know that all that flirting with dark forces did end up affecting Frank. But then he'd also had far darker life experiences than Jack, or indeed than any one of us at the time. In the 1970s, from even before I met him to about 1978, Frank had three lovers die on him, all in strange, if not openly suspicious, circumstances. The first died in his sleep; Frank woke up to find a corpse in bed with him. The second choked on a chicken bone. The third, after they broke up, returned to Scotland and hanged himself. No wonder whenever Frank appeared at Flamingo's Black Party, people who only knew his relationships drew back and repeated his nickname, "The black widow." George Whitmore, who visited me at my Fire Island house the summer of the third death, caught enough of the gossip to turn it into a short story of that title, which was published in *Christopher Street* magazine, and which pained Frank—and me, for his sake.

Some years later we were returning to Frank's Manhattan apartment east of Fifth Avenue on Eleventh Street from dinner nearby. When we got to his door, there was something wrapped around the doorknob, a nasty concoction of hair and cloth and poultry bones, with what looked like soot strewn across the doorstep. He lurched back, tried to hide his surprise behind a frown. "*Santeria!*" he murmured. "Voodoo! Someone's put a curse on me." When he didn't move, I grabbed a magazine I was carrying, scattered the soot and removed the crap from the door handle and threw it away, saying, "Well, I don't believe in that and anyway no one's put a curse on me! So it's okay!" He didn't completely believe me but mentioned it to other people for weeks, trying to find out who'd done it.

Several years after we'd not seen each other in a while, we met for coffee on his invitation and Frank began for the first time to open up to me. At first he talked about bureaucratic politics. He'd quit his job at the New York State Council for the Arts during yet another Byzantine intrigue and was now looking into gay political groups he might administer. Believing my reputation and thinking I was far better connected than I actually was and knew far more than I did, Frank wanted my knowledge and advice. I told him what I knew, which wasn't much, but it seemed enough to satisfy him for the moment. Then he changed the subject. It took me a few minutes to see how much. Frank began to intimate to me how he had begun going to a really louche place in my neighborhod called the Hellfire Club, then went on to tell me he'd been surprised to find himself going regularly, not as a master, a sadist, but as a masochist, being flogged and beaten and urinated on by strangers every weekend, men, women, anyone who wanted to. I tried not to seem too shocked, though I was. Frank had been one of the Pines-Flamingo set's most notorious top-men, virtually a rapist. No one went home with him and got out without having some undergarment ripped off and being soundly screwed. I was even more shocked when Frank said he was seeing a psychiatrist once a week, he, Frank Diaz, whom I'd always thought of as so sure of himself, so strong and self-reliant. At the time, I didn't know whether he was telling me the truth or not, or if he was once again—as he'd so often done at the Pines—testing my reactions, seeing if I'd flinch, be disgusted. I hadn't. I'd unjudgmentally replied I hoped he was treating any open wounds against infection and other dopey practical stuff like that. Not too many months after that confession, Frank jumped out of his apartment window and killed himself.

*　　*　　*

Not two days after I had moved myself, two large traveling bags of summer clothing, and my electric typewriter out to Fire Island Pines for the remainder of the summer, I bumped into Jon Peterson at the harbor. He was out too, mostly on weekends, he said, time-sharing a room with a writer whose name I didn't know in a small house on Tarpon Walk, not far from where I was staying. His house-mates were a new couple, bright and good looking, who he thought I would enjoy. I ought to come by for a drink.

Jon was explaining exactly where the house was when the housemates came by, arm in arm, fresh from the Pines Pantry with dinner fixings in grocery bags. Jon's dark eyes glittered, "Aren't they a-dor-able." He introduced me to the two handsome, mousta-chioed men. The older and smaller—my size—was named Nick Rock, the taller and younger, Enno Poerch. To all our astonishment, Nick had just read *Smart as the Devil*. A friend had given it to him a month ago. He very much wanted to talk to me about it and about psychology, which he studied in college. Why didn't I come for dinner tomorrow night?

Halfway up the boardwalk to their house the following evening, I remembered how I knew Tarpon Walk: it was where Jay Weiss and I had trudged and slogged and almost not made it on our long trek to Sam Plaia's house seven years before. However, this time instead of going up, over, and down to Fire Island Boulevard, I remained at the top of the hill and located the painted-on lot number Jon had told me led to their house. I made out the planked entryway through an overgrown beach plum thicket and pushed through to a good-sized deck along one side of the house that wrapped around front to form a narrow strip of deck, and in back to make a fenced porch connected by a steep stairway to a lower deck, large enough for maybe two recliners.

The house Jon shared with Nick and Enno was a single-story cottage with light gray shingles, white molding—including a trellis upon which nothing ever trailed—and a carmine front door. From the living room windows you looked out and down to an identical white house to the left, and beyond that, lower down the hill, to an oceanfront row of closely built together houses, including the one Sam had rented. These were blocked from most pedestrians' eyes by seven-foot-tall wooden fencing, but because of the angle, from up here on the hill at Tarpon Walk, you could see right through their glass expanses, through their living rooms, to the beach and ocean. From the most extreme part of the front deck, an empty space several houses wide provided a small but totally unimpeded view of the beach, with the surf and a volleyball net stretched across the sands.

When I first arrived I peered in the front windows, but the living room and dining room were empty, so I walked around back. Here my breath was taken away. This tiny, otherwise unremarkable house had been set atop one of the most elevated points on Fire Island, the deck at least thirty feet higher than the highest treetops, above any other house around it, and there were few of those. As a result, the view from the back deck was more than 200 degrees around and totally spectacular, encompassing a panorama of the west side of the Pines from the last houses on Sail Walk to the next big hill on Crown Walk that hid the harbor from view, but included most of the Great South Bay and beyond. At the horizon was the distant shoreline of southern Long Island and hundreds of tiny winking lights of now crepuscular towns—Bayport, Sayville, and every dockside village in between up the coast to Bay Shore. As if the view wasn't enough, my first sight of it was with the sun setting, blood red, sinking into the bay waters, drawing after itself an enormous flaming train of sky, a vast garish celestial peacock's tail, a palette of every tint of the warm spectrum, embroidered with burning flecks of electric green.

I was so stunned that it took me a few minutes to realize I wasn't alone. Standing in the back doorway facing the spectacle, arms wrapped around each other and clad only in Speedos, their faces, their bodies reflecting and at the same time appearing to be internally illuminated by the sky's colors, were Nick and Enno. I hesitated. Then Nick said, "Come! Look from here!" and gestured me toward them in the back door. Enno drew me into his embrace, and we three formed a single awestruck person, watching the sun glide under the incandescent bay waters, pulling behind itself an enormous tail of silken sky that appeared to dapple and pulse as it fell in a thousand ever changing, ever darkening hues.

At that moment, I knew I wanted to live here, to have this spectacular view, to experience these sunsets. I didn't have a suspicion how I would achieve that, nor did I guess how quickly my wish would come true, only that it must.

That first evening together was terribly easy, utterly congenial. Nick and I "clicked" so instantly that after we'd eaten and after Enno excused himself to go into his bedroom to work—he was a graphic artist and had set up an easel there—and after Jon decided to go out to the Sandpiper for a drink and "to see what poor innocent might be lurking about," Nick and I remained in the candlelit little living room talking for several hours more.

On Nick's invitation, I returned to the house next afternoon for a casual barbecue, at which I met several more of their close friends, Paul Popham, Rick Wellikopf, Michael Costello. But even before that, I had joined them and their friends on their patchwork of a dozen beach towels in front of the Ozone Walk stairway down to the sand, and so I'd met various other people from surrounding houses that Nick and Enno knew and socialized with. These included Dick Fischer, Ray Ford, Jimmy Peterson—who was managing the little harbor shop Mel Fante had opened called Melbamar (we nicknamed it "Melbingdales")—Julio Velez, Frank Cioffi, and Little Tommy: the group that would later be called "the Ozone Beach Club." Nick and Enno seemed to know everyone who was attractive, creative, glamorous, witty, or popular, and by the end of that summer—i.e., two weeks after Labor Day—through them, or through people I met through them, or through people I met through the people I met through them, I'd become acquainted with maybe another hundred or so men who'd form the core of gay men I'd exist within for the next five years, and more loosely for the next decade and a half.

The truth is, this was the first group I'd *ever* felt I belonged to. I hadn't ever been an outcast or total outsider growing up, as so many gays and lesbians have been. In junior high, I'd been part of a loose-knit gang of four boys. In high school and college, I'd been part of a small, "arty" or intellectual coterie, while summers I hung out with an even looser group of kids on the north shore of Long Island. The difference lay in *how* I was connected. For instance, in the college group, Barry, Alan, Steve, and all their women friends except for Barbara were older. They'd known each other before I came along, and they shared backgrounds and sharply delineated conventions, even though those conventions included being cynical and unconventional and against everything. They held opinions about life and politics and especially about art that intrigued me, but which I didn't share. For instance, for them it was a given that "the novel is dead, film the only viable art form." I loved film equally, but believed the two forms could inform and interact with each other. I'd come late to their group, and while we argued, most often I went along with them.

By the time I'd come out to the Pines this time, however, I was already past thirty, already formed by my own experiences and my own thinking about life. I felt I was an individual, and I was accepted as an individual by other strongly opinioned individuals with their own range of life experiences and their own thinking about life. One of the real joys was to suddenly have someone open up and tell you about some utterly new aspect of his past: Ray Ford describing being in a kindergarten in a San Francisco school as it was severely damaged during an earthquake; or the so-called silly Latino queen everyone called Santa Anna, suddenly revealing how he'd been an unwilling member of a right-wing Argentinian death squad before he fled South America; or Dominic telling you about the Japanese bombing of Shanghai he'd experienced as a small child, while he and his missionary parents fled, hidden by peasants, in a cabbage cart.

For the first time in my life among equals, I felt evaluated and appreciated by qualities I valued, not artificial conventions. These people added up what I considered important about myself: my talent as a writer, my ability for friendship, my love of the beach and all its outdoor sports and entertainments, my intense interest in all the techniques of sexual love, the pleasure I found in handsome men upon whom to practice these techniques, my love of all kinds of music, dancing, architecture, and all of the arts—including fashion and interior design of which I knew nothing but was most willing to learn—as well as a good feeling about being gay and the direction gay politics were headed, and a general optimism toward life.

Like Frank and Jack, whom they knew and occasionally associated with, this large group of gay men were all more or less professional, all more or less successful, and ranged in age in 1975 from about twenty-five to thirty-five years old. They used recreational drugs to one degree or another, loved going out dancing all night to good music about which they were knowledgeable, were extremely physically healthy and often worked out their bodies to look even better, generally possessed high self-esteem, and were sexually liberated and believed that one should share one's self-esteem, worked-out body, and handsome face with as many other handsome faces and worked-out bodies as possible, whether in a couple, trio, or larger gathering. While romances, summer-long affairs, and even long-term "marriages" were much approved of—indeed the ideal—and "golden couples" such as Nick and Enno the examples everyone wished to emulate, shorter-term relationships, including one-nighters, orgies, public sex in the bushes or on the beach, were also considered okay, so long as they were done with some style.

We shared other values too. Gay politics for instance: no matter how "out" you were among family and at work (and there were a surprising number of us who were out publically then) or however closeted you might be—and people like Paul Popham who were still officers (and a legal counselor for court martials) in the Air Force Reserve—were pretty closeted and with good reason—we were staunchly supportive of gay rights and gay politics. Benefits for various gay causes were hosted at the Pines every other summer weekend, considered chic, and well attended. Any cultural offering in our area with the barest smidgen of homosexuality was sup-ported, attended, and discussed in detail, be it play, movie, book, news item, or gossip. Despite our many different careers, interests, and places of origin, we'd all come from the same era, having come to consciousness during the late 1960s as part of or alongside the counterculture, and this led to a certain cohesion of experience and interests. After having sex with a relative stranger, we'd start talk-ing and discover both of us had been at a particular student sit-in, or he'd been on the Student Nonviolent Coordinating Committee buses down South with people I'd known, or I'd been in the same marches for civil rights and against the war in Vietnam as his friends and relatives. After a year or two of going out to the Pines, going to dinners and parties, to the Boatel for Tea Dance and on weekend nights to the Sandpiper and the Ice Palace in Cherry Grove, and after talking, and going to bed together, and tripping on mescaline together on the beach, we all came to know each other well. Thus when Michael Fesco reopened his dance club Flamingo at Broadway and Houston Street in a larger and far handsomer new location, calling it on the invitation to join, "Fire Island in the City—all winter long!" we all showed up, and were pretty much glad to recognize and greet each other.

The "Gay Two Thousand" someone called us a few years after-ward, after Mrs. Vanderbilt's "New York Four Hundred" a century earlier. That number was based on how many people could fit into the ballroom of her Fifth Avenue mansion; ours was based on how many of us went to the Pines on a weekend holiday. A couple of local cops—Julio and "Red," whom we also got to know and partied with—knew the exact number because every ferry passenger or yachtsman or guest docking in the harbor was counted every weekend.

Like Mrs. Vanderbilt's, our group was essentially social, and despite its greater size, as unified. I wasn't the only one who came to use Flamingo—and to a lesser extent Studio 54, Twelve West, and Paradise Garage—as a club. If you were looking for someone you knew but had lost track of, you might expect to see him there on any Saturday night. Or at least find out from someone he knew exactly where out of town he was and when he'd be back. In the same way, if someone new entered who looked interesting, it would take only a half hour of the most casual inquiries around Flamingo's front lounge to find out not only who he was, what he did for a living, who if anyone he was dating, and what his income was, but also what he liked sexually, any scars or birthmarks he might have, and the shape and size of his dick, to the millimeter! It's difficult for gay men today to understand how this could be, but gay life was much more unified then, possibly because it was so much smaller. Our scene was also bicoastal: although San Francisco and Los Angeles had their own "scenes," any time I was in those cities and went dancing at Studio One or cruised in a Castro Street bar, I was sure to find at least four guys I'd lusted after in the Pines, three who'd lusted after me, two I'd had sex with, and one I personally knew.

Yet it was more than people at the Pines, it was landscape and weather and decorations as much as bodies: flags, kites, giant pennants of colorful Japanese fish and flowers fluttering at different elevations from eaves and roofs and poles, enormous hanging graphics covering outer-deck walls, and weird instant beach sculpture constructed overnight, as though by maritime elves. It was also conversations with a stranger at 6 A.M. at the top of the stairs at Ozone Walk after being out dancing all night. And LSD hallucinations along Fire Island Boulevard that made me believe the passing figures of strollers were trees in motion, while stationary objects like plastic bags of garbage seemed to be people. It was sunrises and sunsets, caresses, a broken boardwalk slat, a sudden chat, a sudden spat after which you made up with a kiss.

And of course it was, most decoratively of all, houses. All kinds of houses. None more eerie than that of a handsome bearded sabra, an Israeli architect working and living at the island all summer whom I'd met one afternoon when a strangely warm, all-enveloping yellow fog had covered the beach. We'd subsequently met again and slept together several times, ending up in my bedroom and one time making love and snoozing at the shoreline just above the surf. We wanted privacy, however, and Dov's house had it, he told me, as he was the only person who lived there, so the following Saturday he invited me to visit.

His house was located on the bay side and it seemed to belong to another world entirely. To get there, I'd arrive at the end of a private walk, itself a spur of a sidewalk that seemed to fold back on itself, a path that looked recently macheted through a fen of more than head-high papyrus reeds growing right to the bay's edge, with only his lot number lightly stenciled, barely visible on the deck wood to give any hint that a residence was hidden within. This in turn branched again, once to an eventually solitary and very rickety little dock that looked as though it was last used decades before, or onto another walk even deeper into the fen. The sudden emergence of a mimosa tree with its delicate flame flowers was the only sign that the island had not totally vanished in this sea of reeds. One would ar-rive at last at a tiny square deck surrounded by marsh except for a dense stand of deeper green bamboo and one aged pine tree so bent as to seem a giant bonsai. Under and beyond its distorted branches were six worn steps that led to another tiny terrace that as you as-cended slowly turned to reveal the wall of what looked to be a single-room shed of dark weathered wood. Suddenly you were above the reeds, above a prairie of reeds, and ahead of you the bay waters were glimmering in midafternoon sunlight. It all seemed so forlorn, so far from any other residence, so intentionally private, that unlike other houses at the Pines that I simply walked into, I would always halt here and call out, hoping to hear Dov reply before I'd dare to enter.

Within the entrance to what could have been an isolated clam-mer's shack perched on stilts at the edge of some bog was a glossy modern kitchen and dining room with details straight out of *Archi-tectural Digest*. I'd walk up another half dozen steps into a studio that transformed itself seamlessly into an outdoor courtyard and deck and garden and surrounding cabana bedrooms. Indoor walls would be patterned by shadows, and even the three skylights above seemed woven about with leaves so that more patterns fell on the floors, on the furniture like silken tapestries, like inlaid mosaics. Outdoors, the deck walls were louvered so that I never once saw any person or object in complete sunlight, even at noon on the brightest August day, but some overhanging shelf, some combination of liana and batik, some Balinese puppet on sticks would cast a cool pall on a square yard or so of discolored wood, upon a tiny ceramic vase of newly planted nasturtiums. A shadow world inhabited by a lovely man dark with secrets. Was he in Likud, the Israeli Secret Service, as someone had suggested? Or was Dov on the lam for financial shenanigans? Or was he merely divorced? Whichever, Dov was very beautiful and very sensual, his comings and goings by private boat or on someone's yacht—never the mundane ferry—utterly ungraspable. I saw him for several weeks. Then he was gone, period.

By Labor Day weekend of that first summer I lived at the Pines, Jon approached me again. Was I interested in going into the house with him next year? The writer was planning to stay out in the Hamptons with his new beau. I could time-share for the summer, alternating weeks, or we could alternate larger chunks of time. The latter, I thought, was better. But first I should see what Frank and Jack were up to about next summer. When I asked, they said they'd already decided to go into that house on Beach Hill with their beautiful, morbid friends. That was a relief and left me free to take up Jon's offer to join in the little house high on Tarpon. Only that didn't quite work out as planned either. Instead of me and Jon splitting half, Jon shared with Nick and Enno. This was partly because Enno had gotten an important commission to help design a new amusement park to be built in New Jersey, called Great Adventure, and partly because Jon, who'd broken up earlier that year with his beautiful (but according to Jon, "impossible") Swedish-American model/lover Eric, hadn't yet replaced him at the Pines and wanted to spend some of the coming summer in Europe, explaining "the best lovers are from abroad." Nick and Enno would come out May, June, and

September, Jon the months between. I could stay out all summer, if I wanted.

I thought taking a half share in the house would be financially tight, though it was cheap even by the year's standards. But by late spring of 1976, I had not only sold German-language rights to *Smart as the Devil*, I'd also collected my second payment for paperback rights plus the advance payment for my new novel from Arbor House, so I wasn't doing too badly. On top of that, Joe Madaras, a fun and sexy Aries I'd begun having sex with on and off since the rainy afternoon we'd met in the Pines, was looking for a place to live, and as my rent in town was low, he ended up subletting my apartment from me. When I moved my things out to the Pines at the beginning of the summer, I found I had so much stuff, I needed two trips between the Pines harbor and Tarpon Walk, even using the children's wagon that came with the house. Not only clothing and my electric typewriter, as I'd had the year before, but also a box filled with books I planned to read and cassette tapes I planned to listen to on the pricey portable cassette player I'd purchased that year. It was to be connected to and amplified through my little Advent radio with detachable speakers, which tuned to easily pull in FM radio stations from not only Manhattan but all along the coast from Boston to Philadelphia. Its great tuner was helped by the fact that Fire Island was so out to sea, so far from other interfering radio station transmitters.

By then I'd long finished the second book, *Eyes*, I'd been contracted to write for Don Fine and Arbor House and was working on another novel. I typed up most of the final draft of *Eyes* as I'd planned to do, at Fire Island the summer of 1975, August and September, during weekdays when I was alone at the house, and I completed it in my New York City apartment the weekend of September 21 after the short season on the Pines house I'd shared with Frank and Jack was over.

I'd been so alone so much of the time that early September that at the Pines, I'd gotten into the habit of writing whenever I wanted to, morning at the breakfast table, cooler afternoons outside on the picnic table with the typewriter plugged into a deckside electrical socket, or quite late at night. Sometimes I'd go out to the Sandpiper, have a drink and a few dances with people I'd come to know, come home alone, and work until 3 or 4 A.M. Almost always after work I was far too excited to go directly to sleep, and I'd go out for a walk; usually a short one, up Ozone Walk to sit on the stairway above the strand where I'd watch the moon shimmering over the ocean, or more usually just stare in amazement at the perfect panoply of the Milky Way's stars spread out above for me like a gigantic not fully comprehensible diagram. Occasionally I'd be so restless I'd take longer walks along the sands, where the night's incoming tide cut a distinctive three-foot-high cliff into the beach, then back, meandering past a score of darkened houses along nearly isolated Fire Island Boulevard. Rarely would I meet anyone out so late looking for a sexual encounter, even more rarely would I take him up on his offer. Almost never would I return to the Ozone Walk house except by myself and, at last exhausted, manage sleep.

Back in the city, I found myself either unwilling or unable to alter this pattern, at least until the novel was done. It was a Monday morning, around 2 A.M., on September 22, when I retyped the final page of *Eyes* for the third time and decreed it good enough. I was excited and pleased. The last fifty pages of the book had become far more difficult to write than I'd anticipated, mostly because to make the story of Johanna Poole work, her relationship with Stu Waehner as well as to herself had to become far more believably complex and sophisticated than I'd ever dreamed. For the first time as a writer I'd come down with what Conrad and Henry James would call "a case of nerves." I wasn't at all certain I could pull it off, wasn't at all sure I possessed the authorial craft and skill to write what was next needed. I wasn't even sure what was next needed, and if this anxiety weren't bad enough, the characters and their story had begun to haunt me day and night. I swear I saw a woman in line ahead of me in my bank who was Johanna, and a young man who'd gotten out of a crowded subway car and peered at me through the graffiti-scrawled windows had to be Stu. Both of them looked anxious, harried; both had looked at me as if I owed them something. I did, closure. If, that is, I wasn't going insane.

I'd taken it all bit by bit, a half page at a time, sometimes a paragraph at a time, and somehow I'd worked out a solution, sweating over those last few conversations between my two main characters, working it over and over and over and over. Then, getting an inspiration from a book I'd read in college years ago, Richardson's *Clarissa*, I'd tried to write Johanna's final journal entries as though they were happening at the time one was reading them, minute by minute, like a sportscaster at a prize fight, at a pennant ball game, as Stu got into her building basement on his way to find her, as Stu inadvertently shorted out her apartment's electricity, leaving her to write by candlelight, as Stu knocked on her apartment door, calling her name, as Johanna huddled in the dark, unable to face being found out by Stu, unable to face the knowledge of who she'd been, what she'd been, clutching a weapon with which to defend herself perhaps with which to attack him when he got in . . . Incredibly stagey. Yet, as in that astoundingly popular eighteenth-century novel, it worked! Belief was suspended, you were gripped, frightened, you had to know what happened next. You empathized with someone you'd thought odd, perhaps crazy. You felt the "pity and terror" that Plato said was required for a tragedy to bring on a true catharsis.

Fitting those pages into the manuscript box, reading them one more time, then telling myself "Stop! Enough!" and forcing myself to at last put the lid on the box and just go, I stepped out of my Jane Street apartment into a balmy, early fall night. It had rained on and off most of the day and the streets shone silver and black in the pale, UFO street lights. The rain had puddled ink and jet, looking like tiny poisoned pools amidst the vulnerable, broken, overpocked yellow-gray stone of the sidewalk. Autos along Hudson Street were few, their sodden tires muffled against the soaked tarmac, their steel bodies gleaming from the most recent outburst, water still dripping off fenders and chrome but twisted and perverted into inscrutable runes by bursts of sudden acceleration. It wasn't cool, but strangely summery, unnaturally warm, the air supersaturated with damp. I walked only as far as Abingdon Square before I felt malaise sweep over me. I sat on an oddly dry wooden bench beneath boughs of dripping trees, watching leaves wetly slither off twigs and stir in little cyclones and night swirl around me. Suddenly a young man was sitting across from me. I didn't know if he'd been there all the while or just arrived, but he was quite presentable, and he was staring. Seeing me look back he might assume I was interested in him, and he stood up and began to dawdle around the swings and unfunctioning granite fountain in my general direction. I admired his trim body in jeans and sweater with my glances and he responded by smiling an engagingly crooked-mouth smile and at long last approached close enough to cautiously alight on the park bench to say hello. I echoed him, then he said something else, something banal like "What are you doing out so late?" I knew I was supposed to respond in some suggestive yet equally banal manner, but I so much wanted to tell him, to tell *someone*, what I'd just gone through—the problems, the near defeat, the victory drawn at last from unknown depths. So I did say it, and as I spoke, I saw his face go from interested openness to complete puzzlement to utter distaste. Panicking now, I talked faster, more urgently, explaining more and more, and at the same time trying to listen carefully to what I was saying, as I watched him draw away incrementally, first his arms, then his legs, then his body, at last his face and damn! if even to myself it didn't sound like complete and utter double-talk, total nonsense, not even English really, but some constructed balderdash. "Well, see you," he managed to interrupt me long enough to sign off. Fleeing me, fleeing as though for his life, his sanity. And I continued sitting on that bench, in the now slowly increasing rain, wondering if I'd been guilty of hubris, if in writing this book and in succeeding where I'd sensed only failure, I'd somehow paid the price, lost my mind; or, more accurately, broken that connection between my brain and my tongue, and if so, how long the affliction would last.

Of course I was fine the following morning when I woke up and someone phoned me and we had a normal conversation. Later that day I wondered what had happened. It would repeat, that incident, not exactly as it had happened that night, but in tiny different ways, for years after: it still happens. I'd come to recognize what had happened, what was happening, was not that I'd broken a connection within myself, but between myself and others. With every book or story or poem or play and every challenge I'd successfully overcome I'd find that my ability to explain to even those closest to me what had taken place during the process lessened. Slowly, but now quite definitely, have I learned the lesson of the creator, how with every creation you become more alienated from those around you, more alone. It's cumulative, as the lines of communication between yourself and others fray, then sunder. You cease to discuss anything creative with anyone, even other writers, and finally normal conversations seem banal and worthless, even "important" or "crucial" ones. You become impatient with others, with life, anything at all outside of what you are doing, and can only bear to be involved in that which you are creating.

"I've walked away from so many parties," I once told a friend. The reason was always the same: I had an idea, something to work out about a character or plot in what I was writing. On the dance floor at the Ice Palace or Palladium, I'd see how to solve a narrative, at the height of an orgy at the Crazy Ladies' house on Shore Walk, my limbs and organs entwined with porn stars and the Pines' hottest men, I'd realize what was wrong with a poem and have to get up and rewrite it. Right away, otherwise I'd become distracted in what I was doing, i.e., living, and forget it.

That's the price I've paid . . . I no longer know if it was worth it.

*   *   *

The "wrap" party for *Pumping Iron* didn't happen in the autumn as Dennis thought. The production company ran out of money and the film was put on hold. Dennis went back to the bookstore, Roger began directing an industrial film touting IBM, and Bob collected unemployment and looked for work in the theatre.

I discovered this partly through Dennis, although we talked infrequently that fall and winter. I learned more through Bob Lowe, whom I suddenly began encountering wherever I was, on the subway, on the street near Broadway and Seventy-second Street where I'd come from visiting a friend—Bob lived in an apartment on Seventy-first—in a bookstore, but most often in the Sam Goody's Records with the large, well-stocked classical section and "cut-out" bins at reduced prices, now closed, then near Eighth Avenue, across from the Mid-City Gym where Bob went daily.

Perhaps the third time we met there and began chatting, Bob

asked if I was hungry. He was starving from just working out, he said, and suggested a local Greek diner with good moussaka. My instinct was to say no, but he seemed eager for me to join him. I ordered dessert and coffee; he ordered a three-course meal and ate it all. We talked about the film. Bob had heard George and Charles were trying to reinvest among friends. They expected to get the final shooting money, maybe the film's finishing costs, together soon. Meanwhile, Bob worked as assistant stage manager for an off-Broadway play here and there.

Although he seemed cheerful, he said his future in theatre, which he'd hoped would be his profession, wasn't looking promising. He laughed as he told me about his last solid job, as stage manager for the Vivian Beaumont Theatre at Lincoln Center. One of the heads had liked Bob, even pushed him into directing. Another was after Bob's body. "I put up with his lechery and innuendos and comments for months," Bob told me, "but one day, he lured me up to his Central Park West penthouse apartment on some pretense, and I found myself literally being chased around a table by him as he tried to rip off my clothing!" Bob laughed remembering it, but he was embarrassed and also angry, which I found an interesting emotional mix. "I managed to get away with my virtue intact," Bob said, "but the next day at rehearsal, the lousy so-and-so was so pissed off, he yelled at me in front of everyone. I knew I had to quit."

Bob moved to a smaller theatre company, which he'd liked, until they ran out of funding. Then he'd found the film job. But there weren't enough film sets to support him in New York City, and after all, he had studied theatre.

I suggested he try part-time work at the gay clubs to supplement his unemployment checks. Flamingo was always interested in guys who looked good with their shirts off. It was every Saturday. If he wanted, I'd connect Bob up.

He demurred, admitted he'd been offered and turned down gay work, ranging from modeling nude for magazine photos to bartending at a high-paying popular leather bar in Chelsea. "I had a male lover in college, but I'm not into the whole gay thing," Bob said. He'd known he was homosexual since he was ten years old; when he was in high school in Longmeadow, Massachusetts, a suburb of

Springfield, he'd developed crushes on guys, but he'd fought his feelings. In college, mostly because of peer and parental pressure, he'd had a girlfriend, Japanese, very sweet, shy, not at all demanding. One night she'd arranged it so that they'd been alone together at a friend's house. Bob had gone through with it, had sex with her, then panicked totally. "As soon as I was done, I went into the bathroom and stayed all night. She kept banging on the door, asking what I was doing. I was showering, over and over, I felt so . . . !" He shuddered as he told me.

In his third year at Colgate, Bob had been "stormed" by Rodney Griffith, one of the stars of the music and arts department, who'd gone on to become founder of and choreographer for American Dance Theater and have his dances performed by the Pennsylvania Ballet and the Martha Graham Company. "He took his time with me, and I didn't find sex with him disgusting. We became boyfriends," Bob said. "My best friend at school, Michael, also said he was gay. We were at the center of this arty gay set despite how conventional Colgate was."

His mother somehow got word of the affair with Rodney. Bob spoke of her as a force of nature, powerful, unceasing, indomitable. When he was home from school for the holidays, she listened in on his phone calls, confronted him about being homosexual, told him how terrible it was, and dragged him to a psychiatrist who believed it could be "cured." Bob hated the sessions, but went through with them until aversion therapy was recommended. Bob said that before he'd undergo that he'd quit college, leave home, and become a hobo. His mother relented. She fixed him up with one "presentable girl" after another, saying his homosexuality was only a "phase" he'd get over. "But I'd had sex with both. I found one repugnant, the other natural," Bob concluded.

He held his ground. Because, if his mother was an unstoppable force, Bob—born under the sign of Taurus the bull—could become when necessary the only thing that could resist her: an immovable object. She'd also been mollified by his high honors when he graduated, as well as by his Rhodes scholarship to study theatre at Oxford. He'd gone to school there for a term, but although Bob was Anglophilic he said he hadn't fit in and been quite surprised to encounter unapologetic antisemitism in England. He'd pursued his studies in Asian Theatre to one source—New Dehli—an amazing experience, then he'd returned to London and connected up with the Royal Shakespeare Company, where he'd stage managed their hit production of Joe Orton's *Loot*. At the green age of twenty-three, Bob had become assistant stage manager to the Royal Ballet during its greatest period in history, when Nureyev and Fonteyn were performing *Romeo and Juliet*, *Swan Lake*, *Giselle*, *La Bayadére*, and *Les Sylphides*, replaced by dancers some thought even better, Dowell and Sibley. Bob stayed for the next few years, living in a flat off Sloane Square in Chelsea, around the corner from where I'd house-sat an American couple's townhouse a few years before. He followed the company to the 'States on tour, to New York where Rodney was then living and they had resumed their affair. When the Royal Ballet went home, Bob chose to stay in New York. He worked as assistant stage manager for various ballets and companies, including the production of *Thumbelina* my friend Jerry Blatt had written. "I thought Jerry was the most blatantly gay man I'd ever seen," Bob confided, "and I'd been in the ballet!"

Though Bob and he had worked together, the jobs Rodney brought didn't pay enough. "Anyway our affair was over. We shouldn't have tried to revive it." Even so, Bob was living in the same apartment. "We're friends. I've got my own bedroom and my own cat, 'Max, . . . You Sly Puss.'"

"From *All About Eve!*" I exclaimed.

"You're only the second person I didn't have to explain the allusion to." Bob beamed. "The first was my best friend in college, Michael Lasalle."

I told Bob about my upcoming share at Fire Island, how I'd be going there to live all summer. He ought to come. "Besides the guys and the gay scene, it's a beautiful place. Wild deer in my backyard and on the surf at dawn licking the sand for salt. The weather's elemental. The view from the house is great. I've made so many friends. Wonderful, smart, talented. I'll go out in early May."

Bob seemed unsure. He was unsure about many things: he had no idea where his life was going. But he'd think about it. He insisted we exchange phone numbers, though I said we could reach

each other through Dennis any time, adding, "I have no secrets from Dennis."

Bob did contact Michael Fesco, who liked him and gave him work at Flamingo, helping set up for the Saturday night dances. I saw him there putting out enormous bowls of fruit and Bob would tell me about the artwork Michael was featuring in the club's lounge that week which Bob had helped hang. "Aren't you hot," I'd ask, "with that shirt on?" No one wore a shirt at Flamingo, and I cajoled him into taking his off. At first Bob was shy about exhibiting the body he'd worked so hard on, but he did take it off when I told him he'd be a cynosure if he didn't. I wasn't the least bit surprised how guys suddenly began coming closer and hanging around nearer, longer. Bob usually left the club early, and he'd never dance, no matter who asked, explaining, "I never learned how to do this sort of thing." So, I didn't push it.

Suddenly it was mid-April, 1976. Filming on the documentary was done. A few weeks earlier, someone in the Museum of Modern Art—perhaps Sam Wagstaff, who curated photography—had come onto the set of *Pumping Iron* and had been so impressed by the rushes, or by the bodies, that he'd arranged an exhibition at the museum called "The Body as Art" with Lou Ferrigno and Arnold Schwarzenegger posing. Dennis was ambivalent: "The media will come only to make fun of it." But he and Bob and I went anyway. A gallery held a single plinth in front of classically draped curtains that opened to reveal a movie screen. It was already filled with people when we arrived, many from local gyms where the event had been advertised, others from the uptown art crowd, gay division. I recognized them from when I'd gone around with Edward. Although the short "informational" slide show and film on bodybuilding in art that the curator and George had cobbled together—Muybridge, Eakins, Bellows, Cadmus—was interesting, the show didn't take off until Ferrigno and especially Schwarzenegger stepped out onto the plinth and began to throw bodybuilding poses. Someone offstage was reading a scholarly paper, but we couldn't hear what was being read, because the crowd went absolutely wild. There were cheers, whistles, shouting, camera flashbulbs going off, and Arnold, knowing the crowd, played to it. The event was so successful, *The New York Times* printed a piece in its arts pages on it.

That article mentioned the upcoming film four times, increasing the likelihood the wrap party would be well attended. So there we were, in the loft belonging to Charles and his wife again, huge vases of calla lilies, tables groaning under rounds of cheese the size of tractor tires next to terrines and pâtés big as televisions, wine, liquor, and a kilo of cocaine mounded on a cutting board. On the street, as my agent Jane and I arrived, weren't the usual two waiting limos but at least a dozen. Jane commented, "Good thing I brought the Fleetwood." As might be expected, everyone connected with the film was present, but unexpectedly, dressed—even Lou and Arnold—in at least a sports jacket. Even Bob, who could only stay long enough to attack the comestibles, wore a blazer. It was Saturday night. He was expected at Flamingo to help set up and to later on be a piece of "standing art" wearing a jockstrap, leather hat, boots, and chaps, up on a platform as all-night decoration for the annual Black Party, which had become the most exciting, dark, and depraved event of the club's season.

Jane and I were on our way to Flamingo later on. She'd dressed in black jodhpurs, thigh-high riding boots, and a black brassiere-blouse right out of Frederick's of Hollywood, which for this earlier party would remain hidden beneath a buttoned-up silk jacket. I was in a black T-shirt, sports jacket, and denims, with black cowboy boots. We took turns playing with her mean-looking riding crop, and naturally we got attention. Especially from one incredibly pretty, tall young woman who was in the kitchen when we wandered in. When she asked why we were dressed in black, I wasn't sure what to say. Jane came right out and said we were on our way to the Black Party at Flamingo. "Farrah goes there!" the model said, meaning Farrah Fawcett, who was in fact a club member and appeared every weekend with what seemed to be a gay couple and another young woman. The model turned to her companion. "Farrah said the Black Party was the wildest. I want to go. Please! Can we go tonight, Warren?" At which point, Jane and I realized that the slender man leaning against the double sink who'd looked familiar was indeed Warren Beatty. He demurred a while, doubtless thinking he'd prefer spending the night in the sack with her rather than leaping about with a bunch of faggots, but when he finally said sure, sure, would we leave his name at the door, I had to say they could only get in if they came with us: members and guests only. He didn't like that, but I said we'd tell them when we were leaving and they could decide then. "If you're worried about being recognized," I said, "don't be. Everyone's on drugs. And everyone there thinks he's a movie star." He laughed. "If it's a big party, there'll be people you know there, too," the model was saying, still pleading, as Jane and I left them in the kitchen.

"If they only knew I grew up in a house with a dirt floor in Texas," Dennis giggled as he greeted us. Ordinarily unflappable, tonight he was giddy: "Do you see who all is here tonight? Jesus, it's like the New York Social Register, junior division." As he was pointing out people with famous names, a statuesque young woman stepped over, and to Jane and Dennis's surprise, gave me a big kiss. "Where on earth have you been?" she asked. Before I could answer, she continued, "Someone told me you'd published a book. Do you know George and Chas? How are you connected with the film? Are you an investor?"

She was someone I'd not seen in sixteen years, someone I'd necked and "petted" with at picnics and clambakes when we were both fifteen when my family had spent summers in that enormous house belonging to some wealthy man in Locust Manor, on the north shore of Long Island. She immediately told me who else I'd known as a teen was here, said how everyone had pitched in when George had told them the movie had gone over budget, so they'd become investors in the film. That explained why he'd seemed familiar. We must have met when we were younger. "What do you think?" she asked, meaning how good an investment did I think it. "It'll take a while, but eventually, you'll make a profit," I prophesied. Which proved true.

She and I spent the next ten minutes catching up, before a guy named Gil, who'd been one of the cuter if more know-it-all boys from our group of summer teens, came to where we'd thought we were hidden. "Holy shit! Is that Picano? Where've you been? Under a log?" Gil called over others I'd known and for the next half hour I was among people I'd last associated with when I'd escorted one girl or another to one debutante ball after another, renting a tux an entire winter, running around Manhattan visiting huge apartments and vast townhouses, seldom seeing an adult who wasn't a servant or occasional grandparent, dining at balls, supping afterward better than I'd ever eaten before, and drinking champagne every night, though I never had ten dollars in my pocket and had to get to this sophisticated high life by an hour-and-a-half-long bus and subway ride from extremely bourgeois, utterly suburban, Twin Ponds.

Gil, who must have inhaled an ounce of coke by this time, and his date, who was much younger and whom I didn't know, talked themselves into joining us at Flamingo. "Jesus, Picano! An author! A homo! If I'd known you were this wild, I would have kept in touch!" my wealthy-but-never-very-close refound pal whispered in my ear while we waited for Jane and Mindy to freshen up. Warren and the model at the last minute begged off, so I phoned Flamingo and said I was bringing two guests. It helped that they were wearing black. Jane drove and the others followed in their own car. We arrived at the club just before it got really crowded, and once in, we hung around a while with Gil and Mindy, who were gaping at the crowd and decor, which included besides the guys on platforms, others done up in leather and rubber, trussed, masked, gagged, and hung from wallracks and other unpleasant looking structures, as well as performers like the fire-eater/fire-fucker, the snake charmer with his very anal boa constrictor, and an over-the-hill female stripper. Finally we lost them.

I saw Gil twice more that night, once dancing wildly with Mindy. She had braided her long hair onto her head and was holding her dress hem in her teeth as she stamped her feet in fandango. He'd stripped off his jacket and had taken out his shirt studs and cufflinks. The rolled-up sleeves revealed bigger arms than I'd remembered, and the ruffled shirt opened to the navel showed a nicely muscled, blond-downed torso. Much later during the party, as I was checking out the line of guys along the long wall in the "back room" who were getting blow jobs from another line of guys kneeling in front of them, someone grabbed me. It was Gil, virtually naked, his shirt off, pants and shorts around his ankles. With the fellator between us, Gil held my face and pulled it toward himself, I

thought to say something to me over the music. But instead, he suddenly began to tongue kiss me hard. I was so surprised, I nearly fell
over and had to grab onto the wall—and Gil's shoulder—to retain
balance. He moved both hands onto my shoulders so in seconds I
could feel him writhe, then shudder, in what must have been a
pretty serious orgasm. He kept holding me, his body still shaking,
even after the guy between us got up and left. Finally Gil said
"Whew!" He let go of me but insisted I wait while he located his
clothing and got dressed.

"Nothing personal, you understand," Gil said, as we got back out
onto the dance floor. "I just like to kiss when I come."

Not a hint of so-called homosexual panic there.

"That your first time with a guy?" I asked, suspecting it wasn't.

"I get blown by TVs at that bar on Eighth Avenue every once in a
while. What's it called, the Gilded Grape? Guys give the best head,"
Gil added casually. Then, "Now what in the hell did I do with
Mindy?"

We found his date amidst a group of young queens from F.I.T.
who'd befriended her in the front lounge by telling her how much
they loved her Chanel dress. She was barefoot by now, her pumps
somewhere on the floor. Eventually, Gil located them and he and
Mindy left the club. I located Jane and she left, and at last Bob was
allowed to come down from his platform and I made him dance a bit
to loosen up his body. He did so by standing in one place, raising his
arms and sort of swinging them slowly. "Oy," I thought, "he *cannot
dance.*" Something else to teach him. Odd, I thought, what great
natural attractions he held. Yet he seemed unformed, unpolished,
like a chunk of the best Carrara marble that had been well carved
but required a few deft strokes of refinement, like a mathematical
formula that needed a few more stages to be more fully, more elegantly solved. I could see what had to be done. It wouldn't be difficult. He seemed to trust me to do it. But why should I bother? He
was nothing to me. He was Dennis's friend! And even if I did bother,
when would I have the opportunity?

*   *   *

Finished copies of *Eyes*, my second published novel, arrived in late July of 1976. As I'd planned, I was living in the little house on the hill on Tarpon Walk all summer, so I walked to the harbor to meet the 10 A.M. ferry, signed for the registered package, and took it home. The cover of the novel was better, much stronger than that on my first book. It had large title lettering in red and yellow above illustrated binoculars through which staring eyes could be seen, against a black background, with white lettering for my name and "Author of *Smart as the Devil*" on the bottom. The back cover had praising quotes for the first book from the *Los Angeles Times*, *Publisher's Weekly*, and a half dozen other reviews. The book was handsome. I loved my photo, a head shot cropped from a Zeb Freeman picture taken on the beach last summer. It was terrific and I was happy with it. Throughout the day and night I kept picking up the book, admiring its paper, its design, reading a page here and there, pleased.

It wasn't until much later that first night the book was in my possession, as I was going through reading chapter headings, that I stopped. Where was chapter twenty, the story of Mrs. Remora? I didn't have my manuscript with me, but despite how I searched the finished book, I couldn't find the old woman's story.

It was crucial that it be in the book, exactly where I'd placed it. Although the novel was about a relationship between two young people, I'd learned much from reading late Dickens, and the novel's resonance, its meaning beyond itself, derived from the world I'd peopled it with surrounding the central pair. Johanna's lubricious boss, her promiscuous woman friend, her down-to-earth gay hairdresser, even her horny delivery boys; Stu's womanizing best male friend, his female co-workers, his interfering spinster downstairs neighbor, and most crucially Mrs. Remora, represented not only various permutations of heterosexual love and how it worked for good or ill, but they also composed Johanna and Stu's moral universe. Remove a single piece, say, Mrs. Remora's pocket biography, and with it the motivation behind her all-important action that turns the plot, the whole structure of the novel was mortally damaged, ready to topple.

I phoned Jane the next morning in a panic, hoping the missing chapter might be only in the copies I'd gotten. But when she checked her box of books, it was missing from all of them too.

She called Don Fine and he told her he'd taken the chapter out, explaining he believed it was unneccessary. Jane reminded him that the manuscript had gone through several stages: it had been edited, and neither he nor Andrea had suggested it be taken out; the book had been copyedited, typeset, and proofread—three more opportunities—again no one suggested it go. Why had it been taken out so late—without our knowledge? Jane couldn't get a satisfactory answer out of Fine, and we were forced to conclude that printing that four-page chapter would have meant another costly signature of pages; it had been removed to shorten the book, to cheapen the unit cost.

To say that I was angry and depressed cannot come near to how I felt. Betrayed comes close. I immediately sent Fine a registered letter saying he'd altered my book without my permission and I considered the company to be in violation of contract. Furthermore, I considered the book he'd published to not be my work. I wanted all copies of the "damaged" book removed from sale. Or if it did go on sale, I wanted my name removed wherever it appeared.

Dozens of panicked phone calls ensued between Arbor House, my agent, and our lawyer. Fine's books were at that time under distribution by another publisher. That company's sales force had taken the orders. Their warehouse held the books and were shipping them. We were told the sale of the book could not be stopped. Although both my lawyer and agent suggested compromise with Fine, telling me to try for much more money or something for the next book, I wouldn't hear of it. I was appalled. I hated my book. I refused to do publicity, refused to have anything to do with Don Fine, aside from making his life as miserable as he'd made mine. He kept phoning me at the Pines, and I kept hanging up on him. Finally he yelled, "You have to talk to me."

"What can you possibly say to defend your actions?"

After a half minute, "I edited Joseph Heller! I edited *Catch-22!*"

Which to him seemed to mean he could do whatever he wanted.

"I don't care if you edited the *Holy Bible!* In the original!" I replied. "See you in court!"

The following days were complete turmoil. But in their midst, good news arrived. Dell had already issued its paperback of *Smart as the Devil* in April and sales in paperback were extremely brisk. So good, in fact, that Linda Grey, who'd bought it, was also buying paperback rights to *Eyes* and for thrice the amount of money she'd paid for the first novel. Because we'd set up payments of any subrights as due to me thirty days after Arbor House received it, I'd have a nice little nest egg when I returned to the city in the autumn. I didn't have to sell my new novel—not to Fine who had a contracted right to read it and refuse it first—not to anyone, if I chose.

Jane and Bruce suggested that I continue holding the threat of a lawsuit over Fine's head, continue writing the next book, and meet with several editors, who were now very interested in my work, and see which I'd prefer. They argued that it was a far more powerful place to be in than any I'd dreamt of. I saw that. I also saw that nothing could be done about the missing chapter in the hardcover, anyway, no matter how much I sued Fine. It was in bookstores—no one but us knew about the missing chapter—selling twice as fast as the first book.

When I spoke to Linda on the phone, I was still so glum about what I considered to be "a priori censorship" and the emasculation of my work that she asked to see the missing pages. I sent them and she phoned back and said, "I can see no good literary reason why he took these pages out. I believe the book is better with them in. I'll put them back in the paperback version."

My heroine!

A few weeks later, Linda mailed me the sketches for the cover art of the *Eyes* paperback, because I'd complained about the paperback cover art for *Smart as the Devil*, and this looked great, better even than the hardcover. "In-house" support was very strong at Dell for the second book. She said they all thought it would become a bestseller. *Eyes* was officially published in September 1976 (despite its copyright date of 1975, another screwup), then May of 1977 in paperback. A week later, it was on paperback best-seller lists all over the country, and was the third best selling paperback at two of the country's largest bookstore chains. It went into multiple printings, totaling 400,000 copies, and was reprinted again in 1984. Rights were sold again to the Mystery Guild, where it did respectably, to New English Library in London, and to publishers in Germany, Argentina, Spain, Brazil, and—a first for me—Japan.

Another first was that I got to see a book of mine being read all around New York City, on subways, in parks, anywhere I went. That was exciting. Equally thrilling and different from my first book, *Eyes* early on became a perennial candidate for film adaptation. Since its publication two decades ago, the book has been under film option all but maybe fifteen months, and I've cowritten two versions of unfilmed screenplays based on the novel, including a draft written with director Frank Perry, a fascinating experience.

Aside from his share of the sales, Don Fine's action to save a few bucks cost him an author—and work that would get me far more attention. After showing about half of the next novel to four editors later that fall and meeting and discussing what I planned to do with the book with each of them, and asking for their ideas in return, I chose Linda Grey, who then published my next three books as hardcovers through Delacorte and paperbacks though Dell. Her dedication, faithfulness, and understanding of my work equaled her willingness to take risks with my work. It took years for me to recover when she left Delacorte and I was left in the hands of other editors.

That early bad experience with *Eyes* somewhat prepared me for some of the many complicated things that could go wrong with publishers and books. Not all, by any means: I'd have my share of horrible surprises in the future. It also taught me an important lesson: to never compromise with people who fuck you over, to never accept their unethical actions, to proclaim them when you can (sometimes you cannot) because that may bring important new allies who more closely share your view of life, and your own integrity.

*   *   *

A few months before *Eyes* came out, I'd been asked to write an essay by the editor of a young women's magazine. My essay, printed that spring, was titled "The Lady May Be Watching Too!" and while it explained some things behind my writing of the book, it didn't detail the actual incident.

The simple facts were as I wrote them: I returned to the United

States from living in Europe in the late 1960s and moved into an apartment I had meanwhile sublet to a newly married couple, friends I'd known in college. They'd subsequently moved to Princeton, where he was getting a graduate degree and she was doing social work. I had never lived in the fourth-floor, front-right studio apartment on Jane Street before I went abroad, so it was as though I were a new tenant.

I've written in *Men Who Loved Me* about the people I associated with at this time, most of them through becoming sexually involved with Bob Herron, who lived at 43 Jane Street when I lived at number 51. I *didn't* write about many of the odd things that happened to me during the year I lived in that studio before I moved into Bob's building. My out-of-body experiences, for instance—a half dozen times, and real doozies. In each case, I'd suddenly wake up and see myself below, lying on the daybed, the floor and rug and furniture where the ceiling was supposed to be, all the pictures and posters upside down, and when I got over my initial shock and was able to look around more, I'd see my back was flat on the ceiling, feet pointed to the open window. Between me on the ceiling and me on the daybed calmly staring, was a connection, a twisted, barely visible yet sparkling iridescent, umbilical cord, seemingly from my navel on the ceiling to my navel on the daybed. The first time I went out of body, it was brief, a second later I was looking *up* at a bare ceiling. But as I became more accustomed to finding myself floating on the ceiling—always in a slightly different location—I'd remain apart longer, I'd try to fly, to float, to drop, to move along the ceiling. Once I slipped toward the open studio window and the next thing I knew I seemed to be outside the building, floating by the studio window, looking in on myself. There was a strong breeze pulling me away from the window, and I didn't know how far the cord would stretch before it broke and what would happen if it did—if I'd ever get back to my body! The total oddness of it got to me. I had no idea what would happen next if I went along with the experience. I became frightened, began fighting the wind, trying to claw at the bricks around the edges of the window to hold on, to crawl back in, to reconnect . . . as suddenly as before, I was in my body again, on the daybed, looking up. I jumped up, and rushed to close the window, and stood there, my heart pounding, feeling I'd just escaped an awful unknown fate. That was my last time out of body.

I began experiencing other weird dislocations while lying reading on my daybed, especially physical "drops." It was as though someone had pulled the mattress from under me, the mattress, the bed, and I was about to fall, fall, fall! I'd grab the bed, the mattress, grasping it for life, and when I'd steadied myself, leap off the bed, scramble to my feet, my heart pounding, my temples throbbing.

A third species of experience was even more frightening. I found myself awakening after a full night or from catnaps only to discover myself paralyzed: my body still asleep, but my mind totally awake. I'd be unable to move a muscle. I'd try to move, say, my little finger, knowing the second I did so, I'd break through the paralysis. But I'd be so panicked, it would often be four or five minutes by the very visible clock to will any muscle, even my little finger, into motion. And all the while, naturally enough, I'd believe that I would remain paralyzed for the rest of my life, eyes open and staring, hearing the telephone ringing, people going up and down the stairs, yelling on the street, everyone and everything around me moving while I remained absolutely frozen.

I have no idea why all this happened when it did or where it did. I wasn't using drugs at the time, and it never happened again, not anywhere else. So, given how completely weird all that was, when the phone calls began, they were by comparison very light stuff. Although enigmatic enough, they didn't induce panic. The calls were from a young woman with a British accent. She knew my name. Where I worked. Somehow she knew my habits, my hours, my comings and goings. At first I thought she was someone who worked where I was employed, or as that staff was so small, in another office on the same floor, and she'd seen me in the elevator, found out my name, looked me up in the phone book. But as we talked, I mentioned names and it became apparent that she didn't know any place near my midtown office, in fact, she only really knew places around the West Village, and then in a circumscribed area around Jane Street.

Our conversations were casual. She gave a name for herself I thought bogus. We played a lot of "Do you go here? Do you know so and so?" which she seemed to enjoy. She'd always call when I wasn't busy, so I had no problem talking with her. She said little about herself. She'd flirt a bit. Usually she had to hang up, suddenly, as though she were working, though she phoned in the evening. She was British, and I'd lived in London, so we had things in common. I'd traveled to Edinburgh and Glasgow, Liverpool and Brighton, Bath, and even Dublin, although she had not. I thought her a lonely young woman in the big city too shy to meet people face to face. She said she was, and I accepted it—and her calls. As I accepted the idea that someone would find me attractive enough to call.

I can't recall when it was, nor precisely what it was, that tipped me off to the fact that my phone caller could see me, *did* see me! When I did realize it, it didn't bother me that much. Indeed it explained what had remained inexplicable till then. I did begin keeping my window shades pulled down a lot more when I was home, even when she teased me about it. I also found myself scanning the many rows of windows of the redbrick building twenty stories high that rose behind the line of brownstones directly across Jane Street from my apartment whenever I'd go out. Even so, I wasn't too perturbed. Not when she revealed to me that the man in the third-floor-right apartment shared my taste in men—meaning she'd seen me bring home someone, or had seen me having sex before I'd begun putting the shades down.

Our phone relationship might have gone on longer but for an incident that suddenly gave me a glimpse of how important to my caller I'd become and how potentially dangerous the situation could become.

This girl I'd liked and palled around with in high school—let's call her Elena—was pretty, easygoing, a brilliant student, and a good sport. We'd gone to various cultural events together with groups of students, up to Tanglewood to hear the Boston Symphony Orchestra and to Jacobs Pillow Dance Festival to see dances by Alvin Ailey and Merce Cunningham, or as a couple to the Metropole Café in Manhattan where we'd heard Allen Ginsburg and his lover Peter Orlovsky read poetry and the brilliant—and at that time still beautiful—young Chet Baker singing and playing cornet with his band. We'd gotten tickets to the Old Met and watched a thrilling production of *Turan-*

dot with Birgit Nilsson and Franco Corelli, and as stunning, of Alban Berg's *Wozzeck*. After high school, Elena had gotten a scholarship to Brandeis University, and from there, I'd heard she had traveled around Europe, settling on a kibbutz in Israel.

Suddenly she was back in the United States, had heard about me from a mutual friend, and called me. As I was always pleased to hear from Elena, we met at my place, went for dinner nearby, returned to my apartment, and talked the night away, catching up on our years and our varied and substantial adventures since high-school graduation. Since we'd always been open with each other, I naturally told her I'd gone to Europe to become gay and how I'd succeeded, and Elena told me about the married man she'd fallen for and all the craziness surrounding that. It was perhaps 4 A.M. when we were done talking. Elena was staying with her parents in the depths of Queens and it would take hours to get home this late by subway and bus, so I suggested she sleep on my daybed, and I'd sleep on the floor. She went home the next morning, leaving with me when I went to work.

That evening my mysterious caller phoned and though I was distracted at the time—clearing out kitchen cabinets, cleaning and spraying against cockroaches—it was evident she was upset. She kept needling me about one thing or another, until it came out that she'd seen Elena, perhaps when she'd first arrived, or when we returned to my apartment, but at any rate, she definitely knew Elena had slept over. Now I was almost certain my caller had seen me having sex with guys because she had more than once coyly hinted at it: athletic, no-holds-barred sex. I doubted, though, if she'd ever seen a woman alone with me in my apartment, which should have left her in no doubt as to my sexuality. Also I told her Elena was an old school friend, even told her Elena was infatuated with an Israeli man. It made no difference. To my phone caller, Elena was suddenly a "whore" and a "tart" and all sorts of things. Naive me, it had taken me maybe fifteen phone calls from her and now a good ten minutes to realize that she was insanely jealous, that she'd fantasized about me, who knew, fantasized I was bisexual or that she could turn me straight or some totally false crap people sometimes convince themselves of, despite all proof to the contrary. When I did all of a sudden recognize this, and also how desperate and sick the relationship was—a relationship I'd all along thought was just me being nice to a lonely woman out of her element—I felt manipulated and used. I got angry. I told her to never phone me again. I pulled down the shades to the window's edge and kept them pulled down the rest of the two months I lived in the studio—though that meant my plants wouldn't get enough sunlight and died—and I moved as soon as I could, into a place down the block with windows on the backyard: so if she saw me at all, thereafter, it was merely coming and going.

I'd told this story to my agent Jane over dinner, early on, before she'd sold *Smart as the Devil*, and in telling it, I had myself said, "What if I weren't gay? What if I were straight and found myself deeply involved with this woman. I never found out who she was. I might easily have picked her up in the Village, in the singles bar on Hudson Street and gone home with her and not even known it was the same person. I might have ended up having a double relationship with her. Especially if she was still calling me up." At which point both of us realized simultaneously that I'd just laid out the plot line of the book. At first I called it *Eyes Across the Street*, but for some reason I can't recall, perhaps because single-word titles were then faddish, it was changed to *Eyes*.

The story would have been intriguing enough, but I've come to believe what made the book popular, for both male and female readers, was that I wrote it from the point of view of *both* the voyeur and the man she watches and phones. I could do this because having young women friends around me, Jane and Elena and Susan, I had a pretty good idea of what they were going through: their hopes and dreams, their hassles and difficulties and fears. It was a newly feminist time, and the women I knew were struggling with the independence they felt they deserved, the right to be a man's equal, at the same time as they were having to deal with men who refused to treat them equally, as independent, or serious in their profession. And, as I never tired of pointing out, unlike other examples of oppression, these heterosexual women slept with, lived with, had emotional relationships with, and *married* the very people who most oppressed them.

FELICE PICANO

Having the sexual tastes I did, I could identify myself as a voyeur obsessed by a beautiful, unobtainable man and see the complexities of the situation. And, I could imagine being on the other side, since I actually had *been* a watched male and knew what was entailed in that ambivalent position. I decided to write the book not precisely symmetrically: the voyeur tells her own story in the first person, in letters, journals, all in her own voice. But the man she watches has his story told more obliquely, through a narrative device I'd begun to use in *Smart as the Devil* which I called "camera on the shoulder," less than omniscient but more capable of authorial distance than first person. I needed unequal perspectives to ensure that the story's turns would be surprising yet feel inevitable; and so the reader would come to understand why Johanna becomes a voyeur, how and why Stu allows her to become his caller, and the effect of the relationship upon themselves and each other as they become more deeply enmeshed.

While this strategy would end up working well for the novel, giving it complexity and readability, it ended up doing something I couldn't predict: it made the story highly desirable as a film property and at the same time, given the industry, unfilmable. The story of *Eyes* works only if you accept that a man can be as desirable as a woman. But commercial feature films exist in a male-dominated hierarchy (even when women produce and direct) where women, not men—even the most beautiful men—are the sex objects. So while it may be terrifically exciting for a man to want to be voyeuristically desired, even watched, by a woman, at the same time few men are willing to accept being objectified or being manipulated by a woman. Another problem is that movies, especially love-story movies, require happy endings. And this story cannot have a happy ending. It's a closely reasoned formula showing the impossibility of heterosexual love. If the Phaëton myth was the basis of *Smart as the Devil*, *Romeo and Juliet* was the forerunner of *Eyes*. It's an argument against mixed-gender love in our society. And so, by reversal, my first gay novel.

*　　*　　*

The first hint something was physically wrong with me was so minor I barely paid attention to it. Early in the summer of 1975, a few days before I'd gone out to Fire Island to live for the first time, I noticed a sudden red eruption on the skin of my left flank. If it weren't located where it had to rub against my underwear and jeans I might not have even noticed it. After a few days it still hadn't gone down, despite the application of various lotions, so I swabbed the area and crushed it open. There was a surprising amount of discharge from such a tiny thing. I swabbed it, bandaged it, and forgot about it.

The following February, another eruption, exactly similar to the first, showed up on my left thigh, on the inside, which might partly explain why it had already developed to a much larger size before I noticed it. I tried the newly available over-the-counter-hydrocortisone lotion on it, but that didn't help. Instead it swelled, and the following day began to hurt, making me aware of it constantly. I once again swabbed it and broke it open. Again, it was surprisingly deep with, this time, a nasty-smelling discharge. The edges were rough, so it took longer to heal, but again healed completely, leaving no scar.

The third appearance was when I was living at the little house on Tarpon Walk, the summer of 1976. The pimple began higher up and back on the inside of my left thigh, so I could only see it with difficulty. One day I noticed it and said to myself, "Oh no! Not again!" The next day it was the size of a half dollar, not just a pimple, but swollen. And it hurt. A lot. It pulled the skin tight and was red and nasty. I mentioned it to my housemates who said it sounded infected and should be looked at by a doctor and perhaps be lanced open. No doctor was at the Pines that day, so I suffered. The following day I woke up in pain, amazed by how such a relatively small thing—though swollen to egg-size, twice the size of the day before—could so rapidly focus all my attention.

The Pines' doctor's office was on the other side of the harbor, in the Community House, half a mile away from Tarpon Walk and, because there were no vehicles in the Pines, could be gotten to only by walking. So I walked. Slowly, and with increasing pain. The last hundred feet I had to stop and catch my breath every few steps because it was so terrifically painful. I was shaking, in a cold sweat despite the warm temperature, when I finally stepped into the waiting room, and leaned against the wall, my body exhausted by pain. At last the doctor saw me. He was a Scotsman (given his brogue) studying in the United States evidently doing his residency at the local hospital. He poked, he prodded, he listened to me. He wanted to give me antibiotics and wait a few days. No, I said, I was in such pain I needed relief now. With much hesitation, he agreed to lance the infection. Both of us were amazed by the quantity and foulness of what came out. I mentioned the previous manifestations. He made me wait to drain the wound while he saw other patients. When he looked at it again, he didn't seem happy. He instructed me to soak the entire area a half hour every day in hot water with epsom salts, and keep squeezing the wound until it ran blood.

"What is it?" I asked. "What's causing this?"

He didn't know exactly, but he knew the infection ran deep, and given its angle toward my lower torso as well as the locations of previous outbreaks, he thought it might have an internal origin.

"Meaning what?" I asked, but he didn't answer.

I did as he told me, soaking and squeezing till it ran only blood and began to heal. The same resident was at the Pines' clinic the following Thursday, looked at my wound, and pronounced it healing well.

As he was sending me out he said, "I went through my books and consulted colleagues, and as I suspected, this infection might prove to be nothing, or might be the manifestation of a far more serious pathology. Should it recur, I suggest you not wait but immediately get yourself to an internist. A specialist in gastrointestinal problems. Take every test to make sure."

"Make sure of what?" I asked.

To which he replied, "You might go directly to an oncologist."

When I got back to the little house on Tarpon Walk I took out my paperback *Webster's Dictionary* and looked up the word *oncologist*: it signified one who specialized in cancer.

I was thirty-two years old, looking better than I'd ever looked in my life, feeling healthier than ever, among people I liked and felt comfortable with. I was at last doing the kind of work I'd struggled to do for years, and getting money for it, making a name for myself,

A House on the Ocean, A House on the Bay

living the life I had dreamed about living for decades. I had no intention of anything stopping me. I distinctly remember speaking out loud my attitude toward even his mere suggestion: "I don't have cancer! Fuck cancer!"

*　　*　　*

I'd been in Manhattan no more than one or two days a month since mid-May 1976, when I'd begun my first full summer living at Fire Island Pines. Yet during each short visit, I'd managed to bump into Bob Lowe, despite being so busy I'd not had the chance to get near a bookshop or record shop, where we'd previously met. Each time we re-encountered, I reinvited him to the Pines. Still, I was surprised when he phoned me in early August and said he would like to come out. The temporary job, the latest in a series of temp jobs all year, had ended. While he wasn't flush, he had both time and spare cash. What was my schedule like?

It was fine, I said. In terms of work, I'd had a rather busy spring and early summer. I'd written four poems and a completely gay-themed short story I'd titled "The Interrupted Recital" (published in *Gaysweek*, then in my 1985 book of short stories). I'd also finished another, longer story (unpublished to this day), titled "Song Without a Score: The Lost Immortal Composer, Caspar Xavier Mensch." It was a comic "biography" of a made-up nineteenth-century romantic musician with a particularly unfortunate destiny: all his many compositions had been lost or destroyed, each in a fashion more horribly bizarre than the previous. Except, of course, for those of his works that survived because they'd been "stolen" by other composers and passed off as their own work: Isolde's "Liebestod" for example, from the Wagner opera; the middle movement of Mahler's *Symphony of a Thousand*; and Brahms's entire Fourth Symphony.

Earlier that year, Dennis and I had begun to collaborate on what we called a "video-drama" titled *Lust for Tomorrow*, a take-off on soap operas, in which all the characters had WASP-y names like Bryce and Wylie and Tish and were blithely, at times criminally, perverted. We got as far as a five-page treatment and a first short episode, which we tried, without success, to hawk to the TV industry. Although we failed in this, I'm noting it here, because our work preceded by some years others that followed, not only *Soapdish* but also Tom Eyen's series, "Mary Hartman, Mary Hartman."

My little catalogue of works also lists for this period, and for the first time ever, three nonfiction pieces, two commissioned: the essay on my book *Eyes* for the short-lived *New Dawn* magazine, and an essay titled "A Very American Day" for the bicentennial issue of the equally short-lived *Islander* magazine. There was also an unpublished "article" that ended up serving as a book treatment and outline. It appears in my catalogue as "Hypnotism—Some Notes for the presentation of *The Mesmerist and Mrs. Lane.*"

That, of course, is what I was provisionally titling what had begun to look to be my next book, the third to be published based on that story headlined in the St. Patrick's Day issue of the turn-of-the-century *New York Journal* I'd received as a gift. After long discussions with my agent and a few other people, after some thought and a great deal of diddling around with various characters in the story and even with loosely drawn plot outlines, I'd come to believe that although the material would have made an excellent nonfiction work as I'd at first intended, I needed much more documentation to do it that way—and documentation was precisely what was missing. On the other hand, everyone who heard the story was fascinated by it. They wanted to know how it had happened and better yet, what happened next. That's all a fiction writer really needs to hear to envision a book as a reality.

I'd given that essay treatment to Jane, who'd read it and said it looked good. She needed me to prepare a few chapters to go with it, especially because I had told her I'd wanted to make certain I felt comfortable writing dialogue in the language of the period without being too obvious about it, which is why most novelists fail with historical novels. More importantly, I wanted to write from the point of view of people who possessed a far poorer (because pre-Freudian) vocabulary for psychological manifestations: which is where even more novelists fail (Caleb Carr's *The Alienist*, for example). Both elements would subtly influence the book's narrative language and determine its style, which as a result would be different from the more contemporary almost "non style" of *Eyes* or *Smart as the Devil.* By mid-July I had three chapters written to my satisfaction, proving it could be done in a natural manner, i.e., without being either "antiquey" or anachronistic. I sent these to Jane and was now awaiting her response.

That was when Bob Lowe called to take up my invitation to the Pines. It was during Jon Peterson's time-share, but as he only came out to the house on weekends, his room was free during midweek. I called Jon and asked if Bob could use it while he wasn't there, and Jon agreed. The plan was for Bob to arrive on a Tuesday at noon or so, and stay out until Friday night, when Jon would arrive. He usually came in on the 6:15 seaplane that let him off in the shoals near Floral Walk on the Bay, the closest connecting walk to Tarpon, with his pants cuffs rolled up, his lace-tied shoes slung over his shoulder.

Over the course of the long, lovely, restful summer, and somewhat as a way of counteracting how much time I was now immobilized sitting at the typewriter, I'd begun to explore my new home. During the previous summer, I'd begun getting to know Fire Island Pines, first by using alternative routes to and from the house and "downtown." When I was too restless to stay on the beach, I'd get up and walk around, come to know the different walks, to look at houses, to check out the views. This year, living at the Pines since before Memorial Day weekend, I'd had ample time when the resort was vacant to see some of its private areas, where I might ordinarily feel I was trespassing. Especially in those months when the weather still had a chill to it, or when it was clouded over or rainy, I'd get out the little map printed on stationery one could buy at the Melbamar and plan where I'd visit that day. As a result, I became quite familiar with the town, not only where various walks and houses were, but I also came to know its natural attractions in a way people who went out only on weekends or for only a two-week vacation seldom did. I found out where the deer hid out during the day, where they slept, in what section of Midway Walk they took their siesta, hidden in the coolness of trees from the hot sun, which walks they used at dawn to the ocean to lick salt off the receding tidal sand. I came to discover where the long, thick black snakes that looked like garden hoses nested, and once saw a pair of them mating. I found tiny ponds and marshy areas behind the forest ranger station where snapping turtles lived. I spotted a family of red foxes, espied raccoons in trees swinging their tails as though fanning themselves. Since the Pines was designated part of the protected National Seashore, as well as a bird sanctuary, and they were everywhere, for the first time in my life I became a bird-watcher. I'd phone Nicholas, my friend Joe's lover, in Manhattan and describe the woodpecker I was watching or read him a list of birds I'd seen the day I'd been to the Sunken Forest. Nick would tell me the names and tell me about the birds, either from his own knowledge or from a Petersen's guide.

Even with all the obvious uniform identity of the island, I began to notice differences that became as clear to me as how a cold afternoon's gathering around a Franklin stove in someone's house in mid-May was different from the sudden showers at night—tropical, relentless, capricious—in late July that thundered upon the roofs so hard I thought I'd never fall asleep, yet awaken to clear skies, sun riding high, not a plank of decking wet, as though that too was a dream. It commenced with location. On a forested strip of sandbar scarcely a quarter mile wide, you wouldn't expect such diversity, but it was evident from the moment I turned off the boardwalk, the straps on my backpack from my nylon bag beginning to dig into my flesh, whenever I'd arrive at the island, arrive at the little Tarpon Walk house, from the moment I entered floor-to-ceiling glass, and flung open all the doors and caught the dampness or the hot must or the inner cool that told me what had happened during my absence, however brief. From the moment I dropped my bag on the bed and pulled back the bedroom curtains and looked out, I might be anywhere really on the island, but that moment told all, somehow, pre-ordaining what new experiences or people awaited me. Brightness first, the sun striking and reflecting off the sand, the surf's phosphorescence, the silvered shingles of wooden houses, the white lines that defined the boardwalks, sunlight dappling all in a general glitter. Then the sound of the surf, even when calm, rolling so long, so full, so unstoppable, that it would end up dyeing my days like an unconsciously heard drip of a faucet, an ink that seeps in without your being aware yet never again departs. Brightness and the surf and the horizontal—soft irregular dunes pierced by clumps of grass, the slatted, cinnamon-painted fence protecting the sand, holding in the gray-green grass, lifting itself into little cliffs from the cooler sands of the tide, a serpentine fence folding in on itself like a lawn hose half thrown, half purposely coiled, but horizontal for its height, for all of its intertwinings. The horizon itself was my vista, ocean and bay, the point of apex without point, and with it, a promise: of wildness, of view, of something possibly attainable.

As the summer rolled on, I became more daring in my explorations, spanning out to include Cherry Grove in my walks, so that in time I would come to know its features and differences almost as well as the Pines. Invariably I'd visit the "meat rack" between the two communities, mostly in the late afternoon, when it was empty, though there would always be one or two stragglers, and once, memorably, someone dancing to "Lady Marmalade" by himself in the sand, as his small black transistor radio swung from the branch of a tree. I was there as much really for exploration, for what natural life I could see, as for the casual sex that infrequently could be obtained.

Beyond the Grove lay the Sunken Forest, a curious garden patch a football field in area, a dozen feet below sea level, wrought of many different kinds of odd biota: succulents, alien looking flowers. Beyond that, after a long trek over rough scrubland or on the wooden path that was sometimes visible but more often covered by sand, I'd happen upon other island communities, some—like Onleyville where I visited Steve Lawrence and David Watt—a handful of houses without electricity, water from wells, nicely primitive. Others, Point O'Woods, closed communities, with large brick houses surreally enclosed in a cyclone fence, protected from what? The sand? The scrub? Complete with repaired concrete sidewalks, an edifice that might be a restaurant, another resembling a dock: five blocks of Syosset secretly dropped onto the island by helicopters at night.

I also explored the other direction, west, toward the big straight single-scene community of Davis Park, which I reached only once. The linking dirt path barely negotiable by utility trucks and police cars we'd come to call the Burma Road was more forested; the branches almost met overhead, with barely enough space between trees for a view of the Great South Bay. A fifteen-minute walk down this road where the island was narrowest, barely a city block wide, the bay and ocean simultaneously visible, was Barrett Beach, where no one lived. The only structures were changing rooms and the ferry dock, which in summer accepted boatloads of families, church groups, and somewhat supervised children from onshore camps. On the bay, paved parks had been installed, looking like those little parks I'd known in Queens—slides, jungle gyms, sandboxes, two kinds of swings—along with tennis courts, a softball diamond, and picnic areas.

The next community along the Burma Road was also tiny, a dozen houses or less. It was known as Water Island and was just getting electrical hookups and water pipes from Patchogue. Very private, it had no public areas save the beach. People used private boats to get there, or landed at Barrett Beach and walked in from there. Not even food was available at Water Island: people brought it from the mainland or came shopping in the Pines. Those in Water Island tended to be older, along with a few celebrities looking for hideaways, photographers like Peter Beard and Bruce Weber. In time, it became a chic hangout for artists and models.

I was walking back to the Pines about three one Saturday afternoon in early July. I'd just visited someone who was staying at Water Island. We'd been on the beach while the people in his house had lunch, then gone up to the house to screw while they were at the beach. He went back to them, and I headed home, deciding to walk the Burma Road, thinking I'd avoid the by now extremely hot midday sun that was strongest at the water's edge. I'd just passed Barrett Beach when the first mosquito began to buzz me. I was wearing nothing but a Speedo and a sun visor, so I was vulnerable. I'd been dawdling, so I now picked up my pace. The mosquito became two, three, and I began to hurry despite the rough road. In minutes, I was surrounded. I took off the visor and began batting them away, then I ran a few feet. Behind me a swarm of mosquitoes had formed: there must have been a thousand of them! In an instant they were at me. I began to run, batting them away with hands and visor, still being bitten over and over. The road ahead was suddenly filled with more mosquitoes turning to join these. I felt like someone in a Farmer

Gray cartoon I'd seen on TV. It was ridiculous, but at the same time I was being bitten, swarmed, I could barely see ahead. I could picture myself stumbling, falling, trying to fight them off until I blacked out from the effort and pain, being stung to death as I lay there, my blood drained by thousands of starving, breeding insects. What had Farmer Gray done to escape? Of course! He'd jumped into the lake. I swerved off the road, through the woods, up the hill, pursued by an immense cloud of mosquitoes, stumbling over rugged terrain where succulents grew close together, tripping me up. But finally there was the ocean! I ran into the surf. The mosquitoes followed. I swam out, out, out, and began diving, barely coming up for air, diving again and again, until when I came up I couldn't see insects. On shore they'd fanned out, the swarm enormous, but those over the water were gone.

I swam leisurely, enjoying the cool ocean water, until I could see the roofs of the Witch House, what we called the last house in the Pines, east.

Jon was at home on Tarpon Walk when I got back. "What happened to you?" he said when I strode on deck, scratching myself all over. I told him, not believing it myself, and he followed me inside as I got out calamine lotion and began to slather it on myself. "Let me do that," Jon said. He took the bottle from me and began putting lotion on the bites, which were on my hands, feet, arms, legs, thighs, shoulders, chest, neck, face, ears, between my toes, and between my fingers. At the same time he was counting the bites.

He'd reached 200 and I was encased in pink goo and despite that I felt awful, my body was a single huge throbbing itching burning mosquito bite, when Jon stopped his ministrations. "You're shaking!" he said. He felt my forehead. "It's cold. How do you feel?" "I feel like I'm going to faint," I said. He managed to get me into my bedroom. I passed out.

What I thought was a few minutes later, but was actually a half hour later, I woke up and Jon and our next door neighbor Herb were looking over me, going in and out of focus. Herb was giving me pills, telling me they were benzedrine, and would make the pain go away, and Jon was holding a glass of water and helping me swallow the pills and drink the water, looking more worried than I'd ever seen him. I woke up hours later, ten at night, stumbled to the bathroom, urinated, and looked at myself in the mirror. I was red, puffy, and swollen everywhere—a mess.

I could hear Jon talking to guests in the living room. He knocked on the bathroom door and looked in at me. "Better take more benzedrine. It'll counteract the bites." My forehead was normal temperature, he said, but I still felt awful. I could barely swallow water, my neck was so sore from being bitten. Jon soaked a towel in cold water and wrapped it around me, then escorted me to bed, where he put a sheet over me. I went to sleep instantly. I slept through Sunday, waking at three in the afternoon, when Jon again made me take benzedrine and wrapped me in wet towels and put me back to bed. I slept through his leaving, woke at midnight and staggered to the john, then looked in the refrigerator. He'd made dinner for Herb and Bill Schwab and his lover and there were leftovers. I picked at them without appetite, until I was sleepy again. I covered myself in calamine lotion, took the benzedrine he'd left for me, wrapped myself in a wet towel, and went back to bed.

Tuesday afternoon I began to feel semihuman. I continued to take the benzedrine, but external signs of insect poisoning were healing, swelling was gone from my head and face, and I was numb from the medicine. Jon phoned, concerned, and seemed gratified. That evening Bill and a friend who'd been a male nurse brought food for me. He looked me over in my bedroom and declared me okay. I continued to take the benzedrine till it ran out. It had one side effect, swelling at the lymph glands located in my groin. As a result, my genitals were swollen to three times their usual size. Thinking I had to get something positive out of this nasty experience (and the loss of close to eighty hours of my life), I took full advantage of the aberration the very next time I appeared on the beach. I wore my Speedo filled with these useless, desensitized, gargantuan things, parading myself in front of every attracive guy on the beach, sometimes merely standing in profile to them a few minutes, before ambling on. By Friday evening when Jon came out again, I was back to normal.

The only other potentially perilous experience of my island explorations was nipped in the bud. I'd been to the Grove dancing at the Ice Palace on a Saturday night and when I decided to leave, I couldn't find my red zipper sweatshirt where I'd left it. Outside it was cool, especially on the beach along which I'd planned to walk home, but substantially warmer, because less windy, along the boardwalks. So I took one walk and hopped off where it ended at the Grove "meat rack." Although it was a dark moonless night, I figured between my knowledge via afternoon forays and the white markings on the trees, I'd easily be able to find my way though the maze.

I had not counted on how dark it was, nor how stoned I still was, nor how distracted I became because of various sexual couplings and group scenes I moved into and out of, all of which seemed to involve poppers. At one point I was in an area that while still populated was far less so, where I couldn't see white-marked trees. I headed through what seemed to be a path, and ended up at a marsh. No way out. I retraced myself and found another path and took that, only to end up at another marsh, this one with head-high reeds, evidently opening directly to the bay, since I saw what must be the distant lights of Great River, Long Island. I retraced my way and again got lost. And again. And yet again. Totally frustrated and admitting I was completely lost in these woods, far from the "meat rack," I stopped and calmed myself. I tried to listen for the surf to locate in which direction the ocean lay. But because I was in a shallow, bowl-like depression, the sound of the ocean seemed everywhere and yet nowhere specific. I continued to wander, until I finally saw a dark figure ahead.

"Wait," I called out.

"Me?" he asked back.

"Yes! I'm lost. Do you know the way out of here?"

He'd come closer and I could see that he was tall with wide shoulders and slender. Had a beard. "Maybe," he temporized.

"Would you help me find my way to the beach?" I asked.

"What's it worth to you?" he asked back in a seductively teasing voice. He thought I was kidding, that this was a come-on. Great! Just what I needed.

Still, he said he knew the way out. So I answered, "I'll do anything you want. Let me hold onto you. I've been going in circles for twenty minutes!"

He did lead me out, at least to the edge of the forest, where I could make out white markings on trees and from which, through openings in the branches, I could see sand paths through low bushes that would lead onto the beach. Once there, he demanded a kiss. While we were kissing, someone came along and began touching us, and another guy and another and after a few minutes, I left my guide in the middle of his own orgy, and stumbled onto the chilly but blessedly visible path to the beach and within sight of the lights of houses in the Pines.

*　　*　　*

It had become my habit to go "downtown" to the little harborside commercial area of the Pines every day around 10:30 or so in the morning to pick up a newspaper, do whatever banking I needed in the little Chemical branch located in the Boatel office, and get whatever groceries I needed. That morning I put it off till noon, knowing I'd probably miss the papers, which invariably sold out, and which Bob Lowe had already agreed to supply from town. He arrived on the ferry and looked around with an air of suddenly having arrived in a fairyland—which, let's face it, in several ways it was. Coming out on the ferry from Sayville, he'd met people he knew through other people in theatre, so Bob was relaxed, rather than nervous, about being in a new place. I also think he felt calmer because he'd come over with a small group of people—and their luggage, dogs, cats, and plants—rather than in the middle of the Fire Island weekend rush. He'd mentioned something about that each time I'd invited him, saying he still didn't feel comfortable among the people who'd gone to Flamingo, pretty much the same people who came out to the island. Although this astonished me—these were my friends, my Scrabble and Risk competitors, my one-night stands, my two-week affairs, my potential long-term lovers, a talented and interesting lot—I told him fine, I understood.

Bob had missed lunch in transit and arrived hungry, so I immediately took him to the Cultured Elephant, a little restaurant on the harbor, where we sat on an outdoor terrace in the partial shade of a giant umbrella and he ate one of his usual large meals while I drank a fruit and yogurt concoction. The summer so far had been smashingly beautiful, the entire past month had been perfect weather. Every day was sunny, dry, warm, and breezy, perfect for the beach where I'd go every afternoon by one o'clock after my morning work. Every evening provided a spectacular sunset over the bay. Every night had been clear and star-studded, the progression of the moon through its phases absolutely textbook, its dance with the planets visible in the ecliptic—bright white Venus and tiny Mercury in the evening, greenish Jupiter rising among the Pleiades at midnight—had been wonderful to see. Not since I'd been a child and my family had vacationed half a summer on an estuary on the southwest shore of lower Rhode Island had my life been as content, as calm, as comfortable, and as in my element. This tiny beach town with its few weekday personalities had truly become my new home and I found whatever I needed here. So, as a novelist, I tried to look at the place and people through Bob's eyes as he was first seeing it—deer crossing the boardwalks, lush foliage, houses out of architecture magazines, people wearing little more than bathing suits, tanned, laid-back—at the same time that I also wanted him to like it.

A brief tour ensued as I took Bob to the house on Tarpon Walk along the ocean sidewalk, listened to him rave about the view from the back of the little house, got him settled in Jon's room, and instead of the beach, went with him to find someone at the other end of the Pines, whom Bob was supposed to meet about a full-time night job as bartender in a new club to open in Manhattan.

Before this, the most time we'd spent together was an hour and a half, and while very friendly, even eagerly so, Bob had always struck me as reserved. This might explain my surprise at how quickly and fully he opened up during that visit. On that walk along most of the length of Fire Island Boulevard on a sunny, warm Tuesday afternoon, almost vacant in midday except at the sleepy harbor itself, Bob revealed himself to be a performer: singer, actor, dancer.

I'm not certain how or why, but we'd gotten onto the subject of Cole Porter and I'd said how much I'd enjoyed Porter's music and especially his lyrics. Bob told me he'd stage managed an important London revival of Porter's 1950 musical *Out of This World* based on the Amphitryon legend. It turned out I knew a few songs: the famous ballad, "From This Moment On," also "Use Your Imagination," because they'd been on some chanteuse's album I owned. I gave Bob a few lines I recalled. In return, and totally delighted to be able to do so, Bob gave me the entire show, beginning to end, in *précis*, complete with the madcap action and very detailed descriptions of how it had been costumed, staged, and set designed. He sang all of the songs, including the sublimely witty "Nobody's Chasing Me," and "I Sleep Easier Now," the popular "Let's Do It, Let's Fall in Love," and some of the most inventive and giddy puns in the Broadway literature, most vividly in Bob's rendition—at the corner of Tuna ("Ike & Tina Tuna" this year) and Fire Island Boulevard—of Mercury's boastful love song "They Couldn't Compare to You," in which the Queen of Sheba is described as "mentally an amoeba" and Queen Nefertiti is "a perfect sweetie." By the time we reached the house he was looking for, I was charmed, any ice between us melted. Mischievously Bob said, "Second act after intermission" then literally "put on" his sober face with one hand, as we opened the fence door to go meet his potential new employer.

Even sober he charmed the man, to whom he spoke for only ten minutes inside the house, while I lazed at the pool. Bob was hired as bartender at the new Christopher and West Street club to be called the Cockring. He'd go in Monday to learn the ropes from the manager. When he talked about this, Bob said he liked the idea of a small dance club in the Village with disco-quality music and lights, open to a racially mixed hot gay crowd. That was the original intention for the club, which in the following years became terrifically popular, and my black friends told me, less than open. Bob would become the main barkeep from Thursday through Sunday night for the next two years, adored by his customers, some of whom came onto him, many more of whom idolized him from afar, several of whom gave quite large tips. To his co-workers, Bob became known as The Empress Lowe. This name was explained to me by one of them as "a step beyond being a mere queen." And because of his hangers-on, the appellation was twisted around to be "The Empress of Love."

We at last managed to get to the Pines' beach that afternoon, then went for late-afternoon drinks at the house Paul Popham and Rick Wellikopf were staying at on vacation, a house with a pool on the beach. Bob relaxed more. Back at my house, while I was washing the chicken that would be dinner, he asked, "Have you ever done that Provençal style?" I let him take over the cooking, and he revealed yet another talent: he was a brilliant French chef.

The next afternoon, Bob asked if we could go to Cherry Grove. Someone he'd met in the city named Barbara worked at a clothing shop near the ferry dock. Bob's ex-lover Rodney had begun seeing someone seriously and Bob thought it time he moved out of the apartment they still shared. Bob had met Barbara while bartending at a club named World and she'd mentioned a studio apartment in her building on Horatio Street—not far from where I lived on Jane Street and local to the Cockring where Bob would be working—that she knew was becoming vacant. It was rent-controlled and would cost what Bob was now paying Rodney. He wanted to visit Barbara, have me meet her, find out about the studio, and see for himself Cherry Grove, the part of Fire Island Bob had heard about from theatre people and read of in theatrical histories and biographies.

As we walked the Fire Island shoreline, I pointed out the best-known edifices we passed in the Pines, detailing why—either because of their architect, their celebrity owner, a famous party they'd hosted, or some scandal they'd been the scene of. When we reached that stretch of bare beach between the two communities, I pointed out the trees behind the dunes and explained that the Meat Rack was back there, if he wanted to see it ("Maybe later," he replied), aware that not long ago Edward had given me this same tour, and even more recently, I myself had nearly been forced to spend the night there because I'd been so lost.

We ascended the boardwalk at the spot dominated for a decade by a big beachfront restaurant/bar/dance place I knew, not only from my visit with Edward but also from before when I'd come by Jeep-taxi with my social worker colleagues. The Sea Shack had gone up in flames two years before, just before the summer season started, and everyone said the mob had torched the building. The reason was never explained very clearly to me. Some said it was because the underworld co-owned the big new motel on the bay side with its huge new dance area for daily afternoon teas and weekend night dances. But several years later, through Bob's by then very tight connections with the gay bar and club scene, I met the owners of the Ice Palace, who were simply gay entrepreneurs, and albeit two of the three men were Italian American and all from Long Island rather than Manhattan, they were nice, smart men, and not mob connected.

Barbara worked at a shop called Fancy from Delancey. She was tall and slim and small breasted, with a slightly horsey face, stunningly beautiful dark blue eyes, long auburn hair, a Bacall-deep voice, and a languid manner that went well with her flowing silk pajama outfit. It was clear she adored Bob, didn't know what my relationship to him was, but had good news: the studio apartment was open September first, and she'd already talked to the super about Bob taking the place. Bob took down the information as I looked around the shop. Barbara attempted to get Bob to try on some of the bathing suits they sold. He was shy about doing so until I seconded her efforts. Bob had brought nothing but huge, wide, baggy, hide-everything trunks and he agreed he needed a new bathing suit. Barbara wanted him to try out tiny slip-on thongs, but Bob said no way, his butt was too big, and settled for a generously cut red Speedo, in which he looked terrific.

"Are you sure I'm not too big in the back?" he kept asking, looking at himself in the mirror. "All the time I was growing up, kids in my swimming class called me 'big-butt.'"

"You look fine," I said. Barbara, and a few people who'd come into the shop agreed. We were understating it. Wearing that red bathing suit, with his perfectly proportioned body and nobly shaped head, his curly black hair, his muscles, and his perfect complexion, Bob Lowe at twenty-eight years old looked like a god. Not a month later, the artist George Stravinos would use him as a barbell model for several illustrations in Dennis Sander's *Gay Source* book, capturing in pen and pencil how perfect Bob was then. A few years later, David Martin would use Bob as a model for Ares, Greek god of war, for my own illustrated novella, *An Asian Minor*. For some reason I cannot explain, for me those illustrations encapsulate Bob's looks and attitude, his substantial personal qualities, far better than any, indeed than all of the many photographs taken of him.

Barbara found someone to watch the shop while she took a coffee break and joined us next door at an outdoor restaurant. She talked about the building she lived in, which the local police referred to as "Love, American Style," after the TV sitcom. She also spoke of another resident, her best friend Erica, whom she described to me as "a wild Cubana bitch but a real doll, you know what I mean," as well as Erica's troublesome lover Harry, whom Erica was keeping on her earnings as model. Barbara described him as "45 percent pecker, 45 percent stomach, leaving you can figure out for yourself how much for brains." Bob had met them, and several others Barbara mentioned, at the World, and he sympathized, commiserated, even offered Barbara some advice, all with that complete attention and utter sincerity that I realized is what made me like him so much too.

A week later, I would see Barbara again, on a Saturday night at the Ice Palace—in another flowing silk pajama outfit matching her ice-blue eye shadow—and we'd dance a long set, then chat a long time leaning on the railing overlooking the pool. Two guys in full leather passed behind and made a crack that I missed. Barbara heard and she spat back a reply, then commented, "Those queens are so unsure of their masculinity! That's why they trash me! Real men never do. But the truth is, making 'the change' isn't easy and it isn't cheap."

It was only then that I understood: Barbara was a man, a transsexual in process. She'd gone through hormone therapy and had developed breasts but hadn't yet had her male genitals removed, which required another year of psychological counseling and a lot more money for the operation. I realized that Erica, whom I'd met in the meantime and who was phenomenally attractive, and indeed many of the women Barbara talked about, must also be transvestites or transgendered. I was astonished because most drag I'd seen was so obvious. I always knew they were men. But Barbara and Erica seemed to be in an entirely other state of existence from drag, not only because of how intrinsically feminine they looked and acted, but by how much they treated themselves as women, by how much they appeared to think, feel, and act in relationship to others—not like the gay men I knew, but like women I knew.

For example, Erica and I met on Eighth Avenue outside the newspaper stand. She was on her way to work at Lord & Taylor where she's a runway model. We talked, she said she's late, stepped into the street, lifted her skirt to reveal one long, well-shaped, dark-nyloned leg and three, I swear three, taxis all but crashed into each other as they swerved to the curb in a brake-screeching halt to be the cabbie that would take Erica uptown. Unlike Barbara, however, Erica had no intention of ever being fully female, despite the implant surgery that had given her nice-sized breasts. "Harry likes to have my handle to hold onto while he fucks," she explained. "Most of the guys I'd go out with and who'd go out with me like that I've still got a dick."

To show how far Erica had gone mentally into femaleness, several years later, shortly after the Mariel Boat Lift from Cuba, Erica called Bob in a panic. She'd gotten a phone call from her younger brother. He and her mother had gotten out of Cuba and were in Miami with relatives. They wanted Erica to come visit. "And I want to go," Erica said. "I haven't seen my sainted mother in twenty years." So go, we told her. "You don't understand," Erica moaned. "The last time they saw me I weighed two hundred pounds, wore a size forty-four suit, was dressed in army fatigues, and had a beard!" After we'd gotten done laughing, Erica came over and we tried to butch her up for the trip. No matter how masculine the clothing we put Erica in, no matter how little makeup she wore, or how macho she tried to walk and act, Erica still looked like Marlene Dietrich trying to pass as a man. Luckily, Erica was only in Miami for two days, and the family was so thrilled to be reunited, they didn't care how Erica dressed or what Erica looked like.

*   *   *

Jon arrived Friday night and was in an unusually mellow mood. That mood was even more soothed by the haute cuisine meal prepared by Bob and me, and by how charmed Jon was by Bob's looks and company, about which Jon wasn't at all shy. When dessert was over and Bob went to go pack, Jon turned to me: "If he doesn't *have* to go back to the city, why not invite him to stay over?" I said Bob didn't have to go back, but asked Jon where he would sleep. Jon made an indescribable face. "He can sleep with me. He can sleep with you," he said as if it were beyond question.

A House on the Ocean, A House on the Bay

"No, he can't. He's Dennis's boyfriend. I've got that small double bed. Two people have to be intimate to sleep in it. But if you don't mind him on the other bed in your room . . ." Jon had Nick and Enno's room, with its single beds lashed together as one. Before I was done, Jon was calling out "Oh-hhh, Bob!"

Bob wouldn't dream of incommoding Jon or letting him suffer a second without the complete privacy he'd already paid for in the house. But he did obviously want to stay rather than go back to an apartment full of ex-lover and ex-lover's new beau, so we talked him into sleeping on one of the daybeds in the little living room. We put up a sheet to completely darken the room, because it faced where the sun rose, often quite blindingly, through thin curtains.

Bob slept over another night too. Temperamental and unpredictable as Jon could be, he was utterly smitten by Bob that second day as well. While Jon and I didn't do a great many things together at the Pines despite being housemates, we did usually place our towels together on the beach, at our usual spot at the Ozone Beach Club, and as I had come to know so many more people, we often had our sheet enlarged by appended beach towels of visitors or perched on by guests from out of the passing promenade along the water's edge which—like Tea Dance and Saturday night Ice Palace—seemed to have become yet another of the Pines's new weekend social "musts." With Bob on our beach towel, we attracted muscle men, bodybuilders, and dancers. When he'd arrived a few days before, Bob had asked where in the Pines he could find weights, and I'd phoned Frank Diaz and asked if Bob could use his gear. I'd walked Bob to their place to introduce them, and they'd all gotten on well. So Frank and Jack came by our beach sheet on Saturday, as well as some men Bob knew from the Mid-City Gym in Manhattan and by midafternoon, Jon was floating on air, giggling girlishly, trying to gird with both his hands yet another enormous bicep, lathering generous suntan oil on yet another hugely muscled thigh.

Jon was put in such a good mood by all this, by the second *cordon bleu* meal of the weekend he didn't have to cook, and by how attentive everyone had been to him at Tea Dance later on Saturday afternoon, that he decided to go to the night dance at the Sandpiper despite sudden rain. Bob and I begged off. We were exhausted by all our activities that day and dissuaded by the rain. It was a long walk, and it looked as though it wouldn't stop storming. So we stayed in, listening to music and talking till Bob dropped off, I covered him up, and went to sleep.

Neither of us heard Jon come in early the next morning, and it was past noon the next day and we two had already been up for hours, gone to the harbor (when the continuing rain let up a little), gotten Sunday papers and fresh bagels and had already eaten breakfast when we heard a loud thump from Jon's room. Another fifteen minutes passed before Jon's bedroom door opened and he limped out, holding onto the wall, groaning, "Coffee, please, coffee! And a doctor too! I think I've broken my leg."

It turned out that despite the incessant rain the night before, there had been enough people out at the Sandpiper for Jon to have met someone, gone home with him, and had rather naughty sex. Upon leaving the house, he lost his balance on the slippery wooden walkway and fell hard. Jon got up, swearing mightily, and had managed to get home, where he'd collapsed into bed.

We inspected his leg and it was quite swollen. After his coffee, Jon took a handful of aspirin but remained in some pain. Bob and I were delegated to locate a doctor, which we did, in a house down the hill at Tarpon. When he finally arrived—he'd been out even later than Jon and looked quite hung over—he said it didn't look like a break or fracture, more like a large-muscle sprain, painful but less serious. He wrapped it and advised Jon to get an X-ray anyway, to stay off the leg, and to keep it warm for the next two days.

Jon phoned a doctor in Manhattan with an in-office X-ray machine who would see him that evening at 5 P.M., and we phoned for a car service to meet Jon at the Sayville Ferry. But there was still the very large problem of how to convey Jon along the quarter mile or so of boardwalk or beach in a light but steady rain from our house to the Pines harbor to that waiting ferry. Poor Jon, it's a good thing he had been well fed, well attended, and well laid already that weekend, because that ride in our little Radio Flyer wagon up the hill and down again at Tarpon, and along Fire Island Boulevard couldn't have been easy—or painless. Of course all he did was sit in the wagon with his wrapped leg sticking straight out on one side. But he also

A House on the Ocean, A House on the Bay

had to hold onto his weekend bag, the sides of the wagon, and an umbrella. While we—wearing shorts, T-shirts, and bright plastic ponchos against the rain—had to actually push and pull Jon without tipping him over or causing him too many jolts. The hill was the worst part, of course, a real epic. It reminded me of scenes from the film *The Guns of Navarone*. But after we'd managed to get him more or less horizontal again, Bob and I began singing "I Loves Ya Porgy" all the way into the harbor, where even Jon was sort of thrilled to arrive in the midst of a large Sunday afternoon ferry-boarding crowd, and to be lifted and carried on board by the two of us, and once he'd been settled, to be sent off with another rousing chorus of the Gershwin song, joined by people on the ferry, as the boat pulled out of the harbor and Jon, laughing and crying at the same time, waved good-bye.

This incident, which showed Bob and I to each other as calm, cheerful, useful, and totally cooperative in an emergency, more than anything solidified our new friendship. It was weeks before Jon could get around without a cane, so it also meant that Bob could use his room at the Pines whenever he had the free time. Once the Cockring opened in the Village, and Bob began bartending there on weekends, his visits became limited to a few days in the middle of the week. But if that meant I had the Tarpon Walk house to myself on weekends, it also meant I came to know Bob a lot better, because he came out to relax and the Pines was usually a great deal calmer without the weekend crowds and pressures.

What I learned of Bob's life baffled me, and at the same time that it somewhat explained his oddly inappropriate attitude toward himself. His family were Russian Jews who'd emigrated to America at the turn of the century. "Goluba, or something like that," was their original name, changed by an immigration official to Lowe. The family of four brothers grew up in poverty on the Lower East Side with so many of their countrymen, and like many of them became involved in the clothing goods business. Two brothers were ambitious and somehow they ended up in Providence, Rhode Island, with a clothing business. By the time Bob's father was old enough to become a partner, it had expanded into a block-sized department store: The Peerless.

I remembered the Peerless shop downtown in the state capitol from visits when I was a child (both of my parents came from Rhode Island) and what I didn't remember, Bob recalled for me, describing the two-story-high ceilings and long sweeping escalators, the tall tapering columns, the large doors that surrounded the central elevator shaft on each floor, the vast selection of carpeting with rolls of rugs piled high, the miles of dark copper pneumatic tubes for message sending threaded through the store, circling light fixtures, cutting through walls, diving to semicircular mahogany counters, their open mouths with air currents you could feel tugging the palm of your hand. The Peerless Company made the Lowe family a fortune. Bob was born in North Providence when the family lived there, but the remaining brothers sold the business by the time Bob was ten and his father moved the family to Longmeadow, where he opened a successful car dealership and they lived in a large mock-Tudor house girded by lawns like the houses of chums near where I'd grown up in Hollis.

Although this explained Bob's air of solidity and worth, it didn't in any way explain his remarkable lack of self-esteem. That was physical in focus, and according to him derived from two sources: his poor health as a child, and his dominating mother's endless critical remarks about Bob. Among the usual childhood diseases, Bob had also suffered a near-fatal collapsed lung (the incisory scar through which it had been drained and pumped up again was barely visible). And after that Bob had been so thin, so constantly ill and so made aware of it by his mother, that when they'd moved to Longmeadow, he'd followed the advice of a gym instructor and begun a regimen to build himself up, particularly through diet and weights. This was why Bob was now an Adonis—to everyone but himself. He couldn't look in a mirror or put on a piece of clothing without finding fault in himself. One day at the Pines he came out of the bathroom with a tiny blemish on his face and began moaning about it. I joined in, exaggerating it, saying how terribly disfiguring it was and how he couldn't possibly go out to the beach in his condition, etc. Bob stopped and looked at me and said, "Is it really that awful?" I replied, "What's the difference what I say? Since *you* think it is." He thought for a second, then said, "To hell with it, let's go to the beach."

A House on the Ocean, A House on the Bay

No one noticed it, and he began telling me of the years'-long campaign of criticism and intimidation and harassment—physical, intellectual, and moral—he'd endured under his mother.

"I'm sorry, but she's wrong," I said. "I'm an excellent judge of people, and in my estimation you're smart, handsome, and altogether wonderful! And in fact, I'm prepared to detail how wonderful you are. I'm also prepared to tell you that you're wonderful every time I see you, whether you like it or not."

He laughed. But that was exactly what I did thereafter, figuring I'd counter her negative campaign with a positive one. Ten times to twenty times a day, more sometimes, indeed whenever I'd see Bob— if he was coming back into the house from having just worked out, or if I were encountering him in the kitchen cooking, or if I went out to the sundeck and saw him reading in a chaise lounge, or after we'd just met someone at the Pines' harbor—anywhere and everywhere I saw him, I would tell him "You're wonderful." And after a while of hearing it so constantly, Bob ceased that tiny flinch of response which meant he didn't believe me, which meant that hearing it pained him, and he began to accept my compliment as I intended it, as fact, and in turn to tell me I was wonderful too. One day, on the beach, when he'd just told me how while living in New Delhi he'd solved some seemingly impossible challenge while he was living in New Dehli, having to do with foreign languages, strange customs, and a Byzantine bureaucracy, I said, "You see! That proves it! You're wonderful, officially wonderful!" His response was a sort of Cheshire smile: it did prove it, even to him. But the next time I said he was wonderful, Bob immediately countered by singing back to me Cole Porter's song "You're the Top," with all the by then just-dated-enough-to-be-amusing contemporary allusions. And in years to come, as we found ourselves in various places around the hemisphere, at resorts, on yachts, by beaches, high in mountains, Bob would suddenly turn to me and out of nowhere suddenly say, "You're a Shakespeare sonnet," or "You're the smile on the Mona Lisa," or my all-time favorite, "You're the National Gallery. You're Garbo's salary! You're cellophane!" It would take many more years to undo the decades of maternal damage to Bob's psyche and it wasn't ever a complete victory, as I would later discover to my sorrow, but by hearing me call him wonderful over and over again and mean it, Bob slowly began to believe in himself. Of course, it helped that he was being adored by others four nights a week in the Cockring, but he let me know that what I thought of him was far more important.

*　　*　　*

Whenever we spoke on the phone, Jon put off coming to the Pines yet another week and made fun of me. He thought I should go after Bob, saying "He can't be *that* involved with Dennis if he's out there with you several days a week." But I had made a new friend and for me that was important, especially as my last close friendship, with Jay Weiss, seemed to be fraying badly at the edges.

Many factors were involved in this, not the least being Jay's intense ambition as a painter and his relative lack of response from the outside world, although his paintings and drawings were clearly more exciting and finer with every passing day and Jon and I and a few other collectors snapped up whatever he painted that we could afford. All Jay's energetic and imaginative attempts at getting publicity, any attention, not to mention shows of his work, seemed to promise a very great deal, just before they would vanish into thin air. And simultaneously with Jay's career disappointment was my own all too visible success as a writer, which by late 1976—with increasing reviews and sales of my books and ever larger contracts with more prestigious publishers—was becoming increasingly evident to even the most self-involved around me.

Attempting to counteract that and to do something nice for Jay, I tried inviting him out to the Pines. After a month of being asked, Jay at last came one weekend, along with his cat and his paints, his easel and canvases—none of which he never touched while he was there. In fact, Jay acted altogether weirdly once he'd arrived and was a grand dame all weekend, complaining that the house was small, it was too far from the harbor, it was on the "wrong side of the Pines," (though his friend Sam's place was right in front, and that had been stylishly enough in location), at the same time making demands for things not obtainable on the island, wanting to be waited on. He didn't have time to be with me as I'd hoped so we might talk and correct any wrong impressions. Instead, he left his cat and boxes of paints and went off without me with other people he knew for lunches and dinners.

Naturally enough after that kind of treatment, I didn't invite him again. People he'd visited at the Pines who we knew in common said that Jay—at the very time he'd been my guest—had bad-mouthed me behind my back, telling anyone who'd listen that I'd sold out as a writer, wasn't any good as a writer anyway, and only wanted money. That embarrassed our friends, who were supportive of my work and who could see how transparently envious and treacherous Jay was. It made me draw away even more. I was left thinking that as long as we'd been equals—both "starving artists"— I was okay. But even my small success had thrown into relief Jay's lack of the same, and for that I could not be forgiven!

I continued to loan him money for the next few years whenever he asked and I had it, and also to buy art from him, using the loans as down payments so he wouldn't have to pay me back. Then an incident occurred that showed how little he valued me and our friendship, how much Jay had come to see me as a patron: someone to be used. My agent had admired Jay's work in my home for years and I finally took the hint and asked if she'd like a Weiss as a wedding present. She said yes, and we made an appointment to go to Jay's studio and pick one out. I had already loaned Jay a certain amount of money some months before, the exact amount he usually charged for a watercolor or pastel, and when making the appointment, I told him Jane's gift would pay back this debt. Jay said that was fine; he saw Jane as a potential new customer, maybe even a patroness. He showed her pastels and watercolors, i.e., work costing the amount of money he owed me, and everything seemed fine. When Jane had chosen a pastel and he'd wrapped it and we'd begun walking out, Jay stopped me at the door and asked for $200 more. I protested. He said he'd raised his prices. I told him I'd mail him the money. The following day I sent a check for the balance he had insisted on—and didn't speak to him again for the next ten years.

Once he realized how hard I'd taken his shill, Jay's response sealed the end of our friendship. He didn't apologize, didn't say he'd been wrong, or desperate for the money, which might—though it's doubtful—have brought me around. Instead he defended his action to others by going around telling everyone who'd listen—especially my old pals in California who couldn't know better—that *he* had stopped seeing *me*. Why? Because I wouldn't listen to Jay when he'd told me, for my own good, that the man I was seeing was a hustler who didn't care for me but was only out to rip me off for all I was worth. The name of this so-called hustler—my friend Bob Lowe.

The truth is, I was relieved Bob wasn't to be a romantic interest. I could see how much work he still needed to do on his self-esteem and how badly that could screw up any relationship. But I was also content for the first time in years to myself play the field. Although I was never a beauty of the Pines-Flamingo set, the few photos of me from those years show a tanned, bearded, exotically appealing fellow, slender, smiling, and relaxed. I was acceptable enough physically, in my personality, in my intelligence, and, increasingly, in status thanks to my rising career, and those factors were considered important, at times crucial, in friendships and relationships among this allegedly "lookist" superficial crowd.

Especially once Jon was incapacitated and I was left alone in the Tarpon Walk house on weekends, I found more than enough interesting men to socialize with, plenty of desirable men for sleepovers, weekends, or week-long affairs. After the chain of romantic disasters I'd undergone in the past decade I thought this might be a good time to forget about relationships and to concentrate instead on work and try to write the best possible books I could. I'd have an infatuation here and there: a few weeks with dark-haired satyr-like Hal Seidman, with his beautifully worked-out body; a month or two with tall, strong, slender, blond, handsome-as-a-1920s-Arrow-shirt-ad-illustration Ray Ford; or with long, lanky, sensuous beyond words, strawberry-blond-haired Jeffrey Childs, discharged from a VA hospital because of wounds from Vietnam; or with smaller, tight-bodied, Jewish-Prince-cute Neal, who'd been married only two years before and who only a short while after our intense affair entered another long-term relationship with a woman. Or with one of the many models from all over the world who made their appearance at the Pines around August first: WASP-y Greg, say, who was as nice and as smart as he was good-looking. Or the sweetly nutty Swedish Italian American, Ed, who when I first met him claimed to have little homosexual experience—a problem I soon rid him of—and who proved to be an eager pupil and eventually an ardent and accomplished top.

Because Fire Island itself was so relaxed, so pleasant and tranquil, yet at the same time its atmosphere was so sexy, and because of the influence of various recreational drugs we used so often, I would suddenly find myself not only re-encountering but also somehow ending up in bed making love with people I'd met previously in merely social contexts, including several guys I'd met through Jay—David Watt, Steve Lawrence, even Zeb Freedman. These sexual bouts might be repeated or might not, but no matter how frequent they were, this sharing of bodies seemed only natural, and often led to closer friendships. During this time there were guys both in the Pines and in Manhattan who began and remained nothing but sex buddies, men I'd sleep with whenever we saw each other, which usually wasn't that often because they had a lover, or lived in New Jersey, or thought they might be straight, or just didn't care to get involved. With all this, I usually had a presentable date Saturday nights, or to be seen with at the Pines parties, and I had sex and the frisson of romance, without the reality—that so often had been a downer.

Because I thought myself single, I wasn't aware of how often I was paired up, because I seldom took those pairings seriously, until one afternoon a few years later at the Boatel Tea Dance someone I didn't know but recognized as also being from the "Class of '75" said, "I don't get it. You're nothing special to look at. How is it whenever I see you, you're always with a gorgeous guy?"

I might have taken offense. Instead I replied, echoing his supercilious tone, "Well, honey, *someone's* gotta fuck 'em. Might as well be me."

*   *   *

How good a friend Bob could be was quickly made clear to me on two occasions toward the end of that summer: one difficult, the other nearly impossible. The first situation began midweek, a Tuesday morning, in late August of 1976. Bob had come out to the Pines Sunday after closing the Cockring at 4 A.M. and having a light breakfast. Though he'd tried to sleep in the car full of co-workers he'd driven out with, he was exhausted when he arrived and even thought he might be coming down with a cold. As the weather was dreary—sunless yet hot and still—all Sunday afternoon and even cloudier and more stifling on Monday—we'd hung around the house on the one deck that presented a small breeze. Film critic and gay politico Vito Russo and his new boyfriend Jeffrey from San Francisco were staying in the Grove and we'd run into them at the Pines harbor when we'd fially gotten up the energy to walk there for groceries. We invited them for dinner Monday night, which had been pleasant but late.

It was 10 A.M. when I awoke and thought I heard voices at the back door. Bob and I came out of our bedrooms and went to see who it was.

Just inside the back screen door, always kept unlocked in those days, were Julio and "Red," the Pines cops. "Sorry to wake you. We have a hurricane alert. It's a big, nasty one. Slated to hit the island around two P.M. We're evacuating everyone. You've got to pack up and leave. The last boat will be at one o'clock."

After they left to find and alert any one else still in the area, Bob and I looked at each other in disbelief at what we'd just heard. While I made coffee he turned on the radio and finally found a station from Philadelphia that gave more information. The hurricane had skipped along North Carolina's Outer Banks the day before, then headed out to sea. But last night it had suddenly veered inland and gained in strength. It was headed for Long Island, due to land at Patchogue, which meant the eye of the hurricane was coming directly at us.

Unable to fully believe it, we made breakfast, and afterward lifted things off the floor, unplugged the stereo equipment and toaster oven, and placed them and clothing and books and cassettes high on a closet shelf. We stocked up water because that might not be available if and when we could return, packed other clothing, and continued to listen to ever worsening, ever more emergent radio reports of the oncoming storm. They were now predicting the storm would hit the Pines at high tide.

I felt a real sense of doom as I prepared to leave what had for the past four months become my home, a place I really loved. Despite how high the house was, I was afraid tornado spin-offs could easily rip it apart. Indeed, I was afraid the whole Pines, which I had come to see and to love as my town, my neighborhood, would be completely torn apart. There was ample evidence it could happen, especially the 1938 hurricane, also with a high tide, that had flooded the island, cutting so deep that the Pines and Cherry Grove were separated for years by water.

Despite hurrying, we made by only a few minutes the crowded last ferry out of the Pines harbor, dropping our bags in a heap downstairs while we went up to the open deck, where few remaining seats were left. We had to go up, to see what might easily be a last look at the place we were leaving.

The usually calm bay waters were completely new, high and rough, sharply tossing, flecked white with spume, so even the broad-keeled, fully laden *Fire Island Princess* rocked on long swells and swept down into trenchlike gullies. The sky we were heading toward over Long Island was dark and rough. Streaks of lightning darted out of the high masses of pewter-colored clouds. Rain had begun sporadically, and we stood on that rain-drenched open boat deck among people and pets and bags, wrapped in wind-twisted raincoats and ponchos, as though posed for some photograph for the United News wire—"Last Fugitives Escape Destruction of Great Hurricane"—so awed by the sudden present, so uncertain for the future, we didn't dare speak above a murmur, a whisper, even though we would have to shout to be heard over the noise of the wind and water, holding onto one another, feeling the backs of our necks prickle with some electromagnetism gone utterly mad, as we looked back to the ever receding shore of Fire Island where we could now descry an eerie yellow glow that hovered menacingly over the highest houses on the topmost hills of the Pines as though marking them out for destruction, while above the entire length of the island stretched so vulnerably before us, and the hurricane itself could now be seen approaching, monstrously vast, like the ill-defined prow of some cyclopean juggernaut, fueled from behind from horizon to horizon by a sky-filling turbulence, powerful and dimensional, made more ominous because it felt aimed, intentional, coming at us, and because among all the lurid colorations that periodically swept through its dark enormity was, I swear to you, an overall impression of the most sickly green, as though something unspeakably huge and vile was about to be vomited by a terminally nauseated planet.

We still saw it, still felt it closing in behind us, as the ferry landed at the Sayville Ferry dock, as we rode in connecting taxi-vans through the beachfront town, where the sense of panic and approaching doom was if anything even greater, cars speeding, honking horns, people rushing around everywhere we looked, closing up, tying up, battening down doors and taping up windows, and already huge trees were noisily whipping themselves into a fury as though in fanfare. We could still see that vomitous green fill the entire sky over the Sayville railroad station, punctuated by the drenching silver of stilettolike rain that began to fall in distinctive shapes, cones, twisted sheets, as we huddled away from the crackling and rumbling ambuscades of thunder like enemy cannon, the bright cold zippers of lightning opening the alien air, the deafening pounding of hail upon the inadequate protection of the patterned metal-roofed station shed where we awaited our train. We could still see the storm's lashing fury throughout most of our journey home on that early-afternoon railroad car—as filled with soaked and sodden people as any rush hour—although aside from the thunder and the train's own sounds, it was a silent ride, virtually devoid of noise most of its way, save for now and again a retriever's anxious, questioning bark to its owner, quickly hushed, or a passenger remembering and unable to restrain a half exclaimed, "Oh no! I forgot to . . ." as we wended our two-hour way into Manhattan.

Once we got to town, the hurricane had already hit and even in the middle of the city the weather was horrendous. Bob insisted we grab a taxi up to Rodney's apartment, to which he still had keys, and where his cat Max . . . You Sly Puss still lived, though Bob had moved. Rodney and David wouldn't be there, however, because they were out of town. There we had tea and watched television news and weather reports the rest of the evening with their grim details of the preparations and evacuations, complete with someone's film of us getting on board that final ferry, and ever more precise and dire predictions of the storm's landfall. We had a depressing dinner thrown together from the cupboards and fridge, watched more news on television, and finally fell into anxious sleep, fully expecting to awaken the next morning with the news that Fire Island had been wiped off the face of the earth.

When we woke up, sunlight entered the windows, and the radio and television news wasn't too bad. The capricious storm had veered yet again before making landfall, turning out to sea once more and not hitting hardest where predicted but farther out, at the fork of Long Island, slashing across the Hamptons before it had swerved again, headed toward Martha's Vineyard, already battened down and evacuated. The film showed enormous trees felled, telephone poles down for blocks at a time. But even with high tides, Fire Island had escaped the worst.

I couldn't wait, but had to see for myself, to know all was well. We returned to Fire Island that afternoon, riding the Long Island Railroad into a perfectly beautiful sunny summer day. Sayville had lost its oldest, largest oak trees: the taxi had to detour around its usual route to the ferry station. There too, we noticed signs of the storm's ferocity: boats lashed together mast to mast, others taken out of the water altogether, shoved against each other, tumbled under inadequate tarpaulins, a vertical row of shingles torn off one wall of the dockside café, the entire dock area looking sandless eerily clean. Once we arrived at the Pines, it seemed even less affected. Oh, a few of the older, more gnarled pine trees at the harbor had lost branches, and all the wagons chained up nearby had been tossed and tumbled into all kinds of odd stand-up angles and combos, but the hurricane doors and wooden window slats were already taken off most of the commerical buildings and two waiters at the Boatel were in shorts, dancing on the deck as our ferry glided along the glassy waters of the Pines harbor.

The little house, we were relieved to discover, was almost unaffected, with only a great slash of silt across the front window, evidently somehow driven up this far and flung—a single rude gesture by the storm. The potted geraniums and impatiens that we'd hidden beneath the house for safety had been tossed every which way, utterly disordered in the wind, so that while they recovered, thereafter they always grew somewhat twisted and bizarre. After opening and cleaning and inspecting the house, airing it out, taking out the lawn furniture to where it lived on the decks, we went down Ozone Walk to look at damage to the beach. It was immediately apparent: the strand had lost the extra two to ten yards of sand that had built up the shoreline slowly during the clement summer, allowing sandbars to suddenly rear themselves under your feet when you were standing in the surf seeking a long strong wave to bodysurf upon, or along the beach, where tide pools accompanied by tidal estuaries had reformed every afternoon, creating brand-new ponds of the clearest water over jacquarded patterns in sand for children to dive and bump their plastic boats together in and for large dogs that had just spent ten minutes rolling themselves in the sand to splash through, rinsing off, and for me—on a long jaunt—to wade through, at times thigh-high, and cool off. All gone. In their place, wrack and refuse: entire shoals full of bladderwort and seaweed on the shore, entwisted with stinking scores of torn starfish, battered horseshoe crabs, mangled lobsters, cracked clams, dead fish.

Bob and I reurned to Tarpon Walk in time to watch another spectacular sunset—this one more fiery than usual—over the bay from our back deck.

It wouldn't be until later, over the next few days as I wandered around the Pines, almost on an inspection tour, and looked much more closely, that I would come to see greater evidence of destruction: windows broken by flying objects; unstowed lawn furniture heaped in a broken mess; the top halves of the beach plum bushes all along the ocean side browned, as though blowtorched by the passing storm; spider webs pulled apart; broken trees and branches everywhere; bird nests tumbled out of trees, eggs broken and emptied; clumps of protecting beach grass wind-pulled from sand dunes; small reptiles and animals thrown stunned and dead onto boardwalks and decks; an imprudent seagull strung up amid the twisted coils of a torn-off-its-hook clothesline; small depressions of land, seemingly protected because right in the middle of the island, where plants or bushes had been ripped out by the wind, filled instead with brackish-smelling, salty liquid—evidently from some water funnel had managed to churn itself this far inland. Tiny things but changes that remained—at least until the next big storm—reshaping, re-forming, redefining the physical place, marking itself and at the same time endearing it all the more to me.

*　　*　　*

The second occasion for Bob to show his worth happened less than a month later. I'd come into Manhattan on business, to bank the large advance against royalties check I'd gotten from Delacorte/Dell for my third book and to have dinner with my new editor, Linda Grey, and to discuss various elements of being a new author with that publisher—then one of the most prestigious and exciting fiction lines in the business, with authors like Kurt Vonnegut, James Baldwin, Richard Yates, Timothy Findley, James Jones, Irwin Shaw, Tim O'Brien, and Jayne Ann Phillips.

My first two years as a published author with Arbor House had been difficult, but as though that had been a needed apprenticeship, the following seven years that I was a Delacorte/Dell author would prove to be far better: not only more profitable for me financially, but also artistically more freeing. This was partly a result of Delacorte's far larger resources, its greater distribution, and subsequently its power in the book marketplace. But it was also because of the staff, both in and out of the editorial departments, many of them young, some but by no means all of them gay, who had a glimmering that American literature was changing. The "old guard" whom they published so well were being replaced by bright young authors, among them women and gay men. Besides Linda Grey, I'll mention Ross Clairborne, Bill Grose, Chuck Adams, and Pat Cool, people with talent, energy, and vision who provided the ambience for me to pursue what would end up being an enormous change in my literary career.

What that change was exactly and how far it would go, I didn't yet know in the summer of 1976, although by the following summer I had a better idea: the creation of something called gay literature. At the time I had no idea that it would so alter my life. When

I'd begun writing I was perceived as a commercial novelist with the skills and abilities of a "serious stylist," an odd combination even in those days. Within a decade after my first novel was printed, not only was I identifying myself as a gay writer, but others were too, and I'd successfully made the nearly impossible switch from a "commercial" to a "serious" writer.

These terms of course never meant anything to me, or in fact to most other writers (unless they were deeply enmeshed in the grant, grad school, writing class, awards nexus) but those terms did and probably still do mean something to many in the publishing and book media industries. And at any rate, what I had slowly become interested in doing during these first years of being published seemed so far out from either category that I found I had many other, more insistent, and more confusing artistic problems to face. I had been writing gay-themed poetry and short stories for various magazines that began popping up around the United States such as Winston Leyland's *Gay Sunshine* in San Francisco and Andrew Bifrost's New York–based poetry quarterly, *Mouth of the Dragon*. I also wrote for *Gaysweek*, a New York paper with a monthly arts and letters section. *Christopher Street, After Dark, The Advocate,* and an earlier *Out* magazine were all far more open to belles lettres, fiction, and poetry than the MTV clones they've subsequently become. And I was commissioned and fairly well paid by gay "body mags" like *Drummer, Mandate,* and even *Blueboy* for short stories.

All of which led me to several conclusions: 1) I liked the immediate—i.e., days or weeks rather than months and years—response to my work that periodicals provided, 2) there really did seem to be a widening and evolving marketplace for gay poetry, stories, and probably novels, and 3) I was in a financial position to do something about that: i.e., to start a small press myself to put out gay books of poetry, plays, and stories. I did some asking around and discovered it would cost about $4,000 to $5,000 to start up my own publishing company and put out a book in an edition of 2,000 or 3,000 copies.

That there would be a need for such a press was confirmed for me in the middle of 1977. I'd heard that gay writers I'd met, Edmund White and Larry Kramer, were publishing novels through St.

Martin's Press and Random House. An editor at William Morrow was already talking about a brilliant gay novel they planned on putting out in the fall of 1978, titled *Dancer from the Dance* by a then unknown named Andrew Holleran. Rita Mae Brown's *Ruby Fruit Jungle*, originally put out by a small press called Daughters Inc., had been rereleased by Bantam paperbacks in 1976 and was a big hit. And I'd sold Delacorte a gay novel, a literary thriller, which I had already begun writing, for more money than all three previous novels. It was to be published in 1979. But with all this activity, gay and lesbian poetry and stories and drama remained orphaned. Seeing how the publishing industry was increasingly geared toward big books, it was clear someone could do quite well taking up the slack in this burgeoning market of lesbian and gay literature. As a result, by February 1977, on my thirty-third birthday, I offically set up the SeaHorse Press.

And so it was that one day a few months later, I had planned to see Bob for dinner and because of the new press, that I'd planned to lunch with George Stavrinos, an artist I'd met in the Pines with whom I was interested in discussing an illustrated story or novella. The previous evening, as I'd stood up from the table at some expensive little place—La Tulipe, I think—I'd felt a sudden sharp pain in my lower back, near my left buttock. It vanished instantly, however, when I'd walked Linda to her apartment building a few blocks away, then home, I tried to locate the source of that little shock, and to my extreme annoyance, I'd found another one of those dangerous inflationary pimples. By the next morning it was already swollen and full as the previous ones had been after three or four days. I phoned my doctor uptown for an apppointment but was told that he was out of the country, on vacation, in Rio de Janeiro, his homeland, where he kept a second home.

He phoned me an hour later and I told him what was wrong. We'd already discussed these infections a few weeks before at my most recent checkup. He said he'd have his secretary call an internist he knew, also South American, who was connected with St. Vincent's Hospital near me in the Village. He'd have her arrange for an appointment for me.

That noon I stepped into his office on Twelfth Street only to be told the doctor was working in the hospital's emergency room all afternoon, and I should go there; he was expecting me. I was dressed in a light jacket and tie, with my version of an attaché case, on my way to have lunch with an illustrator uptown at 1 P.M. The doctor was friendly, and said it was quiet in the E.R. and he could take care of me immediately. He made me take down my pants and bend over a leather table, where I teased, "But Doctor, I hardly know you!" He teased back as he poked and prodded, then asked me about previous instances. He didn't like how close this manifestation was to the last one in time (only a month), nor how near it was to sensitive, infectable areas like the rectum and colon.

"I'll be honest with you," he said, "I've seen this kind of thing before in children and in adults. In children it's usually nothing. In adults . . . I want to lance it now before the infection can travel to where it can be perilous, and because your physician won't be back for two weeks, I'd like to check you in to the hospital and keep you for a few days while we run a series of tests."

My breath was taken away. "Now?!" I managed to get out. "I have a lunch appointment."

"Cancel it," he said. "There's a pay phone in the hallway. But you come right back, you hear? We'll be getting everything ready here." He turned to a male nurse and said, "Prepare a booth and a mobile bed for surgery and prepare this patient with a local anesthetic."

Stunned, I pulled up my pants, located the phone, and called George, who wasn't in. I left a message with his answering service, then phoned my own answering service—this was before we had machines to do it—and told them that when Bob called, they should tell him I was in the hospital and that the doctor or nurse in the E.R. might know where exactly.

Five minutes later, I'd been stripped and my clothing folded into a bag that helped served as a pillow for my head on the mobile bed. I was supine, in one of the E.R. booths, my lower body taped to the sides so I wouldn't move, the topical anesthetic slathered over the area, and a rolled-up wad of gauze shoved into my mouth, like a bullet put between the teeth of a cowboy about to have a bad wound probed into. The doctor said, "This might sting a little."

I'll say it stung. Twice, but for less than ten seconds. As he worked, he explained that he wasn't merely lancing the infection, he was cutting deeper into the capillary that housed and carried the infection, to keep it from spreading. He bandaged it loosely, then he and the male nurse turned me over, put me in an open-back hospital frock, raised the back of the bed, inserted two intravenous tubes into my right hand, one attached to a pouch dripping with liquid sugars, the other with a potent antibiotic, and handed me back my book to read.

"Finished," he said. "I want that to drain. In about an hour, I'll take another look. Meanwhile someone will check you in."

I was registered and a room prepared for me, and I'd read another ten pages of my book, when he returned. He turned me over halfway, took another look, said he wanted it to drain more, turned me back over, and rolled me into the E.R. hallway, where he said an orderly would come take me up to my room. He'd come by for another look tomorrow morning.

That was how and where, Bob found me when he arrived a half hour later. In fact, he arrived—breathless, frightened—at the same time the orderly moving me did, so Bob came with us upstairs to my private room, and helped settle me in. Once I was settled in and nurses had come and gone, dithering over this and that, I said to Bob, "Is that a yogurt? I missed lunch. I'm starving!" Bob was happy to sacrifice his snack, but was very anxious for me, especially when I told him I was here for "tests," which ones I didn't know, and especially when a resident came around and said, "Yogurt's okay. But no solid food. You're slated for a barium enema, a CAT scan, and . . ." giving me an entire list of what I'd be undergoing over the next two days. This really began to panic Bob until I said to him, "Listen, this is all just precautionary. It doesn't mean anything." And Bob asked the resident, who asked, "Are you a family member?" To which I replied, "Yes. My stepbrother. I'm listing him as next of kin. You can tell him anything," to which the resident agreed but added nothing new.

Once he was gone, Bob sat down, looking shocked. He listened, however, to what I needed from home, made a list, took my keys, and got the stuff to me before he went to work at the bar later on. And was back by 11 A.M. the next day waiting for me by the time I'd gotten back to my room from some of my more discomforting tests. Bob brought my mail and made phone calls for me, whatever I needed, and didn't tell anyone where I was but kept them away. He remained worried and proved altogether perfect in my time of need.

Meanwhile, the doctor who'd cut me up came after his E.R. shift was over, looked, and said he wanted me to take sitz baths and further drain. He loosely bandaged the area again, showing me how to care for it once I was home again. Another doctor joined him and it was this second man, about my age, tall and not bad looking, who told me why I was there, what was going on.

"When men your age and of your ethnic background come in with this type of recurrent infection it often indicates a much more serious pathology—cancer of the colon." As I absorbed that nasty shock, he went on, "I've seen it dozens of times already. It might merely be in its beginning stages or it might be more advanced. No matter which, it's very serious. You're healthy and active and that will not help you. It'll work against you. Colon cancers feed faster on healthy young men than on the old and weak. They eat you alive in a matter of months. If we find a malignancy and even if we manage to cut it all out, we'll have to check you every two weeks, possibly every week for new growths, because it metastasizes so rapidly. These first tests will locate any polyps, tell us all about them, and after we biopsy them we'll better know what's next. I cannot overestimate how dangerous this is, nor how fast this can run through your body. I've seen football players walk in here off the playing field with what you've shown us and be gone in less than a year. In six months."

When I was alone again, I looked outside where it was a beautifully sunny late-summer day. Treetops on West Eleventh Street were just below my fourth-floor window and sparrows were circling what must be a nest of hatchlings, squeaking and singing. I lay there unable to think of the next step. I was deeply shocked by what he'd told me. He seemed so certain that this was my problem, and no one else had had a clue up until now, and it was such a terrible thing he was proposing. So sudden, so final! Nor was he even really the first to suggest it. Hadn't that Scottish resident at the Pines earlier this summer told me to see an oncologist? And wouldn't this explain why my

doctor, who as a rule was casual with me to the point of being dila-
tory, had mobilized so instantly, from 8,000 miles away, to get me
looked at? And why his choice here at the hospital had operated on
me ten minutes after I'd first met him? And had made me check in
and forced me to have these tests done? Certainly never as a child,
and possibly only once as a young adult—when I'd blacked out on a
bus leaving college and awakened in a room at a nearby hospital,
with wet bandages blinding my eyes, informed I had German
measles—had I experienced doctors and nurses moving this quickly.
Then, too, it had been serious, though that crisis was soon over. As
much as what the physician actually said, that rapidity, among people who in my experience didn't move fast, frightened me.

On the other hand, I was an adept of yoga and especially in the
past year and a half, and after spending time in such an intensely
physical place as Fire Island, I felt myself closely in touch with my
body from daily *asanas* and meditation: that being after all what
yoga is, literally yoking the mind and body together. So while I believed that there definitely was something wrong with my body,
ergo these infections, I couldn't for the life of me believe it was cancer. It just did not feel like something bad was growing inside me.
But then, wasn't that how this most surreptitious and insidious of
illnesses worked? By not seeming to exist until it was too late?

The next morning, I began the tests. I was folded over a square
metal cube, which stood on one slightly squared-off point, and even
with a variety of analgesics, I felt the incredible pressure of a long
tube—attached I was told to a camera—inserted into me from behind. Once I got my breath back, I was able to look at what the camera was seeing inside me on a tiny little black-and-white television
above my head, as the tube probed my colon, sigmoid, and lower intestine two feet in. The video was taped and looked at by various
medics and technicians before it was removed.

My second test was the CAT scan. I was made to drink glass after
glass of something truly vile, then wrapped into a sledlike object
that closely resembled one of those foot measurers they make you
stand up on in shoe stores. That object was in turn slotted into the
circular opening of a long, noisy machine where I endured immobil-
ity and boredom and sound torture for a good forty-five minutes.

The barium enema was reserved for the next day. I had to drink yet another two bottles of lemon-flavored citrate of magnesia that operated like a depth-charge torpedo in my stomach, exploding out of me whatever liquids I'd taken in that were still remaining in my poor body. For the test itself I had to drink only one glass of something different if equally nasty to what I'd taken for the CAT scan. This drink would radioilluminate my insides. I was then photographed or x-rayed or fluoroscoped in and by various machines for another hour or two, my body again twisted and turned into various angles and distortions by technicians and nurses.

The afternoon of the third day, the hospital doctor and the oncology specialist arrived together in my room as I was eating my first solid food in days: two pieces of savory toast and two heavenly poached eggs.

"The good news is we've found nothing definite," the doctor said. "Nothing in your lower gastrointestinal tract. Nothing that looks bad via the CAT scan. By the way, did you ever break or fracture a rib?"

"Three. When I was ten. I fell off a cliff a hundred feet high. Broke lots of things. Cheekbone, leg, arm, three ribs."

"That showed up as knit marks. But I still don't think we should celebrate yet. There's obviously something wrong in your GI area or you wouldn't be getting these infections. The barium enema tests aren't all in, but two of them show something strange in one specific area of your lower intestine." He pulled out two black-and-white photos that looked to me not like my intestine but sections of some "sea" on the far side of the moon charted by the Apollo crew before they'd landed.

"See these? Same spot. We've got to keep an eye on that spot." He went on in this manner and with other sobering stuff for a while.

Bob came and helped me check out and carried all my gear. Although I lived only four blocks from the hospital, we rode in a taxi. And once there, he insisted that I stay on the sofa, while he did things for me. He tried like hell not to ask me, so once we were settled in my living room and drinking coffee, I said, "All the tests were negative, so far. But there are more to come and I'm not out of the woods yet."

I would continue to get those infections every few months, continue to be lanced, continue to sitz bathe them as they drained, continue to get a battery of tests taken during hospital stays for two days twice a year, knowing that at any moment it could all turn against me and the dreaded colon cancer be discovered: and then—quite simply—my time would be up. It was a constant, unceasing threat, time and again, repeated year after year, undercutting what otherwise was the happiest, most fulfilling, and as I have now come to understand, the most love-filled, time of my life, causing me intense physical pain and costing me an enormous amount of money in medical bills: enough to have used as a down payment on a house or condo.

*   *   *

The weather continued warm and sunny and beautiful that early fall, as though following the hurricane, or because of it, the summer refused to end. I returned to the Pines sooner than my doctor thought wise, but as soon as I felt recovered, and I remained until the third week of October. I was working hard on my new novel, and I didn't want to lose more time, or more importantly, lose the sense of pace I'd already achieved writing the book. Whenever people tell me how "productive" I am, I always reply, "I'm actually pretty lazy. What I am is efficient. I try to do as much as possible when I have to."

There's another element involved although I'm not certain what to call it. It's like recognizing the "tides of creation," or seeing and following "writing flow patterns." I have no idea what these patterns are, nor where they came from; whether they were always here within me like some power line just waiting to be tapped, or if they were first released, as the universe was said to have been, during the "big bang" of my first explosion of writing of that still unpublished novel in 1971. These currents or flows in no way determine the content of what I write, I believe, but they are distinctive, not only by virtue of their varying length and strength, but also because some flows tend to be better for poetry, others for fiction, others for dramatic works, and still others for essays and reviews. It's up to me to sense their character, length, and strength, then work every day while they're flowing. If I misgauge their strength, I'll be forced to stop in the middle of a long work and put it aside. Perhaps to pick it up again at the next flow. If I've contracted for work and there's no flow waiting, like an air current to be ridden by a sky glider, woe is me, the work won't be done. I've learned not to contract for work when I don't feel a flow coming, while if I'm in the midst of a particulary strong flow, I'll take on more work than I'd planned, because often the flows prove longer and stronger than I'd at first guessed, and I'll finish a novel with revisions and still have "juice" left over for a story, some poems, an essay.

I often wonder how finite this creative flow is, how limited. I also wonder if other writers don't, didn't, experience the same thing. Thomas Mann writes in his journals of finding an anecdote turn itself into a novella, a novella into a long four-volume novel. Or what about that paragon of productivity, Balzac, who surely meant something like this flow when he wrote to Mme. Hanska, his confidante. He even wrote a novel, *Le Peau de chagrin*, about it: more precisely about a magic skin that brings good fortune but shrinks every time it's used. Was that the same? And is this current the same thing as the "inspiration" ancient poets like Horace and Hesiod prayed to the muse for? That Petrarch and Dante thanked Laura and Beatrice for? Its indeterminacy the bane of all authors?

At any rate, I was hard at work back at Fire Island Columbus Day weekend and the place was as populated as though it were midsummer. Hal Seidman, who'd gone from boyfriend to friend that year, had a very attractive young guest on his beach towel, someone, it turned out, I'd first met on beach towels earlier that summer on the Bank Street Pier, in the Village. Then, he'd been dating my friend Jerry Blatt and I'd chatted with them, and when Jerry had to leave to meet Bette, I'd remained a while talking with Don, and had been even more interested in what he had to say than in his very nicely muscled body or his pale blue eyes in which micalike chips of yellow and green and white were so arranged that they looked starburst, the way Brenda Starr's eyes are drawn in the comic strip.

Don Eike was Bob's age, just two weeks older and thus a few years younger than me, and he was as intelligent and thoughtful and yet as much fun to be around as I'd recalled from that hour or so on

A House on the Ocean, A House on the Bay

the Village dock. So, I took up Hal's invitation and dined at their house that evening, then went dancing with them. I hung out with Hal and Don on the beach the following day and once Hal left the beach, had another long talk with Don. We three went out dancing again the following night. Once I was back in town for good that autumn, I again bumped into Don at Twelve West, a disco that had opened on the West Side Highway a few blocks from where I lived, and I invited Don the next weekend to Flamingo, which he'd never been to and which he immediately liked. It wasn't until around the Christmas holidays of that year that Don and Bob first met.

Besides being a bookkeeper by day, Don was a singer. Like so many young people, he'd come to New York from St. Louis to be in musical theatre. For some reason that hadn't worked out, and he'd found work as an administrative assistant, learned bookkeeping, and become an accountant. But he continued to sing. He auditioned for parts, which might have been how he and Jerry had met, took roles in small productions of musical revivals around town, and was part of a church choir. Indeed, he was soloist baritone at a holiday program given at St. Thomas Church at Fifth Avenue and Fifty-third Street, where I dragged Bob to hear him. The main piece on the program was one of my favorites since a boyfriend had given me an LP of it years before, the Duruflé *Requiem*. Don sang beautifully and was able to really show off his baritone equipment—and his technique—when he sang a Handel aria. Afterwards, the three of us went to dinner and Don and Bob liked each other instantly as I was sure they would, so the three of us began to associate together, going out together whenever Bob wasn't working at night, to concerts and movies and plays.

Jon decided to drop out of the summer share on Tarpon Walk the following summer and Nick and Enno—whom I also continued to see in the city—were planning to live there all season as I had, but were taking a bigger house on the beach near the co-ops with weekend roommates Paul Popham, Rick Wellikopf, Wes Widener, and John Kohneman. It seemed only natural that I'd suggest to Bob and Don that they together take the second share of what had willy-nilly become my house, the cottage on Tarpon Walk. They agreed, we worked out money, and the summer of 1977 became the year of "Felice and the Supremes."

That name came about early in the summer. All three of us were at the Pines for an early May weekend and went to the Sandpiper that Friday night. The large open-back deck was already crowded when we arrived, people sitting on the side railings, necking, cooling off from dancing, bunched together laughing as they shared a popper, cruising, gossiping as Bob, Don, and I approached the back deck and prepared to go up the three wide stairs. Someone we'd met before or who knew us leaped down a step and put out a hand toward us and in a voice loud enough for everyone to hear, said, "Stop!"

"In the name of love," we three replied, singing out in one voice, also putting up our hands, à la Diana, Mary, and Flo. At which whomever he was fell back and the entire back deck erupted into applause and shouts of "It's the Supremes!" Someone shouted, "They're white! They're boys! But they're here!" And everyone applauded again. Somehow the name stuck, especially as both Bob and Don were so attractive, so desirable, and because that summer we hung out together as much as possible. Later on, whenever Don was having love trouble, Bob and I would sing, "And Flo, she don't know that the boy she loves is a Romeo!" And whenever he was really in the dumps, Don would ironically refer to himself as "the dead Supreme."

There were other names for the three of us that summer. We became a famous trio in the Pines. Not only because of looks. If Bob was sweet, Don was even sweeter. Don smart, Bob smarter. Bob knowledgeable about music and theatre, Don even more so. Don thoughtful and considerate and kind, Bob even kinder and more considerate. And me, well, I wasn't any of that, but by midsummer I was famous, with a best-selling paperback novel, *Eyes*, that everyone was reading in Manhattan and on the train coming out to the Pines, which even the blindest queen could see, and with another book, *The Mesmerist*, due out in hardcover in the fall. No wonder everyone in the Pines wanted us on their beach towels, by their pool, in their pool, in their Jacuzzi, on their back deck, at their party, around their dinner table, with them at the Boatel, the Sandpiper, the Ice Palace, the Monster, at the bar, on the dance floor, and above

A House on the Ocean, A House on the Bay

all, especially, in their bed. Preferably all of us, and if not together, then as many as they could get, even if it meant one at a time.

Because we three were all having such a good time being together, we were like a three-spoked wheel that spins through whatever's there. So we weren't really aware of our tripled reputation until quite late that summer. We were all together on our little back deck, watching another fabulous sunset, when we heard someone shouting at us. At first we couldn't make out what he was saying, then we heard, "Hey, you gods on Olympus! Come down and talk to us mere mortals!"

We located the guy who was shouting. He was directly ahead, in that house about two empty lots away, way down the Tarpon Walk hill, across the dunes and the stream where the deer drank, beyond a copse of trees. Their house was long, with a pitched roof, its windows and deck faced our way. Where we stood and ate lunch on our back deck might have been forty, fifty feet higher.

We looked at each other, amused. I shouted back, "Invite us for cocktails!"

He yelled back, "You're invited! Invited for cocktails! Invited for anything you want that we have."

We thought that a bit excessive, but we trooped down the hill to their deck, from which we could barely see our place—it did look sort of unobtainable and even a little Olympian—and met the four men in the house. Two were American, two were Europeans. They were older, and very nice, and though we maintained our reserve, we drank a cocktail with them and chatted politely. When we left they told us they'd dine out on our visit for the next few months.

When we got home and fixed dinner, we brushed off what they had said, what their words and actions told us about our reputations, and never again referred to it. I suppose it seemed elitist, and we believed that while we were unquestionably special, we were anything but elitist. We had so many friends at the Pines who treated us as equals, we felt ourselves to be no better. By the end of that third summer at Fire Island, I could walk into maybe a dozen houses at the Pines and not feel I was intruding. No, we were no better than anyone else there . . . except maybe those guys in Frank and Jack's new household who we'd partied with and saw around a great deal that summer and who despite their extremely nice bodies and handsome faces, we learned to avoid, and whom we one night nicknamed, "the other seven dwarfs, the ones Disney kept locked away: Sleazy, Druggy, Horny, Pushy, Sweaty, Smarmy, and Jock."

It's difficult to explain how and why we three got along so well. Whenever one of us was blue the other two would, without having to work at it, cheer him up. Whenever one got too crazy about something: some man, say, the other two would remind him about our unwritten but learned-by-heart house rules for the summer:

#1. Nothing is real out here.
#2. Nothing is that important really, Dear.
#3. Nothing—no matter how big it looks in his tight jeans or Speedo—is *that* big.

A typical weekend for the three of us went like this: Don and Bob would usually arrive on Friday evening—afternoon if Don got off early. Sometimes I'd meet them at the ferry dock but more often I'd be trying to finish up my writing for the day before they arrived. We'd hug, kiss, and if it were a nice day, we'd sit outside at the table on the back porch looking at the Pines and the view of the Great South Bay. We seldom went out Friday night, but I usually made dinner and we always ate together and discussed events among our set and in our lives of the past week and listened to music. Despite how quiet this was, we generally never got to bed until after midnight. They usually slept late on Saturdays, giving me a few more hours of writing time. Then breakfast: eggs, toast, cereal, yogurt, fruit, vitamins, juice, coffee. By noon we'd hit the beach. After an hour of sunning and bathing, we'd take the Promenade. That often lasted another two hours. We'd generally get back to the house by four. Bob and sometimes Don and sometimes all three of us would go to Merrill's Gym at Fire Island Boulevard and Cedar Walk, where we'd pump up, exercise, and catch up on all of the Pines gossip. Stop on the way home at the Pines Pantry for dinner, come home, shower, and dress for Tea Dance. All three of us generally hit the Boatel dance floor together by 6 P.M. We'd stay one hour, dance, cruise, chat, meet, and greet. Then home again for dinner. By 9 P.M.

A House on the Ocean, A House on the Bay

we were napping. We'd generally get up by eleven, have a cup of coffee to fully wake up, clean up, dress, take a hallucinogen, smoke some grass or hash to ease its operation, and walk down to the harbor. There, if it were rainy or threatening, we'd stay at the Sandpiper, but if it were clear out, which was 90 percent of the time, we'd wait in front of the ice cream stand for a "lateral" taxi to Cherry Grove. These were either little skiffs with an outboard motor or the bigger Island Water Taxi that could hold a dozen people. We'd get in and be skimmed at top speed across the night-lighted bay waters to the Grove, thumping and bumping amid the spray sheeting up all around us. We'd arrive and pay our way into the Ice Palace and spend most of the night together there dancing and cruising and talking to people we knew, unless one of us wanted to be with someone new. Generally we either split apart by 3:30 A.M. or went home together, two or three of us, walking along the beach, getting back to the house on Tarpon Walk around dawn.

We'd collapse, sleep until noon or one, get up, and while one of us prepared another huge breakfast—including specialties like pancakes or quiche or French toast—the others would go to the harbor for any other food needed and pick up the Sunday papers. We'd generally hit the beach by two. And again bathe, visit, sun, promenade, and in general try to dry out from the night before. A late lunch followed, then we'd clean up, dress, and be off to Sunday Tea Dance, which we seldom missed. If Bob and Don were returning to town that evening, they'd take their shoulder bags with them and stow them with a hundred others in front of the Boatel's bus office window, or once we got to know George, inside the office. We'd have cocktails, dance, cruise, flirt, gossip, then generally by the end of Tea Dance, it would be sunset, and I'd stand on the Boatel deck or up higher, on the balcony of the Crow's Nest, Ralph's little aerie of a clothing shop on the roof of the grocery store, with whomever was remaining in the Pines, and we'd wave good-bye to Bob and Don and everyone else on the ferry as it glided out of the harbor into the bay.

I'd either go home alone for dinner, or join someone else I knew at their house for dinner. Sometimes I'd be writing again that night. Sometimes I'd be making love with someone I'd met, sometimes I'd go out late Sunday night to the Sandpiper, generally a far less hectic evening than Saturday night, when men who'd not been laid so far were more friendly and open—or merely more desperate—where I could see who among the weekend crowd would be remaining out for the week and where the dancing could get quite good. Next morning, I'd wake up, have coffee, write in my journal, and do more work. I'd usually get down to the harbor before 11 A.M. for the daily papers sold at the dock, and meet people who were staying. Everyone met at the harbor, vacationers from California and D.C. and Paris and São Paolo, people who lived at the island all summer, foreigners, movie stars, old boyfriends and former tricks, people you'd not seen in years. It was so small, so central, that one not terribly special weekday morning getting the papers I saw Tommy Tune and James Levine in line ahead of me, as a yacht with Elizabeth Taylor on the back deck—sitting and waving—turned around in the harbor, preparing to go back to the city. Often I'd pick up two papers and stop at Nick and Enno's house, and find them on the deck attaching kites to fly from the housetop rafters or blowing up their rubber raft to take out into the surf, or doing yoga or watering their deck plants or exercising on mats on the shore deck or simply laying out in the sun. I'd spend an hour there catching up on the weekend, the previous day's events at the Pines, before I'd go down to the beach and walk along the shoreline home.

If it seems an ideal life for an out gay writer, it was for me absolutely perfect. It lasted essentially for the next six years before the epidemic began to run like wildfire through the Pines population, ruining everything.

*   *   *

Often after we'd been at Flamingo all night back in New York City we'd still be too hyper to go to sleep and often after a whole night of dancing, Bob and Don would be hungry, so we congregated at various all-night restaurants. The one we came to most favor was the Empire Diner on Ninth Avenue and Twenty-second Street, partly because it was near the Chelsea leather bars on the West Side Highway, partly because it was packed at 5:30 A.M. Sunday morning with all-nighters like ourselves, gay and straight, a real odd, mixed, and colorful after-hours crowd.

We were in the Vampire—as we'd come to call the place for what should be obvious reasons—one morning in late November of 1976, when Hal Seidman and Jimmy Peters joined us. Hal came up with an idea that we throw a Fire Island party in Manhattan.

He'd gone home with someone who lived in a co-op apartment in a very classy building in the lower Forties at Lexington Avenue. The building had public-use top two floors, consisting of a glass-enclosed, Olympic-sized swimming pool, a sauna, a steam room, a weight room, a wrap-around terrace with fabulous views of the city—the U.N. Secretariat Building on one side, the Chrysler Building on the other—and a big lounge complete with fireplace and bar. Hal had asked how much it would cost to rent the space. Only a few hundred dollars, if he did it through his friend. Hal also knew the manager of the new Man's Country baths on West Fifteenth Street. He said he thought he could get them to staff and supply us with towels if we kept their name visible as free advertising. I knew someone who was trying to break into the music/deejay business who'd make a tape for the party just to get his name around, and I could bring in a sound system. Jimmy of course could get the invitation cards printed up. It would be a pool party, nude swimming. We'd throw it in the depths of the winter, when everyone was dying to be at the beach. We selected St. Valentine's Day, and since everyone had at least one bad affair, we cheekily called it "Broken Hearts—an Aquacade." We send out invites that were cards with a heart on it, ripped in half. Between the five of us we had the names and addresses of the 300 hottest gay men in New York. It would be fabulous.

People who were at the party still talk about it. Reporters from *Mandate* and the *Advocate*, alerted by phone callers from on the scene, tried to party crash with their photographers, but were stopped at the street-level lobby by the uniformed doorman, the uniformed concierge, and the bath's manager. I'd come early, naturally, carting in a taxi my own stereo equipment: power amp, receiver, both my own sets and a borrowed pair of speakers and a reel-to-reel tape deck, for which Larry Jacobs had mixed a terrific six-hour-long tape. I'd helped them get it all ready, put notes identifying the various doors, saw the staff in place, the huge concoction of fruit juices, various hallucinogens we three had, and dry ice all dumped into a giant punch bowl. Then I went home to clean up and change. I'd arrived back at ten with Bob and Don and the party was in full swing. I danced, socialized, got high, looked at the city, ended up with most of the people in the huge pool, filled with nude men cavorting and making love, the entire pool area lighted by a score of tiny votive candles and the city's own nocturnal illumination. That night, it seemed that everyone I'd come to know or like romantically, everyone I had slept with, or just socialized with was present. All of us were enjoying ourselves as we did at Fire Island, but somehow more openly, more easily, possibly because we all felt special, chosen, all together, not only physically more open but because we all belonged together, no matter where we might be.

Naturally it didn't go perfectly. But the mishaps were small, and after all that was why we had staff: to handle details. One rather large detail was the man who lived in the building through whom Hal had rented the space. Hal had consistently downplayed how many people would be coming and how huge the thing would be. A half hour into the party, long enough to see what a monster bash it was, the man retired to his apartment and took sleeping pills, hoping he wouldn't awaken to find himself kicked out of the building. His roommate, however, came back up, loved it, and had a terrific time, saying we shouldn't worry, he'd handle Alan—and the building board if neccessary—tomorrow. Naturally our party contained the usual person getting too drunk or too stoned and rowdy and having to be escorted out, all the way downstairs, out the lobby, and into a waiting cab. As well as the person who got sick all over the sauna and had to be cleaned up after. But for weeks afterward I'd hear about the party from people at Flamingo or at the Vampire or on the streets, I'd hear of scenes I'd missed: mini-orgies in the steam room, even in the weight room, sex acts in the pool, people who got into the elevator naked save for a towel and ended up riding with other building residents dressed in evening wear and jewels, not a single one of whom remarked on their oddly attired companion, who said he'd just smiled a lot during the elevator ride and fully intended—had he had been asked—to tell them he'd chased his cat into the hallway and found himself locked out. On the plus side, people had a great time sunning and steaming and swimming in warm water, re-encountered each other, fell in love, fell in lust, went home together. Not a single relationship ended that night, but several did begin, athough I don't know for how long. It cost, I believe, under $1,000.

*   *   *

A decade later, men who'd been at the Broken Hearts Party, men we knew from the Pines or the Grove or Flamingo or the Cockring, would see Bob and I getting out of a taxi, or walking along the Hudson River promenade, stepping into a Korean deli, or standing on the balcony at the Metropolitan Opera, in line at a movie, in a theatre lobby crowd, at the coat check at some opening-night party for yet another new dance club trying to make it, and they would invariably be amazed. "You guys are still together!" they'd say in wonder, shaking their heads at the fact. "After all this time! Still together!"

No one would be more surprised than Bob or me. I've already given some examples of incidents and circumstances by which we grew closer. To explain how we eventually ended up being the closest people in each other's lives would mean describing many further small steps in our lives over the following months and years: many daily small, almost infinitesimally small, yet constant threads that we threw out to each other. Little lifelines you might call them— slowly binding us closer and closer together as they wove a webbing over our lives and our affections. Food, for one, which meant we would cook special dishes for each other. "Serious" music, for another, which meant we'd not only go to symphony concerts and recitals together, but also play for one another new records we purchased. Despite our differing taste in books, we'd pass them on to read and discuss. Plays and movies and even television shows we wanted to see—together if possible. Places and parties we wanted to go to—together. Friends we wanted each other to meet. There seemed to be no end to what it was each other must have.

In the winter of 1990, we were sitting outside on the huge terrace around the pool, alongside the new little wooden dock where a

speedboat bobbed tied up in wait for our use at any time. We were outside Bob's law partner's vacation house on Sapodilla Bay, on Providenciales Island in the Turks and Caicos where we'd taken to going on two-week vacations. Bob would look out at the smooth expanse of the Caribbean and the endless brilliant designs implicit in those shimmering nightly constellations and he would for the first time bring it up, saying, "What I could never figure out is why, with everyone else on the island and in the city making a play for me, you never did." He'd pause as we watched a shooting star glitter a pale green golden arc from the neighborhood of Cygnus to douse itself in the sea, and he'd go on, "At first I thought you didn't like me. But everybody around us said you did like me. And neurotic as I could be, after a while I could see it for myself. So I had to think, maybe you liked me too much to chance ruining our relationship by making it only another sexual encounter, another escapade."

We were stretched out on chaise lounges, a stiff offshore breeze blowing through the papaya trees, ruffling the coconut palms that grew squat and close to the ground on this desertlike island.

"Then I stopped thinking about it," Bob said, "and just let us be. And that was when it happened, wasn't it?" he said, rather than asked. "Now I know no matter what else happens to me or to you, we're together to the end."

Earlier that day while he was out at the gym, I'd watched on cable TV drawn in from somewhere—Rio? Chicago?—the film *The Way We Were*, and at the moment the two men looked back and played "Favorite Year," I thought instantly: summer of 1977: Fire Island Pines. Bob and Don and myself. All of us healthy, surrounded by friends, vivid, involved in the most wonderfully superficial things all summer long, like what outfit to wear going out. When Bob returned from the little gym in town, he saw that I'd been weeping, and I told him I'd been watching the movie. He asked nothing more. Not a word.

Now, hours later, I began to defend myself. "I thought you were Dennis's boyfriend. He all but said you were when he first introduced us."

"I wasn't. We never even slept together."

"I know that now. But I thought you were going out," I said. I wasn't about to explain the many, many reasons—both personal and concerning what I thought best for Bob at the time we'd first met—that were involved in us not beginning an affair but which led to us first becoming friends, deepening our relationship, helping it last through good and bad, for better or worse, in sickness and in health, till death us do part. . . .

"Sometimes thinking the wrong thing makes you behave better, more naturally," I explained. "And sometimes what would be a bad thing leads to something far better."

We sat in silence a while. "By the way," I added, "it's been a while since I told you: You're wonderful!"

Even in the dark I could see a smile play around his lips, and his hand reached for mine. We sat like that a while, listening to the distant incomprehensible chatter of the shortwave radio inside the house on the kitchen table. Then our guest, who'd arrived at the tiny jetport a week after us, stepped out of the house and said, "There you are! I'm ready. And I'm hungry!"

We got up from the chaises and went to meet her, told her how lovely she looked, then headed toward the Jeep. We were driving into the Blue Hills to a local restaurant wrongly—given the glacial pace of service—named Fast Eddies. And all the while he was driving, while she chatted in the seat behind us, I could make out Bob singing, barely audibly, "You're the National Gallery. You're Garbo's salary. You're cellophane!"

We returned to the Pines, Bob and I, not too long ago, in the summer of 1989. We didn't mean to. I'd been invited to be a judge in the Mr. Fire Island muscle man contest one August weekend. Even though we were given a room at the hotel that still houses that shadow of what was once the great Ice Palace, we decided to stay at the home of some media people in the Grove Bob had done legal work for. It was a big house, unlike the tiny cottages that used to be the mainstay there. The contest was held in two sections, Saturday afternoon and Saturday night, and the other judges were a Miss Manners-in-drag and a former Mr. Universe. The entire event was over by Sunday, which turned out to be warm and lovely. After we'd been on the beach long enough, Bob and I decided to walk to the Pines. The Grove had become the loud, crowded, redeveloped, over-populated new hangout for late-1980s young lesbians and their goatee-bearded, close-cropped headed, buff-bodied, hairless young gay buddies from Chelsea and the East Village. By contrast, the Pines seemed vacant. Maybe two people at the harbor, half the shops I'd known closed down, one waiter desultorily talking on the phone inside the vacant, dim Boatel bar.

We walked around, finding nothing to do, no one to greet, no one to recognize, then slowly did a small tour of the central area of the Pines. More people were out on the beach, but they looked to be daytrippers, straight couples, families from Patchogue and Bay Shore who'd come over on the ferry. It was so depressing that we took to the water's edge and walked back to the house in the Grove we were staying at. When someone asked me the next day what the Pines had been like, I had to say like the town surrounding the castle in the story of Sleeping Beauty: everything intact, but inert, as though vines were growing over the walls and boardwalks, the harbor and chained-up wagons, the restaurants, the Boatel, the few people left.

I almost wish it were different, in ruins say, like some city destroyed by a comet, caught in its final moments being purely itself in every aspect for some future archaeologist to dig up again and reconstruct. It is not in ruins, not precisely, but still exists as though in mockery, a mockery more rare because so few of us are still around to perceive it. The others, the "new people" at the Pines, go about seemingly in more or less full enjoyment of what they think the island actually is, or was, or could be. I've been back again and I've caught the stare of an old Pines person, someone I'd seen for years on the boardwalks, at the Sandpiper, yet whom I'd never formally met, or did and forgot his name, and we'll look at some frolic or attitude of the "new people" and smirk sadly across the ferry landing, across the croissant counter, the seaplane dock, as we inwardly see and outwardly remark with our eyes that there was nothing of Pines style left, nothing at all!

Not that style was everything, naturally, but when you were one of the Gay Two Thousand you were consciously aware of it, you would think in advance how best to do a certain thing: how to light a cigarette say for an ex-lover in the midst of a crowded Boatel deck filled with people watching your every move, just before you turned and escorted him inside for a fast dance with his new beau; or the precise angle your faces made against the backdrop of bay and reeds as you kissed in greeting a new roommate at the breakwater's edge, both of you dressed in bright ponchos against a sudden pelting rain just ended, as the twilight cleared as if nothing had happened, the sun splattering persimmon dye across the bay waters, erupting in streaks of purple and pink, as though a color bomb had gone off undersea.

It wasn't merely that other people were watching, evaluating. You yourself were watching, evaluating, and because it seemed disappointing *not* to look as perfect, *not to be* as perfect, as wonderful as possible with that sky, that bay, those dunes, that muscled tanned leg thrown casually over your thigh, those fluttering swimsuits—tiny, striped like sails on children's toy boats—hung out to dry in the late afternoon, you yourself lolling at someone else's pool listening to him indoors on the telephone patiently explaining something to someone over and over again, his voice half drowned out and yet accompanied by the hum of nearby washing machines, as you perused an Iris Murdoch novel and every once in a while glanced at the other double-width chaise where two stunning blond, washboard-tummy model/houseboys flown out for the week from L.A. slowly, almost indifferently masturbated, in rhythm with the complex harmonies of Ray Yeates's "Slow Down" tape.

And so it's no surprise, I suppose, that I sometimes think I exist now only to give testimony to the Pines as it was then, to what it was, and who it was, and to tell the few who were there, and those who say they were, and the very very many who were not—you may despair! For ours was the moment, the irretrievable moment of glory, and now all is decline, ocean side and bay side, what lay between . . . and yes, it is true that one afternoon a Bourbon Pretender turned to me at Tea Dance and said, "*C'est le fin de la race humaine!*" such was the degradation he was personally enmeshed in. Still, he said it with pride on his quaalude-sagging features, with joy in his vodka-slurred speech.

*   *   *

My own health problem—which soon became so minor compared to others around me—would continue to harass me without solution or indeed any kind of conclusion, becoming less frequent and less dangerous until several years had passed. I was on a visit to L.A. and met a man at a party given for me by friends at their house in the Hollywood Hills. I'd seen this man before, each summer for years, in the Pines, usually along the beach or at the Ice Palace, and always with men I hadn't known well. Although we had always smiled at each other and once even spoken, we'd never managed to connect. I made sure we did now. As the party was breaking up and people began going their own ways off to the bars or home, I asked him to stay. He did and it was after we'd had a long and very satisfying session of oral sex that he said, "Don't you ever get fucked on first dates?" He'd made gentle but obvious overtures in that direction, and I'd gently but firmly dissuaded any further exploration. "I used to," I said, "but I get these strange infections around that area, and they're such a nuisance, and possibly dangerous, I've learned to not to. Most guys don't mind too much. Do you?"

He turned out to be a doctor, a surgeon, an internist, and as we lay in postorgasmic semistupor, he asked for the medical history of the infections. I told him in as much detail as he asked, which turned out to be a great deal.

When I was done, he said, "I think I know what the problem is. It's very rare. I heard about it from two doctors, each of whom encountered it only once each, despite having thousands of patients and quite long careers. About a decade ago, without knowing it, you probably ate a piece of glass or sharp metal and before you got rid of it, it cut a tiny hole out of your lower intestine. Your body closed around that opening, and whenever anything managed to get into that hole and escape your intestine, that closure provided a way for it to work its way out of the body, a thread-thick vessel that would eventually open to some vesicular pore on your skin. It's called a fistula. It's extremely rare. One in 100 million or something like that. But it's historical too. It was known as a royal illness, I think because Philip the Fair had one that opened into infections around his upper torso. As the thread is so thin, it's easily moved around by any

A House on the Ocean, A House on the Bay

internal motion of your organs, which is why the infections open up in different places, but always in the same general area."

"How do I treat it?" I asked.

"You don't. It heals itself. That's why the tests showed a spot; that's the scar of the healed cut. Probably the last few times it happened were further apart in time, and much less in severity, and in more or less the same spot?"

They were. Exactly as he'd said it. "They told me it was colon cancer. For years I thought I would get cancer."

He got up and began to get dressed. "In a few years you'll forget all about it. But you're probably right not to fool around in that area until it's completely gone. But when it is, look me up."

It's worked out exactly as he predicted it would. With this one rather ironic twist, given how painful and costly and overwhelmingly frightening and generally daunting it all was: I was infected with an active fistula from the year 1976 to approximately 1982. During those years I was the insertee during anal sex maybe once a year—instead of what would probably have been several score times a year—and always from the same man. This may explain why it is that I still test negative for the HIV virus, while virtually everyone I knew from that time and place has been infected, is symptomatic, or—98 percent of them—is already dead.

"Aren't you glad?" a new acquaintance asked when I'd told him what I've just written.

"Glad? I wouldn't say I'm exactly *glad*! I really resent having been manipulated into a survival I'm not at all sure I'm pleased to have to experience, now that every one I ever loved or who ever loved me is dead. Dead and ashes. Each one, following long years of physical and mental torture. A torture I experienced along with each one of them. A survival brought about by what, after all, has a strange, let's face it, numerically nearly infinite probability against it happening." I paused, trying to keep down the depth of my bitterness, which he being younger would never, could never comprehend, before I added in what I hoped was a more moderated tone of voice, "Besides, I'd have preferred being given the choice."

"The choice?"

"Yes, of knowing I'd have to suffer through this infection and operations and the threat of cancer hanging over my head for nearly a decade and yet surviving. Or, not having the infection, and then dying along with everyone else."

"But . . ." he stammered, "what if you'd made the wrong choice?"

"And which one precisely," I shot back, "would *be* the wrong choice?"

"Why, to not survive."

All I could do was say, "You're so very, *very* naive."

*　　　*　　　*

Ever since, whenever I awaken in strange bedrooms in faraway places, sheets crisp beneath me, light patterns on the otherwise darkened walls slatted or angled like the shadows of a guillotine, I expect to hear the soft distant regular onrolling of the ocean surf.

My hosts might have placed flowers in the room, so exotic a fragrance that I instantly know from the first whiff of frangipane musk that I'm in a louvered duplex off Southard Street in the Old Town of Key West. Or mountain roses, a dozen of them, small and shamelessly open despite the night, so clear and so shy in odor that I don't doubt that if I should go to the bedroom door and open it, I'll find a long cool corridor, paneled wall on one side hung with primitive aquarelles and framed quilts, multipaned windows on the other, giving onto a garden of pine and semi-annuals in full blush, and I know I am in Egremont, in the Berkshire Mountains, in late June.

I open the window to let the night air seep in anywhere I sleep— humid Augusts on West Eleventh Street, with the wet slither of cars on the torrid tar of nearby avenues; the sudden starred chills of Coastlands, where my bedroom hangs aerie high above a small redwood forest, where by day I can make out twenty-five miles of Big Sur coastline—lemon scent wafting up so insinuatingly that on misty mornings I awake with a citrus-flavored dew upon my face and unconsciously lick my lips of it. Not even in the airless high Rocky Mountain resort would I stop to think, wait, here I am, 7,000 feet up in midcountry, the open window rimed a half inch with snow so lacey and icy I could carve patterns with my fingernails

A House on the Ocean, A House on the Bay

from where I lay inside the tiny nest I'd burrowed out of two fluffy comforters.

The desert is the worst, of course, for misrecalling where I am— all that sand breathing and the astray starlight on its billions of crystals; the sky wide and high in the desert, as I had so well known it before. In the desert too there are the occasional, unexplained sounds, always clear yet heard as though through a scrim, and that too is similar.

But it's not the ocean's rolling, not the susurration of surf, not the swish of pine boughs as a quail shifts its berth in nightmare, not the salt-tinged suggestion in air that one is afloat, unmoored, off a coastline that one might see for miles if one stood up and stepped out onto a deck . . . no, not the ocean that filled my awakenings and my dreams of awakening behind latticed windows, curtained windows, screened windows implicit with meshed patterns; that still fills them. . . . No, but the island itself.